# FIRE
## AND
# FURY

# FIRE
## AND
# FURY

### INSIDE THE TRUMP
### WHITE HOUSE

## MICHAEL WOLFF

HENRY HOLT AND COMPANY

NEW YORK

Henry Holt and Company
*Publishers since 1866*
175 Fifth Avenue
New York, New York 10010
www.henryholt.com

Henry Holt® and 🄷® are registered trademarks of Macmillan Publishing Group, LLC.

Library of Congress Cataloging-in-Publication Data is available.

ISBN: 9781250158062

Our books may be purchased in bulk for promotional, educational, or business use. Please contact
your local bookseller or the Macmillan Corporate and Premium Sales Department at (800) 221-7945,
extension 5442, or by e-mail at MacmillanSpecialMarkets@macmillan.com.

First Edition 2018

Designed by Meryl Sussman Levavi

Printed in the United States of America

11   13   15   17   19   20   18   16   14   12

*For Victoria and Louise, mother and daughter*

# CONTENTS

# AUTHOR'S NOTE

The reason to write this book could not be more obvious. With the inauguration of Donald Trump on January 20, 2017, the United States entered the eye of the most extraordinary political storm since at least Watergate. As the day approached, I set out to tell this story in as contemporaneous a fashion as possible, and to try to see life in the Trump White House through the eyes of the people closest to it.

This was originally conceived as an account of the Trump administration's first hundred days, that most traditional marker of a presidency. But events barreled on without natural pause for more than two hundred days, the curtain coming down on the first act of Trump's presidency only with the appointment of retired general John Kelly as the chief of staff in late July and the exit of chief strategist Stephen K. Bannon three weeks later.

The events I've described in these pages are based on conversations that took place over a period of eighteen months with the president, with most members of his senior staff—some of whom talked to me dozens of times—and with many people who they in turn spoke to. The first interview occurred well before I could have imagined a Trump White House, much less a book about it, in late May 2016 at Trump's home in Beverly Hills—the then candidate polishing off a pint of Häagen-Dazs vanilla as he happily and idly opined about a range of topics while his aides, Hope

Hicks, Corey Lewandowski, and Jared Kushner, went in and out of the room. Conversations with members of the campaign's team continued through the Republican Convention in Cleveland, when it was still hardly possible to conceive of Trump's election. They moved on to Trump Tower with a voluble Steve Bannon—before the election, when he still seemed like an entertaining oddity, and later, after the election, when he seemed like a miracle worker.

Shortly after January 20, I took up something like a semipermanent seat on a couch in the West Wing. Since then I have conducted more than two hundred interviews.

While the Trump administration has made hostility to the press a virtual policy, it has also been more open to the media than any White House in recent memory. In the beginning, I sought a level of formal access to this White House, something of a fly-on-the-wall status. The president himself encouraged this idea. But, given the many fiefdoms in the Trump White House that came into open conflict from the first days of the administration, there seemed no one person able to make this happen. Equally, there was no one to say "Go away." Hence I became more a constant interloper than an invited guest—something quite close to an actual fly on the wall—having accepted no rules nor having made any promises about what I might or might not write.

Many of the accounts of what has happened in the Trump White House are in conflict with one another; many, in Trumpian fashion, are baldly untrue. Those conflicts, and that looseness with the truth, if not with reality itself, are an elemental thread of the book. Sometimes I have let the players offer their versions, in turn allowing the reader to judge them. In other instances I have, through a consistency in accounts and through sources I have come to trust, settled on a version of events I believe to be true.

Some of my sources spoke to me on so-called deep background, a convention of contemporary political books that allows for a disembodied description of events provided by an unnamed witness to them. I have also relied on off-the-record interviews, allowing a source to provide a direct quote with the understanding that it was not for attribution. Other sources spoke to me with the understanding that the material in the interviews would not become public until the book came out. Finally, some sources spoke forthrightly on the record.

At the same time, it is worth noting some of the journalistic conundrums that I faced when dealing with the Trump administration, many of them the result of the White House's absence of official procedures and the lack of experience of its principals. These challenges have included dealing with off-the-record or deep-background material that was later casually put on the record; sources who provided accounts in confidence and subsequently shared them widely, as though liberated by their first utterances; a frequent inattention to setting any parameters on the use of a conversation; a source's views being so well known and widely shared that it would be risible not to credit them; and the almost samizdat sharing, or gobsmacked retelling, of otherwise private and deep-background conversations. And everywhere in this story is the president's own constant, tireless, and uncontrolled voice, public and private, shared by others on a daily basis, sometimes virtually as he utters it.

For whatever reason, almost everyone I contacted—senior members of the White House staff as well as dedicated observers of it—shared large amounts of time with me and went to great effort to help shed light on the unique nature of life inside the Trump White House. In the end, what I witnessed, and what this book is about, is a group of people who have struggled, each in their own way, to come to terms with the meaning of working for Donald Trump.

I owe them an enormous debt.

# PROLOGUE:
## AILES AND BANNON

The evening began at six-thirty, but Steve Bannon, suddenly among the world's most powerful men and now less and less mindful of time constraints, was late.

Bannon had promised to come to this small dinner arranged by mutual friends in a Greenwich Village town house to see Roger Ailes, the former head of Fox News and the most significant figure in right-wing media and Bannon's sometime mentor. The next day, January 4, 2017—little more than two weeks before the inauguration of his friend Donald Trump as the forty-fifth president—Ailes would be heading to Palm Beach, into a forced, but he hoped temporary, retirement.

Snow was threatening, and for a while the dinner appeared doubtful. The seventy-six-year-old Ailes, with a long history of leg and hip problems, was barely walking, and, coming in to Manhattan with his wife Beth from their upstate home on the Hudson, was wary of slippery streets. But Ailes was eager to see Bannon. Bannon's aide, Alexandra Preate, kept texting steady updates on Bannon's progress extracting himself from Trump Tower.

As the small group waited for Bannon, it was Ailes's evening. Quite as dumbfounded by his old friend Donald Trump's victory as most everyone else, Ailes provided the gathering with something of a mini-seminar on the randomness and absurdities of politics. Before launching Fox

News in 1996, Ailes had been, for thirty years, among the leading political operatives in the Republican Party. As surprised as he was by this election, he could yet make a case for a straight line from Nixon to Trump. He just wasn't sure, he said, that Trump himself, at various times a Republican, Independent, and Democrat, could make the case. Still, he thought he knew Trump as well as anyone did and was eager to offer his help. He was also eager to get back into the right-wing media game, and he energetically described some of the possibilities for coming up with the billion or so dollars he thought he would need for a new cable network.

Both men, Ailes and Bannon, fancied themselves particular students of history, both autodidacts partial to universal field theories. They saw this in a charismatic sense—they had a personal relationship with history, as well as with Donald Trump.

Now, however reluctantly, Ailes understood that, at least for the moment, he was passing the right-wing torch to Bannon. It was a torch that burned bright with ironies. Ailes's Fox News, with its $1.5 billion in annual profits, had dominated Republican politics for two decades. Now Bannon's Breitbart News, with its mere $1.5 million in annual profits, was claiming that role. For thirty years, Ailes—until recently the single most powerful person in conservative politics—had humored and tolerated Donald Trump, but in the end Bannon and Breitbart had elected him.

Six months before, when a Trump victory still seemed out of the realm of the possible, Ailes, accused of sexual harassment, was cashiered from Fox News in a move engineered by the liberal sons of conservative eighty-five-year-old Rupert Murdoch, the controlling shareholder of Fox News and the most powerful media owner of the age. Ailes's downfall was cause for much liberal celebration: the greatest conservative bugbear in modern politics had been felled by the new social norm. Then Trump, hardly three months later, accused of vastly more louche and abusive behavior, was elected president.

* * *

Ailes enjoyed many things about Trump: his salesmanship, his showmanship, his gossip. He admired Trump's sixth sense for the public marketplace—or at least the relentlessness and indefatigability of his ceaseless attempts to win it over. He liked Trump's game. He liked Trump's impact and his shamelessness. "He just keeps going," Ailes had marveled to a friend after the first debate with Hillary Clinton. "You hit Donald along the head, and he keeps going. He doesn't even know he's been hit."

But Ailes was convinced that Trump had no political beliefs or backbone. The fact that Trump had become the ultimate avatar of Fox's angry common man was another sign that we were living in an upside-down world. The joke was on somebody—and Ailes thought it might be on him.

Still, Ailes had been observing politicians for decades, and in his long career he had witnessed just about every type and style and oddity and confection and cravenness and mania. Operatives like himself—and now, like Bannon—worked with all kinds. It was the ultimate symbiotic and codependent relationship. Politicians were front men in a complex organizational effort. Operatives knew the game, and so did most candidates and officeholders. But Ailes was pretty sure Trump did not. Trump was undisciplined—he had no capacity for any game plan. He could not be a part of any organization, nor was he likely to subscribe to any program or principle. In Ailes's view, he was "a rebel without a cause." He was simply "Donald"—as though nothing more need be said.

In early August, less than a month after Ailes had been ousted from Fox News, Trump asked his old friend to take over the management of his calamitous campaign. Ailes, knowing Trump's disinclination to take advice, or even listen to it, turned him down. This was the job Bannon a week later.

After Trump's victory, Ailes seemed to balance regret that he had not seized the chance to run his friend's campaign with incredulity that Trump's offer had turned out to be the ultimate opportunity. Trump's rise to power, Ailes understood, was the improbable triumph of many things that Ailes and Fox News represented. After all, Ailes was perhaps the person most responsible for unleashing the angry-man currents of Trump's victory: he had invented the right-wing media that delighted in the Trump character.

Ailes, who was a member of the close circle of friends and advisers Trump frequently called, found himself hoping he would get more time

with the new president once he and Beth moved to Palm Beach; he knew
Trump planned to make regular trips to Mar-a-Lago, down the road from
Ailes's new home. Still, though Ailes was well aware that in politics, win-
ning changes everything—the winner is the winner—he couldn't quite
get his head around the improbable and bizarre fact that his friend
Donald Trump was now president of the United States.

* * *

At nine-thirty, three hours late, a good part of the dinner already eaten,
Bannon finally arrived. Wearing a disheveled blazer, his signature pairing
of two shirts, and military fatigues, the unshaven, overweight sixty-three-
year-old joined the other guests at the table and immediately took control of the conversation. Pushing a proffered glass of wine away—"I don't
drink"—he dived into a live commentary, an urgent download of information about the world he was about to take over.

"We're going to flood the zone so we have every cabinet member for
the next seven days through their confirmation hearings," he said of the
business-and-military 1950s-type cabinet choices. "Tillerson is two days,
Session is two days, Mattis is two days. . . ."

Bannon veered from "Mad Dog" Mattis—the retired four-star general whom Trump had nominated as secretary of defense—to a long riff
on torture, the surprising liberalism of generals, and the stupidity of the
civilian-military bureaucracy. Then it was on to the looming appointment
of Michael Flynn—a favorite Trump general who'd been the opening act
at many Trump rallies—as the National Security Advisor.

"He's fine. He's not Jim Mattis and he's not John Kelly . . . but he's
fine. He just needs the right staff around him." Still, Bannon averred:
"When you take out all the never-Trump guys who signed all those letters
and all the neocons who got us in all these wars . . . it's not a deep bench."

Bannon said he'd tried to push John Bolton, the famously hawkish
diplomat, for the job as National Security Advisor. Bolton was an Ailes
favorite, too.

"He's a bomb thrower," said Ailes. "And a strange little fucker. But
you need him. Who else is good on Israel? Flynn is a little nutty on Iran.
Tillerson"—the secretary of state designate—"just knows oil."

"Bolton's mustache is a problem," snorted Bannon. "Trump doesn't think he looks the part. You know Bolton is an acquired taste."

"Well, he got in trouble because he got in a fight in a hotel one night and chased some woman."

"If I told Trump that, he might have the job."

* * *

Bannon was curiously able to embrace Trump while at the same time suggesting he did not take him entirely seriously. He had first met Trump, the on-again off-again presidential candidate, in 2010; at a meeting in Trump Tower, Bannon had proposed to Trump that he spend half a million dollars backing Tea Party–style candidates as a way to further his presidential ambitions. Bannon left the meeting figuring that Trump would never cough up that kind of dough. He just wasn't a serious player. Between that first encounter and mid-August 2016, when he took over the Trump campaign, Bannon, beyond a few interviews he had done with Trump for his Breitbart radio show, was pretty sure he hadn't spent more than ten minutes in one-on-one conversation with Trump.

But now Bannon's Zeitgeist moment had arrived. Everywhere there was a sudden sense of global self-doubt. Brexit in the UK, waves of immigrants arriving on Europe's angry shores, the disenfranchisement of the workingman, the specter of more financial meltdown, Bernie Sanders and his liberal revanchism—everywhere was backlash. Even the most dedicated exponents of globalism were hesitating. Bannon believed that great numbers of people were suddenly receptive to a new message: the world needs borders—or the world should return to a time when it had borders. When America was great. Trump had become the platform for that message.

By that January evening, Bannon had been immersed in Donald Trump's world for almost five months. And though he had accumulated a sizable catalogue of Trump's peculiarities, and cause enough for possible alarm about the unpredictability of his boss and his views, that did not detract from Trump's extraordinary, charismatic appeal to the right-wing, Tea Party, Internet meme base, and now, in victory, from the opportunity he was giving Steve Bannon.

* * *

"Does *he* get it?" asked Ailes suddenly, pausing and looking intently at Bannon.

He meant did Trump get it. This seemed to be a question about the right-wing agenda: Did the playboy billionaire really get the workingman populist cause? But it was possibly a point-blank question about the nature of power itself. Did Trump get where history had put him?

Bannon took a sip of water. "He gets it," said Bannon, after hesitating for perhaps a beat too long. "Or he gets what he gets."

With a sideways look, Ailes continued to stare him down, as though waiting for Bannon to show more of his cards.

"Really," Bannon said. "He's on the program. It's his program." Pivoting from Trump himself, Bannon plunged on with the Trump agenda. "Day one we're moving the U.S. embassy to Jerusalem. Netanyahu's all in. Sheldon"—Sheldon Adelson, the casino billionaire, far-right Israel defender, and Trump supporter—"is all in. We know where we're heading on this."

"Does Donald know?" asked a skeptical Ailes.

Bannon smiled—as though almost with a wink—and continued:

"Let Jordan take the West Bank, let Egypt take Gaza. Let them deal with it. Or sink trying. The Saudis are on the brink, Egyptians are on the brink, all scared to death of Persia . . . Yemen, Sinai, Libya . . . this thing is bad. . . . That's why Russia is so key. . . . Is Russia that bad? They're bad guys. But the world is full of bad guys."

Bannon offered all this with something like ebullience—a man remaking the world.

"But it's good to know the bad guys are the bad guys," said Ailes, pushing Bannon. "Donald may not know."

The real enemy, said an on-point Bannon, careful not to defend Trump too much or to dis him at all, was China. China was the first front in a new cold war. And it had all been misunderstood in the Obama years—what we thought we understood we didn't understand at all. That was the failure of American intelligence. "I think Comey is a third-rate guy. I think Brennan is a second-rate guy," Bannon said, dismissing the FBI director and the CIA director.

"The White House right now is like Johnson's White House in 1968. Susan Rice"—Obama's National Security Advisor—"is running the campaign against ISIS as a National Security Advisor. They're picking the targets, she's picking the drone strikes. I mean, they're running the war with just as much effectiveness as Johnson in sixty-eight. The Pentagon is totally disengaged from the whole thing. Intel services are disengaged from the whole thing. The media has let Obama off the hook. Take the ideology away from it, this is complete amateur hour. I don't know what Obama does. Nobody on Capitol Hill knows him, no business guys know him—what has he accomplished, what does he do?"

"Where's Donald on this?" asked Ailes, now with the clear implication that Bannon was far out ahead of his benefactor.

"He's totally on board."

"Focused?"

"He buys it."

"I wouldn't give Donald too much to think about," said an amused Ailes.

Bannon snorted. "Too much, too little—doesn't necessarily change things."

* * *

"What has he gotten himself into with the Russians?" pressed Ailes.

"Mostly," said Bannon, "he went to Russia and he thought he was going to meet Putin. But Putin couldn't give a shit about him. So he's kept trying."

"He's Donald," said Ailes.

"It's a magnificent thing," said Bannon, who had taken to regarding Trump as something like a natural wonder, beyond explanation.

Again, as though setting the issue of Trump aside—merely a large and peculiar presence to both be thankful for and to have to abide—Bannon, in the role he had conceived for himself, the auteur of the Trump presidency, charged forward:

"China's everything. Nothing else matters. We don't get China right, we don't get anything right. This whole thing is very simple. China is where Nazi Germany was in 1929 to 1930. The Chinese, like the Germans, are the most rational people in the world, until they're not. And they're gonna flip like Germany in the thirties. You're going to have a hypernationalist state, and once that happens you can't put the genie back in the bottle."

"Donald might not be Nixon in China," said Ailes, deadpan, suggesting that for Trump to seize the mantle of global transformation might strain credulity.

Bannon smiled. "Bannon in China," he said, with both remarkable grandiosity and wry self-deprecation.

"How's the kid?" asked Ailes, referring to Trump's son-in-law and paramount political adviser, thirty-six-year-old Jared Kushner.

"He's my partner," said Bannon, his tone suggesting that if he felt otherwise, he was nevertheless determined to stay on message.

"Really?" said a dubious Ailes.

"He's on the team."

"He's had lot of lunches with Rupert."

"In fact," said Bannon, "I could use your help here." Bannon then spent several minutes trying to recruit Ailes to help kneecap Murdoch. Ailes, since his ouster from Fox, had become only more bitter towards Murdoch. Now Murdoch was frequently jawboning the president-elect and encouraging him toward establishment moderation—all a strange inversion in the ever-stranger currents of American conservatism. Bannon wanted Ailes to suggest to Trump, a man whose many neuroses included a horror of forgetfulness or senility, that Murdoch might be losing it.

"I'll call him," said Ailes. "But Trump would jump through hoops for Rupert. Like for Putin. Sucks up and shits down. I just worry about who's jerking whose chain."

The older right-wing media wizard and the younger (though not by all that much) continued on to the other guests' satisfaction until twelve-thirty, the older trying to see through to the new national enigma that was Trump—although Ailes would say that in fact Trump's behavior was ever predictable—and the younger seemingly determined not to spoil his own moment of destiny.

"Donald Trump has got it. He's Trump, but he's got it. Trump is Trump," affirmed Bannon.

"Yeah, he's Trump," said Ailes, with something like incredulity.

# 1

## ELECTION DAY

On the afternoon of November 8, 2016, Kellyanne Conway—Donald Trump's campaign manager and a central, indeed starring, personality of Trumpworld—settled into her glass office at Trump Tower. Right up until the last weeks of the race, the Trump campaign headquarters had remained a listless place. All that seemed to distinguish it from a corporate back office were a few posters with right-wing slogans.

Conway now was in a remarkably buoyant mood considering she was about to experience a resounding if not cataclysmic defeat. Donald Trump would lose the election—of this she was sure—but he would quite possibly hold the defeat to under 6 points. That was a substantial victory. As for the looming defeat itself, she shrugged it off: it was Reince Priebus's fault, not hers.

She had spent a good part of the day calling friends and allies in the political world and blaming Priebus. Now she briefed some of the television producers and anchors with whom she'd built strong relationships—and with whom, actively interviewing in the last few weeks, she was hoping to land a permanent on-air job after the election. She'd carefully courted many of them since joining the Trump campaign in mid-August and becoming the campaign's reliably combative voice and, with her spasmodic smiles and strange combination of woundedness and imperturbability, peculiarly telegenic face.

Beyond all of the other horrible blunders of the campaign, the real problem, she said, was the devil they couldn't control: the Republican National Committee, which was run by Priebus, his sidekick, thirty-two-year-old Katie Walsh, and their flack, Sean Spicer. Instead of being all in, the RNC, ultimately the tool of the Republican establishment, had been hedging its bets ever since Trump won the nomination in early summer. When Trump needed the push, the push just wasn't there.

That was the first part of Conway's spin. The other part was that despite everything, the campaign had really clawed its way back from the abyss. A severely underresourced team with, practically speaking, the worst candidate in modern political history—Conway offered either an eye-rolling pantomime whenever Trump's name was mentioned, or a dead stare—had actually done extraordinarily well. Conway, who had never been involved in a national campaign, and who, before Trump, ran a small-time, down-ballot polling firm, understood full well that, post-campaign, she would now be one of the leading conservative voices on cable news.

In fact, one of the Trump campaign pollsters, John McLaughlin, had begun to suggest within the past week or so that some key state numbers, heretofore dismal, might actually be changing to Trump's advantage. But neither Conway nor Trump himself nor his son-in-law Jared Kushner—the effective head of the campaign, or the designated family monitor of it—wavered in their certainty: their unexpected adventure would soon be over.

Only Steve Bannon, in his odd-man view, insisted the numbers would break in their favor. But this being Bannon's view—crazy Steve—it was quite the opposite of being a reassuring one.

Almost everybody in the campaign, still an extremely small outfit, thought of themselves as a clear-eyed team, as realistic about their prospects as perhaps any in politics. The unspoken agreement among them: not only would Donald Trump *not* be president, he should probably not be. Conveniently, the former conviction meant nobody had to deal with the latter issue.

As the campaign came to an end, Trump himself was sanguine. He had survived the release of the Billy Bush tape when, in the uproar that followed, the RNC had had the gall to pressure him to quit the race. FBI director James Comey, having bizarrely hung Hillary out to dry by saying he was reopening the investigation into her emails eleven days before the election, had helped avert a total Clinton landslide.

"I can be the most famous man in the world," Trump told his on-again, off-again aide Sam Nunberg at the outset of the campaign.

"But do you want to be president?" Nunberg asked (a qualitatively different question than the usual existential candidate test: "Why do you want to be president?"). Nunberg did not get an answer.

The point was, there didn't need to be an answer because he wasn't going to be president.

Trump's longtime friend Roger Ailes liked to say that if you wanted a career in television, first run for president. Now Trump, encouraged by Ailes, was floating rumors about a Trump network. It was a great future.

He would come out of this campaign, Trump assured Ailes, with a far more powerful brand and untold opportunities. "This is bigger than I ever dreamed of," he told Ailes in a conversation a week before the election. "I don't think about losing because it isn't losing. We've totally won." What's more, he was already laying down his public response to losing the election: *It was stolen!*

Donald Trump and his tiny band of campaign warriors were ready to lose with fire and fury. They were not ready to win.

* * *

In politics somebody has to lose, but invariably everybody thinks they can win. And you probably can't win unless you believe that you will win—except in the Trump campaign.

The leitmotif for Trump about his own campaign was how crappy it was and how everybody involved in it was a loser. He was equally convinced that the Clinton people were brilliant winners—"They've got the best and we've got the worst," he frequently said. Time spent with Trump on the campaign plane was often an epic dissing experience: everybody around him was an idiot.

Corey Lewandowski, who served as Trump's first more or less official campaign manager, was often berated by the candidate. For months Trump called him "the worst," and in June 2016 he was finally fired. Ever after, Trump proclaimed his campaign doomed without Lewandowski. "We're all losers," he would say. "All our guys are terrible, nobody knows what they're doing. . . . Wish Corey was back." Trump quickly soured on his second campaign manager, Paul Manafort, as well.

By August, trailing Clinton by 12 to 17 points and facing a daily firestorm of eviscerating press, Trump couldn't conjure even a far-fetched scenario for achieving an electoral victory. At this dire moment, Trump in some essential sense sold his losing campaign. The right-wing billionaire Bob Mercer, a Ted Cruz backer, had shifted his support to Trump with a $5 million infusion. Believing the campaign was cratering, Mercer and his daughter Rebekah took a helicopter from their Long Island estate out to a scheduled fundraiser—with other potential donors bailing by the second—at New York Jets owner and Johnson & Johnson heir Woody Johnson's summer house in the Hamptons.

Trump had no real relationship with either father or daughter. He'd had only a few conversations with Bob Mercer, who mostly talked in monosyllables; Rebekah Mercer's entire history with Trump consisted of a selfie taken with him at Trump Tower. But when the Mercers presented their plan to take over the campaign and install their lieutenants, Steve Bannon and Kellyanne Conway, Trump didn't resist. He only expressed vast incomprehension about why anyone would want to do that. "This thing," he told the Mercers, "is so fucked up."

By every meaningful indicator, something greater than even a sense of doom shadowed what Steve Bannon called "the broke-dick campaign"—a sense of structural impossibility.

The candidate who billed himself as a billionaire—ten times over—refused even to invest his own money in it. Bannon told Jared Kushner—who, when Bannon signed on to the campaign, had been off with his wife on a holiday in Croatia with Trump enemy David Geffen—that, after the first debate in September, they would need an additional $50 million to cover them until election day.

"No way we'll get fifty million unless we can guarantee him victory," said a clear-eyed Kushner.

"Twenty-five million?" prodded Bannon.

"If we can say victory is more than likely."

In the end, the best Trump would do is loan the campaign $10 million, provided he got it back as soon as they could raise other money. (Steve Mnuchin, then the campaign's finance chairman, came to collect the loan with the wire instructions ready to go, so Trump couldn't conveniently forget to send the money.)

There was in fact no real campaign because there was no real organization, or at best only a uniquely dysfunctional one. Roger Stone, the early de facto campaign manager, quit or was fired by Trump—with each man publicly claiming he had slapped down the other. Sam Nunberg, a Trump aide who had worked for Stone, was noisily ousted by Lewandowski, and then Trump exponentially increased the public dirty-clothes-washing by suing Nunberg. Lewandowski and Hope Hicks, the PR aide put on the campaign by Ivanka Trump, had an affair that ended in a public fight on the street—an incident cited by Nunberg in his response to Trump's suit. The campaign, on its face, was not designed to win anything.

Even as Trump eliminated the sixteen other Republican candidates, however far-fetched that might have seemed, it did not make the ultimate goal of winning the presidency any less preposterous.

And if, during the fall, winning seemed slightly more plausible, that evaporated with the Billy Bush affair. "I'm automatically attracted to beautiful—I just start kissing them," Trump told the NBC host Billy Bush on an open mic, amid the ongoing national debate about sexual harassment. "It's like a magnet. Just kiss. I don't even wait. And when you're a star they let you do it. You can do anything. . . . Grab them by the pussy. You can do anything."

It was an operatic unraveling. So mortifying was this development that when Reince Priebus, the RNC head, was called to New York from Washington for an emergency meeting at Trump Tower, he couldn't bring himself to leave Penn Station. It took two hours for the Trump team to coax him across town.

"Bro," said a desperate Bannon, cajoling Priebus on the phone, "I may never see you again after today, but you gotta come to this building and you gotta walk through the front door."

* * *

The silver lining of the ignominy Melania Trump had to endure after the Billy Bush tape was that now there was no way her husband could become president.

Donald Trump's marriage was perplexing to almost everybody around him—or it was, anyway, for those without private jets and many homes. He and Melania spent relatively little time together. They could go days at a time without contact, even when they were both in Trump Tower. Often she did not know where he was, or take much notice of that fact. Her husband moved between residences as he would move between rooms. Along with knowing little about his whereabouts, she knew little about his business, and took at best modest interest in it. An absentee father for his first four children, Trump was even more absent for his fifth, Barron, his son with Melania. Now on his third marriage, he told friends he thought he had finally perfected the art: live and let live—"Do your own thing."

He was a notorious womanizer, and during the campaign became possibly the world's most famous masher. While nobody would ever say Trump was sensitive when it came to women, he had many views about how to get along with them, including a theory he discussed with friends about how the more years between an older man and a younger woman, the less the younger woman took an older man's cheating personally.

Still, the notion that this was a marriage in name only was far from true. He spoke of Melania frequently when she wasn't there. He admired her looks—often, awkwardly for her, in the presence of others. She was, he told people proudly and without irony, a "trophy wife." And while he may not have quite shared his life with her, he gladly shared the spoils of it. "A happy wife is a happy life," he said, echoing a popular rich-man truism.

He also sought Melania's approval. (He sought the approval of all the women around him, who were wise to give it.) In 2014, when he first seriously began to consider running for president, Melania was one of the few who thought it was possible he could win. It was a punch line for his daughter, Ivanka, who had carefully distanced herself from the campaign. With a never-too-hidden distaste for her stepmother, Ivanka would say to friends: *All you have to know about Melania is that she thinks if he runs he'll certainly win.*

But the prospect of her husband's actually becoming president was, for Melania, a horrifying one. She believed it would destroy her carefully sheltered life—one sheltered, not inconsiderably, from the extended Trump family—which was almost entirely focused on her young son.

Don't put the cart before the horse, her amused husband said, even as he spent every day on the campaign trail, dominating the news. But her terror and torment mounted.

There was a whisper campaign about her, cruel and comical in its insinuations, going on in Manhattan, which friends told her about. Her modeling career was under close scrutiny. In Slovenia, where she grew up, a celebrity magazine, *Suzy*, put the rumors about her into print after Trump got the nomination. Then, with a sickening taste of what might be ahead, the *Daily Mail* blew the story across the world.

The *New York Post* got its hands on outtakes from a nude photo shoot that Melania had done early in her modeling career—a leak that everybody other than Melania assumed could be traced back to Trump himself.

Inconsolable, she confronted her husband. Is this the future? She told him she wouldn't be able to take it.

Trump responded in his fashion—*We'll sue!*—and set her up with lawyers. But he was unaccustomedly contrite, too. Just a little longer, he told her. It would all be over in November. He offered his wife a solemn guarantee: there was simply no way he would win. And even for a chronically—he would say helplessly—unfaithful husband, this was one promise to his wife that he seemed sure to keep.

* * *

The Trump campaign had, perhaps less than inadvertently, replicated the scheme from Mel Brooks's *The Producers*. In that classic, Brooks's larcenous and dopey heroes, Max Bialystock and Leo Bloom, set out to sell more than 100 percent of the ownership stakes in the Broadway show they are producing. Since they will be found out only if the show is a hit, everything about the show is premised on its being a flop. Accordingly,

they create a show so outlandish that it actually succeeds, thus doom-
ing our heroes.

Winning presidential candidates—driven by hubris or narcissism or
a preternatural sense of destiny—have, more than likely, spent a substantial
part of their careers, if not their lives from adolescence, preparing for the
role. They rise up the ladder of elected offices. They perfect a public face.
They manically network, since success in politics is largely about who
your allies are. They cram. (Even in the case of an uninterested George W.
Bush, he relied on his father's cronies to cram for him.) And they clean
up after themselves—or, at least, take great care to cover up. They prepare
themselves to win and to govern.

The Trump calculation, quite a conscious one, was different. The candidate and his top lieutenants believed they could get all the benefits of
*almost* becoming president without having to change their behavior or
their fundamental worldview one whit: we don't have to be anything but
who and what we are, because of course we won't win.

Many candidates for president have made a virtue of being Washington outsiders; in practice, this strategy merely favors governors over sen-
ators. Every serious candidate, no matter how much he or she disses
Washington, relies on Beltway insiders for counsel and support. But with
Trump, hardly a person in his innermost circle had ever worked in politics
at the national level—his closest advisers had not worked in politics at
all. Throughout his life, Trump had few close friends of any kind, but
when he began his campaign for president he had almost no friends in
politics. The only two actual politicians with whom Trump was close were
Rudy Giuliani and Chris Christie, and both men were in their own way
peculiar and isolated. And to say that he knew nothing—nothing at all—
about the basic intellectual foundations of the job was a comic understatement. Early in the campaign, in a *Producers*-worthy scene, Sam
Nunberg was sent to explain the Constitution to the candidate: "I got as
far as the Fourth Amendment before his finger is pulling down on his lip
and his eyes are rolling back in his head."

Almost everybody on the Trump team came with the kind of messy
conflicts bound to bite a president or his staff. Mike Flynn, Trump's
future National Security Advisor, who became Trump's opening act at

campaign rallies and whom Trump loved to hear complain about the CIA and the haplessness of American spies, had been told by his friends that it had not been a good idea to take $45,000 from the Russians for a speech. "Well, it would only be a problem if we won," he assured them, knowing that it would therefore not be a problem.

Paul Manafort, the international lobbyist and political operative who Trump retained to run his campaign after Lewandowski was fired—and who agreed not to take a fee, amping up questions of quid pro quo—had spent thirty years representing dictators and corrupt despots, amassing millions of dollars in a money trail that had long caught the eye of U.S. investigators. What's more, when he joined the campaign, he was being pursued, his every financial step documented, by the billionaire Russian oligarch Oleg Deripaska, who claimed he stole $17 million from him in a crooked real estate scam and had sworn a blood revenge.

For quite obvious reasons, no president before Trump and few politicians ever have come out of the real estate business: a lightly regulated market, based on substantial debt with exposure to frequent market fluctuations, it often depends on government favor, and is a preferred exchange currency for problem cash—money laundering. Trump's son-in-law Jared Kushner, Jared's father Charlie, Trump's sons Don Jr. and Eric, and his daughter Ivanka, as well as Trump himself, all supported their business enterprises to a greater or lesser extent working in the dubious limbo of international free cash flow and gray money. Charlie Kushner, to whose real estate business interests Trump's son-in-law and most important aide was wholly tied, had already spent time in a federal prison for tax evasion, witness tampering, and making illegal campaign donations.

Modern politicians and their staffs perform their most consequential piece of opposition research on themselves. If the Trump team had vetted their candidate, they would have reasonably concluded that heightened ethical scrutiny could easily put them in jeopardy. But Trump pointedly performed no such effort. Roger Stone, Trump's longtime political adviser, explained to Steve Bannon that Trump's psychic makeup made it impossible for him to take such a close look at himself. Nor could he tolerate knowing that somebody else would then know a lot about him—and therefore have something over him. And anyway, why take such a close and potentially threatening look, because what were the chances of winning?

Not only did Trump disregard the potential conflicts of his business deals and real estate holdings, he audaciously refused to release his tax returns. Why should he if he wasn't going to win?

What's more, Trump refused to spend any time considering, however hypothetically, transition matters, saying it was "bad luck"—but really meaning it was a waste of time. Nor would he even remotely contemplate the issue of his holdings and conflicts.

*He wasn't going to win! Or losing was winning.*

Trump would be the most famous man in the world—a martyr to crooked Hillary Clinton.

His daughter Ivanka and son-in-law Jared would have transformed themselves from relatively obscure rich kids into international celebrities and brand ambassadors.

Steve Bannon would become the de facto head of the Tea Party movement.

Kellyanne Conway would be a cable news star.

Reince Priebus and Katie Walsh would get their Republican Party back.

Melania Trump could return to inconspicuously lunching.

That was the trouble-free outcome they awaited on November 8, 2016. Losing would work out for everybody.

Shortly after eight o'clock that evening, when the unexpected trend—Trump might actually win—seemed confirmed, Don Jr. told a friend that his father, or DJT, as he called him, looked as if he had seen a ghost. Melania, to whom Donald Trump had made his solemn guarantee, was in tears—and not of joy.

There was, in the space of little more than an hour, in Steve Bannon's not unamused observation, a befuddled Trump morphing into a disbelieving Trump and then into a quite horrified Trump. But still to come was the final transformation: suddenly, Donald Trump became a man who believed that he deserved to be and was wholly capable of being the president of the United States.

# 2

# TRUMP TOWER

On the Saturday after the election, Donald Trump received a small group of well-wishers in his triplex apartment in Trump Tower. Even his close friends were still shocked and bewildered, and there was a dazed quality to the gathering. But Trump himself was mostly looking at the clock.

Rupert Murdoch, heretofore doubtlessly certain Trump was a charlatan and a fool, said he and his new wife, Jerry Hall, would pay a call on the president-elect. But Murdoch was late—quite late. Trump kept assuring his guests that Rupert was on his way, coming soon. When some of the guests made a move to leave, Trump cajoled them to stay a little longer. *You'll want to stay to see Rupert.* (Or, one of the guests interpreted, you'll want to stay to see Trump with Rupert.)

Murdoch, who, with his then wife, Wendi, had often socialized with Jared and Ivanka, in the past made little effort to hide his lack of interest in Trump. Murdoch's fondness for Kushner created a curious piece of the power dynamic between Trump and his son-in-law, one that Kushner, with reasonable subtly, played to his advantage, often dropping Murdoch's name into conversations with his father-in-law. When, in 2015, Ivanka Trump told Murdoch that her father really, truly was going to run for president, Murdoch dismissed the possibility out of hand.

But now, the new president-elect—after the most astonishing upset in American history—was on tenterhooks waiting for Murdoch. "He's one of the greats," he told his guests, becoming more agitated as he waited. "Really, he's one of the greats, the last of the greats. You have to stay to see him."

It was a matched set of odd reversals—an ironic symmetry. Trump, perhaps not yet appreciating the difference between becoming president and elevating his social standing, was trying mightily to curry favor with the previously disdainful media mogul. And Murdoch, finally arriving at the party he was in more than one way sorely late to, was as subdued and thrown as everyone else, and struggling to adjust his view of a man who, for more than a generation, had been at best a clown prince among the rich and famous.

* * *

Murdoch was hardly the only billionaire who had been dismissive of Trump. In the years before the election, Carl Icahn, whose friendship Trump often cited, and who Trump had suggested he'd appoint to high office, openly ridiculed his fellow billionaire (whom he said was not remotely a billionaire).

Few people who knew Trump had illusions about him. That was almost his appeal: he was what he was. Twinkle in his eye, larceny in his soul.

But now he was the president-elect. And that, in a reality jujitsu, changed everything. So say whatever you want about him, he had done this. Pulled the sword from the stone. That meant something. *Everything.*

The billionaires had to rethink. So did everyone in the Trump orbit. The campaign staff, now suddenly in a position to snag West Wing jobs—career- and history-making jobs—had to see this odd, difficult, even ridiculous, and, on the face of it, ill-equipped person in a new light. He had been elected president. So he was, as Kellyanne Conway liked to point out, by definition, presidential.

Still, nobody had yet seen him be presidential—that is, make a public bow to political ritual and propriety. Or even to exercise some modest self-control.

Others were now recruited and, despite their obvious impressions of the man, agreed to sign on. Jim Mattis, a retired four-star general, one of the most respected commanders in the U.S. armed forces; Rex Tillerson, CEO of ExxonMobil; Scott Pruitt and Betsy DeVos, Jeb Bush loyalists—all of them were now focused on the singular fact that while he might be a peculiar figure, even an absurd-seeming one, he had been elected president.

We can make this work, is what everybody in the Trump orbit was suddenly saying. Or, at the very least, this *could possibly* work.

In fact, up close, Trump was not the bombastic and pugilistic man who had stirred rabid crowds on the campaign trail. He was neither angry nor combative. He may have been the most threatening and frightening and menacing presidential candidate in modern history, but in person he could seem almost soothing. His extreme self-satisfaction rubbed off. Life was sunny. Trump was an optimist—at least about himself. He was charming and full of flattery; he focused on you. He was funny—self-deprecating even. And incredibly energetic—*Let's do it* whatever it is, *let's do it.* He wasn't a tough guy. He was "a big warm-hearted monkey," said Bannon, with rather faint praise.

PayPal cofounder and Facebook board member Peter Thiel—really the only significant Silicon Valley voice to support Trump—was warned by another billionaire and longtime Trump friend that Trump would, in an explosion of flattery, offer Thiel his undying friendship. *Everybody says you're great, you and I are going to have an amazing working relationship, anything you want, call me and we'll get it done!* Thiel was advised not to take Trump's offer too seriously. But Thiel, who gave a speech supporting Trump at the Republican Convention in Cleveland, reported back that, even having been forewarned, he absolutely was certain of Trump's sincerity when he said they'd be friends for life—only never to basically hear from him again or have his calls returned. Still, power provides its own excuses for social lapses. Other aspects of the Trump character were more problematic.

Almost all the professionals who were now set to join him were coming face to face with the fact that it appeared he knew nothing. There was simply no subject, other than perhaps building construction, that he had substantially mastered. Everything with him was off the cuff. Whatever he knew he seemed to have learned an hour before—and that was mostly half-baked. But each member of the new Trump team was convincing him- or herself otherwise—because what did they know, the man had been elected president. He offered something, obviously. Indeed, while everybody in his rich-guy social circle knew about his wide-ranging ignorance—Trump, the businessman, could not even read a balance sheet, and Trump, who had campaigned on his deal-making skills, was, with his inattention to details, a terrible negotiator—they yet found him somehow *instinctive*. That was the word. He was a force of personality. He could make you believe.

"Is Trump a good person, an intelligent person, a capable person?" asked Sam Nunberg, Trump's longtime political aide. "I don't even know. But I know he's a star."

Trying to explain Trump's virtues and his attraction, Piers Morgan—the British newspaper man and ill-fated CNN anchor who had appeared on *Celebrity Apprentice* and stayed a loyal Trump friend—said it was all in Trump's book *The Art of the Deal*. Everything that made him Trump and that defined his savvy, energy, and charisma was there. If you wanted to know Trump, just read the book. But Trump had not written *The Art of the Deal*. His co-writer, Tony Schwartz, insisted that he had hardly contributed to it and might not even have read all of it. And that was perhaps the point. Trump was not a writer, he was a character—a protagonist and hero.

A pro wrestling fan who became a World Wrestling Entertainment supporter and personality (inducted into the WWE Hall of Fame), Trump lived, like Hulk Hogan, as a real-life fictional character. To the amusement of his friends, and unease of many of the people now preparing to work for him at the highest levels of the federal government, Trump often spoke of himself in the third person. Trump did this. The Trumpster did that. So powerful was this persona, or role, that he seemed reluctant, or unable, to give it up in favor of being president—or presidential.

However difficult he was, many of those now around him tried to justify his behavior—tried to find an explanation for his success in it, to understand it as an advantage, not a limitation. For Steve Bannon, Trump's unique political virtue was as an alpha male, maybe the last of the alpha males. A 1950s man, a Rat Pack type, a character out of *Mad Men*.

Trump's understanding of his own essential nature was even more precise. Once, coming back on his plane with a billionaire friend who had brought along a foreign model, Trump, trying to move in on his friend's date, urged a stop in Atlantic City. He would provide a tour of his casino. His friend assured the model that there was nothing to recommend Atlantic City. It was a place overrun by white trash.

"What is this 'white trash'?" asked the model.

"They're people just like me," said Trump, "only they're poor."

He looked for a license not to conform, not to be respectable. It was something of an outlaw prescription for winning—and winning, however you won, was what it was all about.

Or, as his friends would observe, mindful themselves not to be taken in, he simply had no scruples. He was a rebel, a disruptor, and, living outside the rules, contemptuous of them. A close Trump friend who was also a good Bill Clinton friend found them eerily similar—except that Clinton had a respectable front and Trump did not.

One manifestation of this outlaw personality, for both Trump and Clinton, was their brand of womanizing—and indeed, harassing. Even among world-class womanizers and harassers, they seemed exceptionally free of doubt or hesitation.

Trump liked to say that one of the things that made life worth living was getting your friends' wives into bed. In pursuing a friend's wife, he would try to persuade the wife that her husband was perhaps not what she thought. Then he'd have his secretary ask the friend into his office; once the friend arrived, Trump would engage in what was, for him, more or less constant sexual banter. *Do you still like having sex with your wife? How often? You must have had a better fuck than your wife? Tell me about it. I have girls coming in from Los Angeles at three o'clock. We can go upstairs and have a great time. I promise . . .* And all the while, Trump would have his friend's wife on the speakerphone, listening in.

Previous presidents, and not just Clinton, have of course lacked scruples. What was, to many of the people who knew Trump well, much more confounding was that he had managed to win this election, and arrive at this ultimate accomplishment, wholly lacking what in some obvious sense must be the main requirement of the job, what neuroscientists would call executive function. He had somehow won the race for president, but his brain seemed incapable of performing what would be essential tasks in his new job. He had no ability to plan and organize and pay attention and switch focus; he had never been able to tailor his behavior to what the goals at hand reasonably required. On the most basic level, he simply could not link cause and effect.

The charge that Trump colluded with the Russians to win the election, which he scoffed at, was, in the estimation of some of his friends, a perfect example of his inability to connect the dots. Even if he hadn't personally conspired with the Russians to fix the election, his efforts to curry favor with, of all people, Vladimir Putin had no doubt left a trail of alarming words and deeds likely to have enormous political costs.

Shortly after the election, his friend Ailes told him, with some urgency, "You've got to get right on Russia." Even exiled from Fox News, Ailes still maintained a fabled intelligence network. He warned Trump of potentially damaging material coming his way. "You need to take this seriously, Donald."

"Jared has this," said a happy Trump. "It's all worked out."

\* \* \*

Trump Tower, next door to Tiffany and now headquarters of a populist revolution, suddenly seemed like an alien spaceship—the Death Star—on Fifth Avenue. As the great and good and ambitious, as well as angry protesters and the curious hoi polloi, began beating a path to the next president's door, mazelike barricades were hurriedly thrown up to shield him.

The Pre-Election Presidential Transition Act of 2010 established funding for presidential nominees to start the process of vetting thousands of candidates for jobs in a new administration, codifying policies that would determine the early actions of a new White House, and preparing for the handoff of bureaucratic responsibilities on January 20. During the campaign, New Jersey governor Chris Christie, the nominal head of the Trump transition office, had to forcefully tell the candidate that he couldn't redirect these funds, that the law required him to spend the money and plan for a transition—even one he did not expect to need. A frustrated Trump said he didn't want to hear any more about it.

The day after the election, Trump's close advisers—suddenly eager to be part of a process that almost everybody had ignored—immediately began blaming Christie for a lack of transition preparations. Hurriedly, the bare-bones transition team moved from downtown Washington to Trump Tower.

This was certainly some of the most expensive real estate ever occupied by a transition team (and, for that matter, a presidential campaign). And that was part of the point. It sent a Trump-style message: we're not only outsiders, but we're more powerful than you insiders. Richer. More famous. With better real estate.

And, of course, it was personalized: his name, fabulously, was on the door. Upstairs was his triplex apartment, vastly larger than the White House living quarters. Here was his private office, which he'd occupied since the 1980s. And here were the campaign and now transition floors—firmly in his orbit and not that of Washington and the "swamp."

Trump's instinct in the face of his unlikely, if not preposterous, success was the opposite of humility. It was, in some sense, to rub everybody's face in it. Washington insiders, or would-be insiders, would have to come to him. Trump Tower immediately upstaged the White House. Everybody who came to see the president-elect was acknowledging, or accepting, an outsider government. Trump forced them to endure what was gleefully called by insiders the "perp walk" in front of press and assorted gawkers. An act of obeisance, if not humiliation.

The otherworldly sense of Trump Tower helped obscure the fact that few in the thin ranks of Trump's inner circle, with their overnight responsibility for assembling a government, had almost any relevant experience. Nobody had a political background. Nobody had a policy background. Nobody had a legislative background.

Politics is a network business, a who-you-know business. But unlike other presidents-elect—all of whom invariably suffered from their own management defects—Trump did not have a career's worth of political and

government contacts to call on. He hardly even had his own political organization. For most of the last eighteen months on the road, it had been, at its
core, a three-person enterprise: his campaign manager, Corey Lewandowski (until he was forced out a month before the Republican National
Convention); his spokesperson-bodyperson-intern, the campaign's first
hire, twenty-six-year-old Hope Hicks; and Trump himself. Lean and mean
and gut instincts—the more people you had to deal with, Trump found,
the harder it was to turn the plane around and get home to bed at night.

The professional team—although in truth there was hardly a political
professional among them—that had joined the campaign in August was
a last-ditch bid to avoid hopeless humiliation. But these were people he'd
worked with for just a few months.

Reince Priebus, getting ready to shift over from the RNC to the White
House, noted, with alarm, how often Trump offered people jobs on the
spot, many of whom he had never met before, for positions whose importance Trump did not particularly understand.

Ailes, a veteran of the Nixon, Reagan, and Bush 41 White Houses,
was growing worried by the president-elect's lack of immediate focus on
a White House structure that could serve and protect him. He tried to
impress on Trump the ferocity of the opposition that would greet him.

"You need a son of a bitch as your chief of staff. And you need a son
of a bitch who knows Washington," Ailes told Trump not long after the
election. "You'll want to be your own son of a bitch, but you don't know
Washington." Ailes had a suggestion: "Speaker Boehner." (John Boehner
had been the Speaker of the House until he was forced out in a Tea Party
putsch in 2011.)

"Who's that?" asked Trump.

Everybody in Trump's billionaire circle, concerned about his contempt for other people's expertise, tried to impress upon him the importance of the people, the many people, he would need with him in the
White House, people who understood Washington. *Your people are more
important than your policies. Your people* are *your policies.*

"Frank Sinatra was wrong," said David Bossie, one of Trump's longtime political advisers. "If you can make it in New York, you can't necessarily make it in Washington."

* * *

The nature of the role of the modern chief of staff is a focus of much White House scholarship. As much as the president himself, the chief of staff determines how the White House and executive branch—which employs 4 million people, including 1.3 million people in the armed services—will run.

The job has been construed as deputy president, or chief operating officer, or even prime minister. Larger-than-life chiefs have included Richard Nixon's H. R. Haldeman and Alexander Haig; Gerald Ford's Donald Rumsfeld and Dick Cheney; Jimmy Carter's Hamilton Jordan; Ronald Reagan's James Baker; George H. W. Bush's return of James Baker; Bill Clinton's Leon Panetta, Erskine Bowles, and John Podesta; George W. Bush's Andrew Card; and Barack Obama's Rahm Emanuel and Bill Daley. Anyone studying the position would conclude that a stronger chief of staff is better than a weaker one, and a chief of staff with a history in Washington and the federal government is better than an outsider.

Donald Trump had little, if any, awareness of the history of or the thinking about this role. Instead, he substituted his own management style and experience. For decades, he had relied on longtime retainers, cronies, and family. Even though Trump liked to portray his business as an empire, it was actually a discrete holding company and boutique enterprise, catering more to his peculiarities as proprietor and brand representative than to any bottom line or other performance measures.

His sons, Don Jr. and Eric—behind their backs known to Trump insiders as Uday and Qusay, after the sons of Saddam Hussein—wondered if there couldn't somehow be two parallel White House structures, one dedicated to their father's big-picture views, personal appearances, and salesmanship and the other concerned with day-to-day management issues. In this construct, they saw themselves tending to the day-to-day operations.

One of Trump's early ideas was to recruit his friend Tom Barrack—part of his kitchen cabinet of real estate tycoons including Steven Roth and Richard Lefrak—and make him chief of staff.

Barrack, the grandson of Lebanese immigrants, is a starstruck real estate investor of legendary acumen who owns Michael Jackson's former oddball paradise, Neverland Ranch. With Jeffrey Epstein—the New York financier who would become a tabloid regular after accusations of sex with underage girls and a guilty plea to one count of soliciting prostitution that sent him to jail in 2008 in Palm Beach for thirteen months—Trump and Barrack were a 1980s and '90s set of nightlife Musketeers.

The founder and CEO of the private equity firm Colony Capital, Barrack became a billionaire making investments in distress debt investments in real estate around the world, including helping to bail out his friend Donald Trump. More recently, he had helped bail out his friend's son-in-law, Jared Kushner.

He watched with amusement Trump's eccentric presidential campaign and brokered the deal to have Paul Manafort replace Corey Lewandowski after Lewandowski fell out of favor with Kushner. Then, as confounded as everyone else by the campaign's continuing successes, Barrack introduced the future president in warm and personal terms at the Republican National Convention in July (at odds with its otherwise dark and belligerent tone).

It was Trump's perfect fantasy that his friend Tom—an organizational whiz fully aware of his friend's lack of interest in day-to-day management—would sign on to run the White House. This was Trump's instant and convenient solution to the unforeseen circumstance of suddenly being president: to do it with his business mentor, confidant, investor, and friend, someone whom acquaintances of the two men describe as "being one of the best Donald handlers." In the Trump circle this was called the "two amigos" plan. (Epstein, who remained close to Barrack, had been whitewashed out of the Trump biography.)

Barrack, among the few people whose abilities Trump, a reflexive naysayer, didn't question, could, in Trump's hopeful view, really get things running smoothly and let Trump be Trump. It was, on Trump's part, an uncharacteristic piece of self-awareness: Donald Trump might not know what he didn't know, but he knew Tom Barrack knew. He would run the business and Trump would sell the product—making American great again. #MAGA.

For Barrack, as for everybody around Trump, the election result was a kind of beyond-belief lottery-winning circumstance—your implausible friend becoming president. But Barrack, even after countless pleading and cajoling phone calls from Trump, finally had to disappoint his friend, telling him "I'm just too rich." He would never be able to untangle his holdings and interests—including big investments in the Middle East—in a way that would satisfy ethics watchdogs. Trump was unconcerned or in denial about his own business conflicts, but Barrack saw nothing but hassle and cost for himself. Also, Barrack, on his fourth marriage, had no appetite for having his colorful personal life—often, over the years, conducted with Trump—become a public focus.

\* \* \*

Trump's fallback was his son-in-law. On the campaign, after months of turmoil and outlandishness (if not to Trump, to most others, including his family), Kushner had stepped in and become his effective body man, hovering nearby, speaking only when spoken to, but then always offering a calming and flattering view. Corey Lewandowski called Jared the butler. Trump had come to believe that his son-in-law, in part because he seemed to understand how to stay out of his way, was uniquely sagacious.

In defiance of law and tone, and everybody's disbelieving looks, the president seemed intent on surrounding himself in the White House with his family. The Trumps, all of them—except for his wife, who, mystifyingly, was staying in New York—were moving in, all of them set to assume responsibilities similar to their status in the Trump Organization, without anyone apparently counseling against it.

Finally, it was the right-wing diva and Trump supporter Ann Coulter who took the president-elect aside and said, "Nobody is apparently telling you this. But you can't. You just can't hire your children."

Trump continued to insist that he had every right to his family's help, while at the same time asking for understanding. This is family, he said— "It's a *leettle, leettle* tricky." His staffers understood not only the inherent conflicts and difficult legal issues in having Trump's son-in-law run the White House, but that it would become, even more than it already was, family first for Trump. After a great deal of pressure, he at least agreed not to make his son-in-law the chief of staff—not officially, anyway.

* * *

If not Barrack or Kushner, then, Trump thought the job should probably go to New Jersey governor Chris Christie, who, with Rudy Giuliani, comprised the sum total of his circle of friends with actual political experience.

Christie, like most Trump allies, fell in and out of favor. In the final weeks of the campaign, Trump contemptuously measured Christie's increasing distance from his losing enterprise, and then, with victory, his eagerness to get back in.

Trump and Christie went back to Trump's days trying—and failing—to become an Atlantic City gaming mogul. *The* Atlantic City gaming mogul. (Trump had long been competitive with and in awe of the Las Vegas gaming mogul Steve Wynn, whom Trump would name finance chairman of the RNC.) Trump had backed Christie as he rose through New Jersey politics. He admired Christie's straight-talk style, and for a while, as Christie anticipated his own presidential run in 2012 and 2013—and as Trump was looking for a next chapter for himself with the fading of *The Apprentice*, his reality TV franchise—Trump even wondered whether he might be a vice presidential possibility for Christie.

Early in the campaign, Trump said he wouldn't have run against Christie but for the Bridgegate scandal (which erupted when Christie's associates closed traffic lanes on the George Washington Bridge to undermine the mayor of a nearby town who was a Christie opponent, and which Trump privately justified as "just New Jersey hardball"). When Christie dropped out of the race in February 2016 and signed on with the Trump campaign, he endured a torrent of ridicule for supporting his friend, whom he believed had promised him a clear track to the VP slot.

It had personally pained Trump not to be able to give it to him. But if the Republican establishment had not wanted Trump, they had not wanted Christie almost as much. So Christie got the job of leading the transition and the implicit promise of a central job—attorney general or chief of staff.

But when he was the federal prosecutor in New Jersey, Christie had sent Jared's father, Charles Kushner, to jail in 2005. Charlie Kushner, pursued by the feds for an income tax cheat, set up a scheme with a prostitute to blackmail his brother-in-law, who was planning to testify against him.

Various accounts, mostly offered by Christie himself, make Jared the vengeful hatchet man in Christie's aborted Trump administration career. It was a kind of perfect sweet-revenge story: the son of the wronged man (or, in this case—there's little dispute—the guilty-as-charged man) uses his power over the man who wronged his family. But other accounts offer a subtler and in a way darker picture. Jared Kushner, like sons-in-law everywhere, tiptoes around his father-in-law, carefully displacing as little air as possible: the massive and domineering older man, the reedy and pliant younger one. In the revised death-of-Chris-Christie story, it is not the deferential Jared who strikes back, but—in some sense even more satisfying for the revenge fantasy—Charlie Kushner himself who harshly demands his due. It was his daughter-in-law who held the real influence in the Trump circle, who delivered the blow. Ivanka told her father that Christie's appointment as chief of staff or to any other high position would be extremely difficult for her and her family, and it would be best that Christie be removed from the Trump orbit altogether.

* * *

Bannon was the heavy of the organization. Trump, who seemed awestruck by Bannon's conversation—a mix of insults, historical riffs, media insights, right-wing bons mots, and motivational truisms—now began suggesting Bannon to his circle of billionaires as chief of staff, only to have this notion soundly ridiculed and denounced. But Trump pronounced many people in favor of it anyway.

In the weeks leading up to the election, Trump had labeled Bannon a flatterer for his certainty that Trump would win. But now he had come to credit Bannon with something like mystical powers. And in fact Bannon, with no prior political experience, was the only Trump insider able to offer a coherent vision of Trump's populism—aka Trumpism.

The anti-Bannon forces—which included almost every non–Tea Party

Republican—were quick to react. Murdoch, a growing Bannon nemesis, told Trump that Bannon would be a dangerous choice. Joe Scarborough, the former congressman and cohost of MSNBC's *Morning Joe*, a favorite Trump show, privately told Trump "Washington will go up in flames" if Bannon became chief of staff, and, beginning a running theme, publicly denigrated Bannon on the show.

In fact, Bannon presented even bigger problems than his politics: he was profoundly disorganized, seemingly on the spectrum given what captured his single-minded focus to the disregard of everything else. Might he be the worst manager who ever lived? He might. He seemed incapable of returning a phone call. He answered emails in one word— partly a paranoia about email, but even more a controlling crypticness. He kept assistants and minders at constant bay. You couldn't really make an appointment with Bannon, you just had to show up. And somehow, his own key lieutenant, Alexandra Preate, a conservative fundraiser and PR woman, was as disorganized as he was. After three marriages, Bannon lived his bachelor's life on Capitol Hill in a row house known as the Breitbart Embassy that doubled as the Breitbart office—the life of a messy party. No sane person would hire Steven Bannon for a job that included making the trains run on time.

* * *

Hence, Reince Priebus.

For the Hill, he was the only reasonable chief among the contenders, and he quickly became the subject of intense lobbying by House Speaker Paul Ryan and Senate Majority Leader Mitch McConnell. If they were going to have to deal with an alien like Donald Trump, then best they do it with the help of a member of their own kind.

Priebus, forty-five, was neither politician nor policy wonk nor strategist. He was political machine worker, one of the oldest professions. A fundraiser.

A working-class kid originally from New Jersey and then Wisconsin, at thirty-two he made his first and last run for elective office: a failed bid for Wisconsin state senate. He became the chairman of the state party and then the general counsel of the Republican National Committee. In

2011 he stepped up to chairmanship of the RNC. Priebus's political cred came from appeasing the Tea Party in Wisconsin, and his association with Wisconsin governor Scott Walker, a rising Republican star (and, briefly—very briefly—the 2016 front-runner).

With significant parts of the Republican Party inalterably opposed to Trump, and with an almost universal belief within the party that Trump would go down to ignominious defeat, taking the party with him, Priebus was under great pressure after Trump captured the nomination to shift resources down the ticket and even to abandon the Trump campaign entirely.

Convinced himself that Trump was hopeless, Priebus nevertheless hedged his bets. The fact that he did not abandon Trump entirely became a possible margin of victory and made Priebus something of a hero (equally, in the Kellyanne Conway version, if they had lost, he would have been a reasonable target). He became the default choice for chief.

And yet his entry into the Trump inner circle caused Priebus his share of uncertainty and bewilderment. He came out of his first long meeting with Trump thinking it had been a disconcertingly weird experience. Trump talked nonstop and constantly repeated himself.

"Here's the deal," a close Trump associate told Priebus. "In an hour meeting with him you're going to hear fifty-four minutes of stories and they're going to be the same stories over and over again. So you have to have one point to make and you have to pepper it in whenever you can."

The Priebus appointment as chief of staff, announced in mid-November, also put Bannon on a coequal level. Trump was falling back on his own natural inclinations to let nobody have real power. Priebus, even with the top job, would be a weaker sort of figure, in the traditional mold of most Trump lieutenants over the years. The choice also worked well for the other would-be chiefs. Tom Barrack could easily circumvent Priebus and continue to speak directly to Trump. Jared Kushner's position as son-in-law and soon top aide would not be impeded. And Steve Bannon, reporting directly to Trump, remained the undisputed voice of Trumpism in the White House.

There would be, in other words, one chief of staff in name—the unimportant one—and various others, more important, in practice, ensuring both chaos and Trump's own undisputed independence.

Jim Baker, chief of staff for both Ronald Reagan and George H. W. Bush and almost everybody's model for managing the West Wing, advised Priebus not to take the job.

* * *

The transmogrification of Trump from joke candidate, to whisperer for a disaffected demographic, to risible nominee, to rent-in-the-fabric-of-time president-elect, did not inspire in him any larger sense of sober reflection. After the shock of it, he immediately seemed to rewrite himself as the inevitable president.

One instance of his revisionism, and of the new stature he now seemed to assume as president, involved the lowest point of the campaign—the Billy Bush tape.

His explanation, in an off-the-record conversation with a friendly cable anchor, was that it "really wasn't me."

The anchor acknowledged how unfair it was to be characterized by a single event.

"No," said Trump, "it wasn't me. I've been told by people who understand this stuff about how easy it is to alter these things and put in voices and completely different people."

He was the winner and now expected to be the object of awe, fascination, and favor. He expected this to be binary: a hostile media would turn into a fannish one.

And yet here he was, the winner who was treated with horror and depredations by a media that in the past, as a matter of course and protocol, could be depended on to shower lavish deference on an incoming president no matter who he was. (Trump's shortfall of three million votes continued to rankle and was a subject best avoided.) It was nearly incomprehensible to him that the same people—that is, the media—who had violently criticized him for saying he might dispute the election result were now calling *him* illegitimate.

Trump was not a politician who could parse factions of support and opprobrium; he was a salesman who needed to make a sale. "I won.

I am the winner. I am not the loser," he repeated, incredulously, like a mantra.

Bannon described Trump as a simple machine. The On switch was full of flattery, the Off switch full of calumny. The flattery was dripping, slavish, cast in ultimate superlatives, and entirely disconnected from reality: so-and-so was the best, the most incredible, the ne plus ultra, the eternal. The calumny was angry, bitter, resentful, ever a casting out and closing of the iron door.

This was the nature of Trump's particular salesmanship. His strategic belief was that there was no reason not to heap excessive puffery on a prospect. But if the prospect was ruled out as a buyer, there was no reason not to heap scorn and lawsuits on him or her. After all, if they don't respond to sucking up, they might respond to piling on. Bannon felt—perhaps with overconfidence—that Trump could be easily switched on and off.

Against the background of a mortal war of wills—with the media, the Democrats, and the swamp—that Bannon was encouraging him to wage, Trump could also be courted. In some sense, he wanted nothing so much as to be courted.

Amazon's Jeff Bezos, the owner of the *Washington Post*, which had become one of the many Trump media bêtes noires in the media world, nevertheless took pains to reach out not only to the president-elect but to his daughter Ivanka. During the campaign, Trump said Amazon was getting "away with murder taxwise" and that if he won, "Oh, do they have problems." Now Trump was suddenly praising Bezos as "a top-level genius." Elon Musk, in Trump Tower, pitched Trump on the new administration's joining him in his race to Mars, which Trump jumped at. Stephen Schwarzman, the head of the Blackstone Group—and a Kushner friend—offered to organize a business council for Trump, which Trump embraced. Anna Wintour, the *Vogue* editor and fashion industry queen, had hoped to be named America's ambassador to the UK under Obama and, when that didn't happen, closely aligned herself with Hillary Clinton. Now Wintour arrived at Trump Tower (but haughtily refused to do the perp walk) and, with quite some remarkable chutzpah, pitched herself to Trump to be *his* ambassador to the Court of St. James's.

And Trump was inclined to entertain the idea. ("Fortunately," said Bannon, "there was no chemistry.")

On December 14, a high-level delegation from Silicon Valley came to Trump Tower to meet the president-elect, though Trump had repeatedly criticized the tech industry throughout the campaign. Later that afternoon, Trump called Rupert Murdoch, who asked him how the meeting had gone.

"Oh, great, just great," said Trump. "Really, really good. These guys really need my help. Obama was not very favorable to them, too much regulation. This is really an opportunity for me to help them."

"Donald," said Murdoch, "for eight years these guys had Obama in their pocket. They practically ran the administration. They don't need your help."

"Take this H-1B visa issue. They really need these H-1B visas."

Murdoch suggested that taking a liberal approach to H-1B visas might be hard to square with his immigration promises. But Trump seemed unconcerned, assuring Murdoch, "We'll figure it out."

"What a fucking idiot," said Murdoch, shrugging, as he got off the phone.

* * *

Ten days before Donald Trump's inauguration as the forty-fifth president, a group of young Trump staffers—the men in regulation Trump suits and ties, the women in the Trump-favored look of high boots, short skirts, and shoulder-length hair—were watching President Barack Obama give his farewell speech as it streamed on a laptop in the transition offices.

"Mr. Trump said he's never once listened to a whole Obama speech," said one of the young people authoritatively.

"They're so boring," said another.

While Obama bade his farewell, preparations for Trump's first press conference since the election, to be held the next day, were under way down the hall. The plan was to make a substantial effort to show that the president-elect's business conflicts would be addressed in a formal and considered way.

Up until now, Trump's view was that he'd been elected *because* of those conflicts—his business savvy, connections, experience, and brand—not in spite of them, and that it was ludicrous for anyone to think he could untangle himself even if he wanted to. Indeed, to reporters and anyone else who would listen, Kellyanne Conway offered on Trump's behalf a self-pitying defense about how great his sacrifice had already been.

After fanning the flames of his intention to disregard rules regarding conflicts of interest, now, in a bit of theater, he would take a generous new tack. Standing in the lobby of Trump Towner next to a table stacked high with document folders and legal papers, he would describe the vast efforts that had been made to do the impossible and how, henceforth, he would be exclusively focused on the nation's business.

But suddenly this turned out to be quite beside the point.

Fusion GPS, an opposition research company (founded by former journalists, it provided information to private clients), had been retained by Democratic Party interests. Fusion had hired Christopher Steele, a former British spy, in June 2016, to help investigate Trump's repeated brags about his relationship with Vladimir Putin and the nature of Trump's relationship with the Kremlin. With reports from Russian sources, many connected to Russian intelligence, Steele assembled a damaging report—now dubbed the "dossier"—suggesting that Donald Trump was being blackmailed by the Putin government. In September, Steele briefed reporters from the *New York Times*, the *Washington Post*, Yahoo! News, the *New Yorker*, and CNN. All declined to use this unverified information, with its unclear provenance, especially given that it was about an unlikely election winner.

But the day before the scheduled press conference, CNN broke details of the Steele dossier. Almost immediately thereafter, Buzzfeed published the entire report—an itemized bacchanal of beyond-the-pale behavior.

On the verge of Trump's ascendancy to the presidency, the media, with its singular voice on Trump matters, was propounding a conspiracy of vast proportions. The theory, suddenly presented as just this side of a likelihood, was that the Russians had suborned Donald Trump during a trip to Moscow with a crude blackmail scheme involving prostitutes and videotaped sexual acts pushing new boundaries of deviance (including "golden showers") with prostitutes and videotaped sex acts. The implicit conclusion: a compromised Trump had conspired with the Russians to steal the election and to install him in the White House as Putin's dupe.

If this was true, then the nation stood at one of the most extraordinary moments in the history of democracy, international relations, and journalism.

If it was not true—and it was hard to fathom a middle ground—then it would seem to support the Trump view (and the Bannon view) that the media, in also quite a dramatic development in the history of democracy, was so blinded by an abhorrence and revulsion, both ideological and personal, for the democratically elected leader that it would pursue any avenue to take him down. Mark Hemingway, in the conservative, but anti-Trump, *Weekly Standard*, argued the novel paradox of two unreliable narrators dominating American public life: the president-elect spoke with little information and frequently no factual basis, while "the frame the media has chosen to embrace is that everything the man does is, by default, unconstitutional or an abuse of power."

On the afternoon of January 11, these two opposing perceptions faced off in the lobby of Trump Tower: the political antichrist, a figure of dark but buffoonish scandal, in the pocket of America's epochal adversary, versus the would-be revolutionary-mob media, drunk on virtue, certainty, and conspiracy theories. Each represented, for the other side, a wholly discredited "fake" version of reality.

If these character notes seemed comic-book in style, that was exactly how the press conference unfolded.

First Trump's encomiums to himself:

"I will be the greatest jobs producer that God ever created. . . ."

A smattering of the issues before him:

"Veterans with a little cancer can't see a doctor until they are terminal. . . ."

Then the incredulity:

"I was in Russia years ago with the Ms. Universe contest—did very very well—I tell everyone be careful, because you don't want to see yourself on television—cameras all over the place. And again, not just Russia, all over. So would anyone really believe that story? I'm also very much of a germaphobe, by the way. Believe me."

Then the denial:

"I have no deals in Russia, I have no deal that could happen in Russia because we've stayed away, and I have no loans with Russia. I have to say one thing . . . Over the weekend I was offered two billion dollars to do a deal in Dubai and I turned it down. I didn't have to turn it down, because as you know I have a no-conflict situation as president. I didn't know about that until three months ago but it's a nice thing to have. But I didn't want to take advantage of something. I have a no-conflict-of-interest provision as president. I could actually run my business, run my business and run government at the same time. I don't like the way that looks but I would be able to do that if I wanted to. I could run the Trump organization, a great, great company, and I could run the country, but I don't want to do that."

Then the direct attack on CNN, his nemesis:

"Your organization is terrible. Your organization is terrible. . . . Quiet . . . quiet . . . don't be rude . . . Don't be. . . . No, I'm not going to give you a question . . . I'm not going to give you a question. . . . You are fake news. . . ."

And in summation:

"That report first of all should never have been printed because it's not worth the paper it's printed on. I will tell you that should never ever happen. Twenty-two million accounts were hacked by China. That's because we have no defense, because we're run by people who don't know what they're doing. Russia will have far greater respect for our country when I'm leading it. And not just Russia, China, which has taken total advantage of us. Russia, China, Japan, Mexico, all countries will respect us far more, far more than they do under past administrations. . . ."

Not only did the president-elect wear his deep and bitter grievances on his sleeve, but it was now clear that the fact of having been elected president would not change his unfiltered, apparently uncontrollable, utterly shoot-from-the-hip display of wounds, resentments, and ire.

"I think he did a fantastic job," said Kellyanne Conway after the news conference. "But the media won't say that. They never will."

# 3

# DAY ONE

Jared Kushner at thirty-six prided himself on his ability to get along with older men. By the time of Donald Trump's inauguration he had become the designated intermediary between his father-in-law and the establishment, such as it was—more moderate Republicans, corporate interests, the New York rich. Having a line to Kushner seemed to offer an alarmed elite a handle on a volatile situation.

Several of his father-in-law's circle of confidants also confided in Kushner—often confiding their worries about their friend, the president-elect.

"I give him good advice about what he needs to do and for three hours the next day he does it, and then goes hopelessly off script," complained one of them to Trump's son-in-law. Kushner, whose pose was to take things in and not give much back, said he understood the frustration.

These powerful figures tried to convey a sense of real-world politics, which they all claimed to comprehend at some significantly higher threshold than the soon-to-be president. They were all concerned that Trump did not understand what he was up against. That there was simply not enough method to his madness.

Each of these interlocutors provided Kushner with something of a tutorial on the limitations of presidential power—that Washington was as much designed to frustrate and undermine presidential power as to accommodate it.

"Don't let him piss off the press, don't let him piss off the Republican Party, don't threaten congressmen because they will fuck you if you do, and most of all don't let him piss off the intel community," said one national Republican figure to Kushner. "If you fuck with the intel community they will figure out a way to get back at you and you'll have two or three years of a Russian investigation, and every day something else will leak out."

A vivid picture was painted for the preternaturally composed Kushner of spies and their power, of how secrets were passed out of the intelligence community to former members of the community or to other allies in Congress or even to persons in the executive branch and then to the press.

One of Kushner's now-frequent wise-men callers was Henry Kissinger. Kissinger, who had been a front-row witness when the bureaucracy and intelligence community revolted against Richard Nixon, outlined the kinds of mischief, and worse, that the new administration could face.

"Deep state," the left-wing and right-wing notion of an intelligence-network permanent-government conspiracy, part of the Breitbart lexicon, became the Trump team term of art: he's poked the deep state bear.

Names were put to this: John Brennan, the CIA director; James Clapper, the director of national intelligence; Susan Rice, the outgoing National Security Advisor; and Ben Rhodes, Rice's deputy and an Obama favorite.

Movie scenarios were painted: a cabal of intelligence community myrmidons, privy to all sorts of damning evidence of Trump's recklessness and dubious dealings, would, with a strategic schedule of wounding, embarrassing, and distracting leaks, make it impossible for the Trump White House to govern.

What Kushner was told, again and again, is that the president had to make amends. He had to reach out. He had to mollify. *These were forces not to be trifled with* was said with utmost gravity.

Throughout the campaign and even more forcefully after the election, Trump had targeted the American intelligence community—

the CIA, FBI, NSC, and, altogether, seventeen separate intelligence agencies—as incompetent and mendacious. (His message was "on auto pilot," said one aide.) Among the various and plentiful Trump mixed messages at odds with conservative orthodoxy, this was a particularly juicy one. His case against American intelligence included its faulty information about weapons of mass destruction that preceded the Iraq war, a litany of Obama Afghanistan-Iraq-Syria-Libya and other war-related intelligence failures, and, more recently, but by no means least of all, intelligence leaks regarding his purported Russian relationships and subterfuges.

Trump's criticism seemed to align him with the left in its half century of making a bogeyman of American intelligence agencies. But, in quite some reversal, the liberals and the intelligence community were now aligned in their horror of Donald Trump. Much of the left—which had resoundingly and scathingly rejected the intelligence community's unambiguous assessment of Edward Snowden as a betrayer of national secrets rather than a well-intentioned whistle-blower—now suddenly embraced the intelligence community's authority in its suggestion of Trump's nefarious relationships with the Russians.

Trump was dangerously out in the cold.

Hence, Kushner thought it was sensible to make a reach-out to the CIA among the first orders of the new administration's business.

* * *

Trump did not enjoy his own inauguration. He had hoped for a big blowout. Tom Barrack, the would-be showman—in addition to Michael Jackson's Neverland Ranch, he had bought Miramax Pictures from Disney with the actor Rob Lowe—may have declined the chief of staff job, but, as part of his shadow involvement with his friend's White House, he stepped up to raise the money for the inaugural and to create an event that—seemingly quite at odds with the new president's character, and with Steve Bannon's wish for a no-frills populist inauguration—he promised would have a "soft sensuality" and "poetic cadence." But Trump, imploring friends to use their influence to nail some of the A-level stars who were snubbing the event, started to get angry and hurt that stars were determined to embarrass him. Bannon, a soothing voice as well as a professional agitator, tried to argue the dialectical nature of what they had achieved (without using the word "dialectical"). Because Trump's success was beyond measure, or certainly beyond all expectations, the media and the liberals had to justify their own failure, he explained to the new president.

In the hours before the inauguration, the whole of Washington seemed to be holding its breath. On the evening before Trump was sworn in, Bob Corker, the Republican senator from Tennessee and the chairman of the Senate Foreign Relations Committee, opened his remarks as the featured speaker at a gathering at the Jefferson Hotel with the existential question, "Where are things going?" He paused for a moment and then answered, as though from some deep well of bewilderment, "I have no idea."

Later that evening, a concert at the Lincoln Memorial, part of an always awkward effort to import pop culture to Washington, ended up, absent any star power, with Trump himself taking the stage as the featured act, angrily insisting to aides that he could outdraw any star.

Dissuaded by his staff from staying at the Trump International Hotel in Washington and regretting his decision, the president-elect woke up on inaugural morning complaining about the accommodations at Blair House, the official guest residence across the street from the White House. Too hot, bad water pressure, bad bed.

His temper did not improve. Throughout the morning, he was visibly fighting with his wife, who seemed on the verge of tears and would return to New York the next day; almost every word he addressed to her was sharp and peremptory. Kellyanne Conway had taken up Melania Trump as a personal PR mission, promoting the new First Lady as a vital pillar of support for the president and a helpful voice in her own right, and was trying to convince Trump that she could have an important role in the White House. But, in general, the Trumps' relationship was one of those things nobody asked too many questions about—another mysterious variable in the presidential mood.

At the ceremonial meeting of the soon-to-be-new president and the soon-to-be-old president at the White House, which took place just before they set off for the swearing-in ceremony, Trump believed the Obamas acted disdainfully—"very arrogant"—toward him and Melania. Instead of wearing a game face, going into the inaugural events, the president-elect wore what some around him had taken to calling his golf face: angry and pissed off, shoulders hunched, arms swinging, brow furled, lips pursed. This had become the public Trump—truculent Trump.

An inauguration is supposed to be a love-in. The media gets a new and upbeat story. For the party faithful, happy times are here again. For the permanent government—the swamp—it's a chance to curry favor and seek new advantage. For the country, it's a coronation. But Bannon had three messages or themes he kept trying to reinforce with his boss: his presidency was going to be different—as different as any since Andrew Jackson's (he was supplying the less-than-well-read president-elect with Jackson-related books and quotes); they knew who their enemies were and shouldn't fall into the trap of trying to make them their friends, because they wouldn't be; and so, from day one, they should consider themselves on a war footing. While this spoke to Trump's combative "counterpuncher" side, it was hard on his eager-to-be-liked side. Bannon saw himself as managing these two impulses, emphasizing the former and explaining to his boss why having enemies here created friends somewhere else.

In fact, Trump's aggrieved mood became a perfect match for the Bannon-written aggrieved inaugural address. Much of the sixteen-minute speech was part of Bannon's daily *joie de guerre* patter—his take-back-the-country America-first, carnage-everywhere vision for the country. But it actually became darker and more forceful when filtered through Trump's disappointment and delivered with his golf face. The administration purposely began on a tone of menace—a Bannon-driven message to the other side that the country was about to undergo profound change. Trump's wounded feelings—his sense of being shunned and unloved on the very day he became president—helped send that message. When he came off the podium after delivering his address, he kept repeating, "Nobody will forget this speech."

George W. Bush, on the dais, supplied what seemed likely to become the historic footnote to the Trump address: "That's some weird shit."

* * *

Trump, despite his disappointment at Washington's failure to properly greet and celebrate him, was, like a good salesman, an optimist. Salesmen, whose primary characteristic and main asset is their ability to keep selling, constantly recast the world in positive terms. Discouragement for everyone else is merely the need to improve reality for them.

By the next morning, Trump was soliciting affirmation of his view that the inauguration had been a great success. "That crowd went all the way back. That were more than a million people at least, right?" He made a series of phone calls to friends who largely yes'd him on this. Kushner confirmed a big crowd. Conway did nothing to dissuade him. Priebus agreed. Bannon made a joke.

Among Trump's first moves as president was to have a series of inspirational photographs in the West Wing replaced with images of big crowd scenes at his inaugural ceremony.

Bannon had come to rationalize Trump's reality distortions. Trump's hyperbole, exaggerations, flights of fancy, improvisations, and general freedom toward and mangling of the facts, were products of the basic lack of guile, pretense, and impulse control that helped create the immediacy and spontaneity that was so successful with so many on the stump— while so horrifying to so many others.

For Bannon, Obama was the north star of aloofness. "Politics," said Bannon with an authority that belayed the fact that until the previous August he had never worked in politics, "is a more immediate game than he ever played it." Trump was, for Bannon, a modern-day William Jennings Bryan. (Bannon had long talked about the need for a new Williams Jennings Bryan in right-wing politics, with friends assuming Bannon meant himself.) At the turn of the twentieth century, Bryan had enthralled rural audiences with his ability to speak passionately and extemporaneously for apparently unlimited periods of time. Trump compensated—in the theory of some intimates, including Bannon—for his difficulties with reading, writing, and close focus with an improvisational style that produced, if not exactly a William Jennings Bryan effect, certainly close to the exact opposite of the Obama effect.

It was part hortatory, part personal testimony, part barstool blowhard, a rambling, disjointed, digressive, what-me-worry approach that combined aspects of cable television rage, big-tent religious revivalism, Borscht Belt tummler, motivational speaking, and YouTube vlogging. Charisma in American politics had come to define an order of charm, wit, and style—a coolness. But another sort of American charisma was more in the Christian evangelical vein, an emotional, experiential spectacle.

The Trump campaign had built its central strategy around great rallies regularly attracting tens of thousands, a political phenomenon that the Democrats both failed to heed and saw as a sign of Trump's limited appeal. For the Trump team, this style, this unmediated connection—his speeches, his tweets, his spontaneous phone calls to radio and television shows, and, often, to anyone who would listen—was revelatory, a new, personal, and inspirational politics. For the other side, it was clownishness that, at best, aspired to the kind of raw, authoritarian demagoguery that had long been discredited by and assigned to history and that, when it appeared in American politics, reliably failed.

While the advantages of this style for the Trump team were now very clear, the problem was that it often—in fact regularly—produced assertions that were not remotely true.

This had led increasingly to the two-different-realities theory of Trump politics. In the one reality, which encompassed most of Trump's supporters, his nature was understood and appreciated. He was the anti-wonk. He was the counterexpert. His was the gut call. He was the everyman. He was jazz (some, in the telling, made it rap), everybody else an earnest folk music. In the other reality, in which resided most of his antagonists, his virtues were grievous if not mental and criminal flaws. In this reality lived the media, which, with its conclusion of a misbegotten and bastard presidency, believed it could diminish him and wound him (and wind him up) and rob him of all credibility by relentlessly pointing out how literally wrong he was.

The media, adopting a "shocked, shocked" morality, could not fathom how being factually wrong was not an absolute ending in itself. How could this not utterly shame him? How could his staff defend him? The facts were the facts! Defying them, or ignoring them, or subverting them, made you a liar—intending to deceive, bearing false witness. (A minor journalism controversy broke out about whether these untruths should be called inaccuracies or lies.)

In Bannon's view: (1) Trump was never going to change; (2) trying to get him to change would surely cramp his style; (3) it didn't matter to Trump supporters; (4) the media wasn't going to like him anyway; (5) it was better to play against the media than to the media; (6) the media's claim to be the protector of factual probity and accuracy was itself a sham; (7) the Trump revolution was an attack on conventional assumptions and expertise, so better to embrace Trump's behavior than try to curb it or cure it.

The problem was that, for all he was never going to stick to a script ("his mind just doesn't work that way" was one of the internal rationalizations), Trump craved media approval. But, as Bannon emphasized, he was never going to get the facts right, nor was he ever going to acknowledge that he got them wrong, so therefore he was not going to get that approval. This meant, next best thing, that he had to be aggressively defended against the media's disapproval.

The problem here was that the more vociferous the defense—mostly of assertions that could easily be proved wrong—the more the media redoubled its attacks and censure. What's more, Trump was receiving the censure of his friends, too. And it was not only calls from friends worried about him, but staffers calling people to call him and say *Simmer down.* "Who do you have in there?" said Joe Scarborough in a frantic call. "Who's the person you trust? Jared? Who can talk you through this stuff before you decided to act on it?"

"Well," said the president, "you won't like the answer, but the answer is me. Me. I talk to myself."

Hence, within twenty-four hours of the inauguration, the president had invented a million or so people who did not exist. He sent his new press secretary, Sean Spicer—whose personal mantra would shortly become "You can't make this shit up"—to argue his case in a media moment that turned Spicer, quite a buttoned-down political professional, into a national joke, which he seemed destined to never recover from. To boot, the president blamed Spicer for not making the million phantom souls seem real.

It was the first presidential instance of what the campaign regulars had learned over many months: on the most basic level, Trump just did not, as Spicer later put it, give a fuck. You could tell him whatever you wanted, but he knew what he knew, and if what you said contradicted what he knew, he simply didn't believe you.

The next day Kellyanne Conway, her aggressive posture during the campaign turning more and more to petulance and self-pity, asserted the new president's right to claim "alternative facts." As it happened, Conway meant to say "alternative information," which at least would imply there might be additional data. But as uttered, it certainly sounded like the new administration was claiming the right to recast reality. Which, in a sense, it was. Although, in Conway's view, it was the media doing the recasting, making a mountain (hence "fake news") out of a molehill (an honest minor exaggeration, albeit of vast proportions).

Anyway, the frequently asked question about whether Trump would continue his unsupervised and often inexplicable tweets now that he was officially in the White House and the president of the United States—a question as hotly asked inside the White House as out—was answered: he would.

This was his fundamental innovation in governing: regular, uncontrolled bursts of anger and spleen.

\* \* \*

The president's immediate official business, however, was to make nice with the CIA.

On Saturday, January 21, in an event organized by Kushner, the president, in his first presidential act, paid a call on Langley to, in Bannon's hopeful description, "play some politics." In carefully prepared remarks in his first act as president, he would lay some of the famous Trump flattery on the CIA and the rest of the sprawling, and leaking, U.S. intelligence world.

Not taking off his dark overcoat, lending him quite a hulking gangster look, pacing in front of the CIA's wall of stars for its fallen agents, in front of a crowd of about three hundred agency personnel and a group of White House staffers, and, suddenly, in a mood of sleepless cockiness and pleasure at having a captive crowd, the new president, disregarding his text, launched into what we could confidently call some of the most peculiar remarks ever delivered by an American president.

"I know a lot about West Point, I'm a person who very strongly believes in academics. Every time I say I had an uncle who was a great professor at MIT for 35 years, who did a fantastic job in so many ways academically—he was an academic genius—and then they say, Is Donald Trump an intellectual? Trust me, I'm like a smart person."

Which was all somehow by way of praise for the new, soon-to-be-confirmed CIA director, Mike Pompeo, who had attended West Point and who Trump had brought with him to stand in the crowd—and who now found himself as bewildered as everyone else.

"You know when I was young. Of course I feel young—I feel like I was 30 . . . 35 . . . 39 . . . . Somebody said, Are you young? I said, I think I'm young. I was stopping in the final months of the campaign, four stops, five stops, seven stops—speeches, speeches in front of twenty-five, thirty thousand people . . . fifteen, nineteen thousand. I feel young—I think we're all so young. When I was young we were always winning things in this country. We'd win with trade, we'd win with wars—at a certain age I remembering hearing from one of my instructors, the United States has never lost a war. And then, after that, it's like we haven't won anything. You know the old expression, to the victor belongs the spoils? You remember I always say, keep the oil."

"*Who* should keep the oil?" asked a bewildered CIA employee, leaning over to a colleague in the back of the room.

"I wasn't a fan of Iraq, I didn't want to go into Iraq. But I will tell you when we were in we got out wrong and I always said in addition to that keep the oil. Now I said it for economic reasons, but if you think about it, Mike"—he called out across the room, addressing the soon-to-be director—"if we kept the oil we wouldn't have ISIS because that's where they made their money in the first place, so that's why we should have kept the oil. But okay—maybe you'll have another chance—but the fact is we should have kept the oil."

The president paused and smiled with evident satisfaction.

"The reason you are my first stop, as you know I have a running war with the media, they are among the most dishonest human beings on earth, and they sort of made it sound like I had a feud with the intelligence community and I just want to let you know the reason you're the number one stop is exactly the opposite, exactly, and they understand that. I was explaining about the numbers. We did, we did a thing yesterday at the speech. Did everybody like the speech? You had to like it. But we had a massive field of people. You saw them. Packed. I get up this morning, I turn on one of the networks, and they show an empty field and I say, Wait a minute, I made a speech. I looked out—the field was—it looked like a million, million and half people. They showed a field where there were practically nobody standing there. And they said Donald Trump did not draw well and I said it was almost raining, the rain should have scared them away, but God looked down and said we're not going to let it rain on your speech and in fact when I first started I said, Oooh no, first line I got hit by a couple of drops, and I said, Oh this is too bad, but we'll go right through it, the truth is it stopped immediately. . . ."

"No, it didn't," one of the staffers traveling with him said reflexively, then catching herself and, with a worried look, glancing around to see if she had been overheard.

". . . and then it became really sunny and I walked off and it poured right after I left. It poured but we have something amazing because—honestly it looked like a million, million and a half people, whatever it was it was, but it went all the way back to the Washington Monument and by mistake I get this network and it showed an empty field and it said we drew two hundred fifty thousand people. Now that's not bad, but it's a lie. . . . And we had another one yesterday which was interesting. In the Oval Office there's a beautiful statue of Dr. Martin Luther King and I also happen to like Churchill—Winston Churchill—I think most of us like Churchill, doesn't come from our country but had a lot to do with it, helped us, real ally, and as you know the Churchill statue was taken out. . . . So a reporter for *Time* magazine and I have been on the cover like fourteen or fifteen times. I think I have the all-time record in the history of *Time* magazine. Like if Tom Brady is on the cover it's one time because he won the Super Bowl or something. I've been on fifteen times this year. I don't think, Mike, that's a record that can ever be broken, do you agree with that . . . . What do you think?"

"No," said Pompeo in a stricken voice.

"But I will say that they said it was very interesting that 'Donald Trump took down the bust, the statue, of Dr. Martin Luther King,' and it was right there, there was a cameraman that was in front of it. So Zeke . . . Zeke . . . from *Time* magazine . . . writes a story that I took it down. I would never do that. I have great respect for Dr. Martin Luther King. But this is how dishonest the media is. Now big story, but the retraction was like this"—he indicated ever-so-small with his fingers. "Is it a line or do they even bother putting it in? I only like to say I love honesty, I like honest reporting. I will tell you, final time, although I will say it when you let in your thousands of other people who have been trying to come in, because I am coming back, we may have to get you a larger room, we may have to get you a larger room and maybe, *maybe*, it will be built by somebody that knows how to build and we won't have columns. You understand that? We get rid of the columns, but you know I just wanted to say that I love you, I respect you, there's nobody I respect more. You do a fantastic job and we're going to start winning again, and you're going to be leading the charge, so thank you all very much."

In a continuing sign of Trump's *Rashomon* effect—his speeches inspiring joy or horror—witnesses would describe his reception at the CIA as either a Beatles-like emotional outpouring or a response so confounded and appalled that, in the seconds after he finished, you could hear a pin drop.

# 4

# BANNON

Steve Bannon was the first Trump senior staffer in the White House after Trump was sworn in. On the inauguration march, he had grabbed the newly appointed deputy chief of staff, Katie Walsh, Reince Priebus's deputy at the RNC, and together they had peeled off to inspect the now vacant West Wing. The carpet had been shampooed, but little else had changed. It was a warren of tiny offices in need of paint, not rigorously cleaned on a regular basis, the décor something like an admissions office at a public university. Bannon claimed the nondescript office across from the much grander chief of staff's suite, and he immediately requisitioned the white boards on which he intended to chart the first hundred days of the Trump administration. And right away he began moving furniture out. The point was to leave no room for anyone to sit. There were to be no meetings, at least no meetings where people could get comfortable. Limit discussion. Limit debate. This was war. This was a war room.

Many who had worked with Bannon on the campaign and through the transition shortly noticed a certain change. Having achieved one goal, he was clearly on to another. An intense man, he was suddenly at an even higher level of focus and determination.

"What's up with Steve?" Kushner began to ask. And then, "Is something wrong with Steve?" And then finally, "I don't understand. We were so close."

Within the first week, Bannon seemed to have put away the camaraderie of Trump Tower—including a willingness to talk at length at any
hour—and become far more remote, if not unreachable. He was "focused
on my shit." He was just getting things done. But many felt that getting
things done was was more about him hatching plots against them. And
certainly, among his basic character notes, Steve Bannon was a plotter.
Strike before being struck. Anticipate the moves of others—counter them
before they can make their moves. To him this was seeing things ahead,
focusing on a set of goals. The first goal was the election of Donald Trump,
the second the staffing of the Trump government. Now it was capturing
the soul of the Trump White House, and he understood what others did
not yet: this would be a mortal competition.

* * *

In the early days of the transition, Bannon had encouraged the Trump
team to read David Halberstam's *The Best and the Brightest*. (One of the
few people who seem actually to have taken him up on this reading assign-
ment was Jared Kushner.) "A very moving experience reading this book. It
makes the world clear, amazing characters and all true," Bannon enthused.

This was a personal bit of branding—Bannon made sure to exhibit
the book to many of the liberal reporters he was courting. But he was
also trying to make a point, an important one considering the slapdash
nature of the transition team's staffing protocols: be careful who you hire.

Halberstam's book, published in 1972, is a Tolstoyan effort to understand how great figures of the academic, intellectual, and military world
who had served during the Kennedy and Johnson years had so grievously
misapprehended the nature of the Vietnam War and mishandled its prosecution. *The Best and the Brightest* was a cautionary tale about the 1960s
establishment—the precursor of the establishment that Trump and
Bannon were now so aggressively challenging.

But the book also served as a reverential guide to the establishment.
For the 1970s generation of future policy experts, would-be world lead-
ers, and Ivy League journalists aiming for big-time careers—though it was
Bannon's generation, he was far outside this self-selected elite circle—*The
Best and the Brightest* was a handbook about the characteristics of

American power and the routes to it. Not just the right schools and right backgrounds, although that, too, but the attitudes, conceits, affect, and language that would be most conducive to finding your way into the American power structure. Many saw the book as a set of prescriptions about how to get ahead, rather than, as intended, what not to do when you are ahead. *The Best and the Brightest* described the people who should be in power. A college-age Barack Obama was smitten with the book, as was Rhodes Scholar Bill Clinton.

Halberstam's book defined the look and feel of White House power. His language, resonant and imposing and, often, boffo pompous, had set the tone for the next half century of official presidential journalism. Even scandalous or unsuccessful tenants of the White House were treated as unique figures who had risen to the greatest heights after mastering a Darwinian political process. Bob Woodward, who helped bring Nixon down—and who himself became a figure of unchallengeable presidential mythmaking—wrote a long shelf of books in which even the most misguided presidential actions seemed part of an epochal march of ultimate responsibility and life-and-death decision making. Only the most hardhearted reader would not entertain a daydream in which he or she was not part of this awesome pageant.

Steve Bannon was such a daydreamer.

* * *

But if Halberstam defined the presidential mien, Trump defied it—and defiled it. Not a single attribute would place him credibly in the revered circle of American presidential character and power. Which was, in a curious reversal of the book's premise, just what created Steve Bannon's opportunity.

The less likely a presidential candidate is, the more unlikely, and, often, inexperienced, his aides are—that is, an unlikely candidate can attract only unlikely aides, as the likely ones go to the more likely candidates. When an unlikely candidate wins—and as outsiders become ever more the quadrennial flavor of the month, the more likely an unlikely candidate is to get elected—ever more peculiar people fill the White House. Of course, a point about the Halberstam book and about the Trump campaign was that the most obvious players make grievous mistakes, too. Hence, in the Trump narrative, unlikely players far outside the establishment hold the true genius.

Still, few have been more unlikely than Steve Bannon.

At sixty-three, Bannon took his first formal job in politics when he joined the Trump campaign. Chief Strategist—his title in the new administration—was his first job not just in the federal government but in the public sector. (*"Strategist!"* scoffed Roger Stone, who, before Bannon, had been one of Trump's chief strategists.) Other than Trump himself, Bannon was certainly the oldest inexperienced person ever to work in the White House.

It was a flaky career that got him here.

Catholic school in Richmond, Virginia. Then a local college, Virginia Tech. Then seven years in the Navy, a lieutenant on ship duty and then in the Pentagon. While on active duty, he got a master's degree at Georgetown's School of Foreign Service, but then he washed out of his naval career. Then an MBA from Harvard Business School. Then four years as an investment banker at Goldman Sachs—his final two years focusing on the media industry in Los Angeles—but not rising above a midlevel position.

In 1990, at the age of thirty-seven, Bannon entered peripatetic entrepreneurhood under the auspices of Bannon & Co., a financial advisory firm to the entertainment industry. This was something of a hustler's shell company, hanging out a shingle in an industry with a small center of success and concentric rings radiating out of rising, aspiring, falling, and failing strivers. Bannon & Co., skirting falling and failing, made it to aspiring by raising small amounts of money for independent film projects—none a hit.

Bannon was rather a movie figure himself. A type. Alcohol. Bad marriages. Cash-strapped in a business where the measure of success is excesses of riches. Ever scheming. Ever disappointed.

For a man with a strong sense of his own destiny, he tended to be hardly noticed. Jon Corzine, the former Goldman chief and future United States senator and governor of New Jersey, climbing the Goldman ranks when Bannon was at the firm, was unaware of Bannon. When Bannon was appointed head of the Trump campaign and became an overnight press sensation—or question mark—his credentials suddenly included a convoluted story about how Bannon & Co. had acquired a stake in the megahit show *Seinfeld* and hence its twenty-year run of residual profits. But none of the Seinfeld principals, creators, or producers seem ever to have heard of him.

Mike Murphy, the Republican media consultant who ran Jeb Bush's PAC and became a leading anti-Trump movement figure, has the vaguest recollection of Bannon's seeking PR services from Murphy's firm for a film Bannon was producing a decade or so ago. "I'm told he was in the meeting, but I honestly can't get a picture of him."

The *New Yorker* magazine, dwelling on the Bannon enigma—one that basically translated to: How is it that the media has been almost wholly unaware of someone who is suddenly among the most powerful people in government?—tried to trace his steps in Hollywood and largely failed to find him. The *Washington Post* traced his many addresses to no clear conclusion, except a suggestion of possible misdemeanor voter fraud.

In the midnineties, he inserted himself in a significant role into Biosphere 2, a project copiously funded by Edward Bass, one of the Bass family oil heirs, about sustaining life in space, and dubbed by *Time* one of the hundred worst ideas of the century—a rich man's folly. Bannon, having to find his opportunities in distress situations, stepped into the project amid its collapse only to provoke further breakdown and litigation, including harassment and vandalism charges.

After the Biosphere 2 disaster, he participated in raising financing for a virtual currency scheme (MMORPGs, or MMOs) called Internet Gaming Entertainment (IGE). This was a successor company to Digital Entertainment Network (DEN), a dot-com burnout, whose principals— including the former child star Brock Pierce (*The Mighty Ducks*) who went on to be the founder of IGE—were sued over allegations of sexual abuse of minors. Pierce was pushed out of IGE, Bannon was put in as CEO, and the company was then subsumed by endless litigation.

Distress is an opportunistic business play. But some distress is better than others. The kinds of situations available to Bannon involved managing conflict, nastiness, and relative hopelessness—in essence managing and taking a small profit on dwindling cash. It's a living at the margins of people who are making a much better living. Bannon kept trying to make a killing but never found the killing sweet spot.

Distress is also a contrarian's game. And the contrarian's impulse—equal parts personal dissatisfaction, general resentment, and gambler's instinct—started to ever more strongly fuel Bannon. Part of the background for his contrarian impulse lay in an Irish Catholic union family, Catholic schools, and three unhappy marriages and bad divorces (journalists would make much of the recriminations in his second wife's divorce filings).

Not so long ago, Bannon might have been a recognizably modern figure, something of a romantic antihero, an ex-military and up-from-the-working-class guy, striving, through multiple marriages and various careers, to make it, but never finding much comfort in the establishment world, wanting to be part of it and wanting to blow it up at the same time—a character for Richard Ford, or John Updike, or Harry Crews. An American man's story. But now such stories have crossed a political line. The American man story is a right-wing story. Bannon found his models in political infighters like Lee Atwater, Roger Ailes, Karl Rove. All were larger-than-life American characters doing battle with conformity and modernity, relishing ways to violate liberal sensibilities.

The other point is that Bannon, however smart and even charismatic, however much he extolled the virtue of being a "stand-up guy," was not necessarily a nice guy. Several decades as a grasping entrepreneur without a satisfying success story doesn't smooth the hustle in hustler. One competitor in the conservative media business, while acknowledging his intelligence and the ambitiousness of his ideas, also noted, "He's mean, dishonest, and incapable of caring about other people. His eyes dart around like he's always looking for a weapon with which to bludgeon or gouge you."

Conservative media fit not only his angry, contrarian, and Roman Catholic side, but it had low barriers to entry—liberal media, by contrast, with its corporate hierarchies, was much harder to break into. What's more, conservative media is a highly lucrative target market category, with books (often dominating the bestseller lists), videos, and other products

available through direct sales avenues that can circumvent more expensive distribution channels.

In the early 2000s, Bannon became a purveyor of conservative books
products and media. His partner in this enterprise was David Bossie, the
far-right pamphleteer and congressional committee investigator into the
Clintons' Whitewater affair, who would join him as deputy campaign
manager on the Trump campaign. Bannon met Breitbart News founder
Andrew Breitbart at a screening of one of the Bannon-Bossie documenta-
ries *In the Face of Evil* (billed as "Ronald Reagan's crusade to destroy the
most tyrannical and depraved political systems the world has ever
known"), which in turn led to a relationship with the man who offered
Bannon the ultimate opportunity: Robert Mercer.

*  *  *

In this regard, Bannon was not so much an entrepreneur of vision or even
business discipline, he was more simply following the money—or trying
to separate a fool from his money. He could not have done better than
Bob and Rebekah Mercer, who had set themselves up as almost professional fools. Bannon focused his entrepreneurial talents on becoming
courtier, Svengali, and political investment adviser to father and daughter.

Theirs was a consciously quixotic mission. They would devote vast
sums—albeit still just a small part of Bob Mercer's many billions—to
trying to build a radical free-market, small-government, home-
schooling, antiliberal, gold-standard, pro-death-penalty, anti-Muslim,
pro-Christian, monetarist, anti-civil-rights political movement in the
United States.

Bob Mercer is an ultimate quant, an engineer who designs investment algorithms and became a co-CEO of one of the most successful
hedge funds, Renaissance Technologies. With his daughter, Rebekah,
Mercer set up what is in effect a private Tea Party movement, self-funding
whatever Tea Party or alt-right project took their fancy. Father and
daughter are far out on the odd spectrum. Bob Mercer is almost nonver-
bal, looking at you with a dead stare and either not talking or offering
only minimal response. He had a Steinway baby grand on his yacht; after
inviting friends and colleagues on the boat, he would spend the time

playing the piano, wholly disengaged from his guests. And yet his political beliefs, to the extent they could be discerned, were generally Bush-like, and his political discussions, to the extent that you could get him to be responsive, were about issues involving ground game and data gathering. It was Rebekah Mercer—who had bonded with Bannon, and whose politics were grim, unyielding, and doctrinaire—who defined the family. "She's nuts . . . nuts . . . full-fledged . . . like whoa, ideologically there is no conversation with her," said one senior Trump White House staffer.

With the death of Andrew Breitbart in 2012, Bannon, in essence holding the proxy of the Mercers' investment in the site, took over the Breitbart business. He leveraged his gaming experience into using Gamergate—a precursor alt-right movement that coalesced around an antipathy toward, and harassment of, women working in the online gaming industry—to build vast amounts of traffic through the virality of political memes. (After hours one night in the White House, Bannon would argue that he knew exactly how to build a Breitbart for the left. And he would have the key advantage because "people on the left want to win Pulitzers, whereas I want to *be* Pulitzer!")

Working out of—and living in—the town house Breitbart rented on Capitol Hill, Bannon became one of the growing number of notable Tea Party figures in Washington, the Mercers' consigliere. But a seeming measure of his marginality was that his big project was the career of Jeff Sessions—"Beauregard," Sessions's middle name, in Bannon's affectionate moniker and evocation of the Confederate general—among the least mainstream and most peculiar people in the Senate, whom Bannon tried to promote to run for president in 2012.

Donald Trump was a step up—and early in the 2016 race, Trump became the Breitbart totem. (Many of Trump's positions in the campaign were taken from the Breitbart articles he had printed out for him.) Indeed, Bannon began to suggest to people that he, like Ailes had been at Fox, was the true force behind his chosen candidate.

Bannon didn't much question Donald Trump's bona fides, or behavior, or electability, because, in part, Trump was just his latest rich man. The rich man is a fixed fact, which you have to accept and deal with in an entrepreneurial world—at least a lower-level entrepreneurial world. And, of course, if Trump had had firmer bona fides, better behavior, and clear electability, Bannon would not have had his chance.

However much a marginal, invisible, small-time hustler Bannon had been—something of an Elmore Leonard character—he was suddenly transformed inside Trump Tower, an office he entered on August 15, and for practical purposes, did not exit, save for a few hours a night (and not every night) in his temporary midtown Manhattan accommodations, until January 17, when the transition team moved to Washington. There was no competition in Trump Tower for being the brains of the operation. Of the dominant figures in the transition, neither Kushner, Priebus, nor Conway, and certainly not the president-elect, had the ability to express any kind of coherent perception or narrative. By default, everybody had to look to the voluble, aphoristic, shambolic, witty, off-the-cuff figure who was both ever present on the premises and who had, in an unlikely attribute, read a book or two.

And indeed who, during the campaign, turned out to be able to harness the Trump operation, not to mention its philosophic disarray, to a single political view: that the path to victory was an economic and cultural message to the white working class in Florida, Ohio, Michigan, and Pennsylvania.

* * *

Bannon collected enemies. Few fueled his savagery and rancor toward the standard-issue Republican world as much as Rupert Murdoch—not least because Murdoch had Donald Trump's ear. It was one of the key elements of Bannon's understanding of Trump: the last person Trump spoke to ended up with enormous influence. Trump would brag that Murdoch was always calling him; Murdoch, for his part, would complain that he couldn't get Trump off the phone.

"He doesn't know anything about American politics, and has no feel for the American people," said Bannon to Trump, always eager to point out that Murdoch wasn't an American. But Trump couldn't get enough of him. With his love of "winners"—and he saw Murdoch as the ultimate winner—Trump was suddenly bad-mouthing his friend Ailes as a "loser."

And yet in one regard Murdoch's message was useful to Bannon.

Having known every president since Harry Truman—as Murdoch took frequent opportunities to point out—and, he conjectured, as many heads of state as anyone living, Murdoch believed he understood better than younger men, even seventy-year-old Trump, that political power was fleeting. (This was in fact the same message he had imparted to Barack Obama.) A president really had only, max, six months to make an impact on the public and set his agenda, and he'd be lucky to get six months. After that it was just putting out fires and battling the opposition.

This was the message whose urgency Bannon himself had been trying to impress on an often distracted Trump. Indeed, in his first weeks in the White House, an inattentive Trump was already trying to curtail his schedule of meetings, limit his hours in the office, and keep his normal golf habits.

Bannon's strategic view of government was shock and awe. Dominate rather than negotiate. Having daydreamed his way into ultimate bureaucratic power, he did not want to see himself as a bureaucrat. He was of a higher purpose and moral order. He was an avenger. He was also, he believed, a straight shooter. There was a moral order in aligning language and action—if you said you were going to do something, you do it.

In his head, Bannon carried a set of decisive actions that would not just mark the new administration's opening days, but make it clear that nothing ever again would be the same. At the age of sixty-three, he was in a hurry.

* * *

Bannon had delved deeply into the nature of executive orders—EOs. You can't rule by decree in the United States, except you really can. The irony here was that it was the Obama administration, with a recalcitrant Republican Congress, that had pushed the EO envelope. Now, in something of a zero-sum game, Trump's EOs would undo Obama's EOs.

During the transition, Bannon and Stephen Miller, a former Sessions aide who had earlier joined the Trump campaign and then become Bannon's effective assistant and researcher, assembled a list of more than two hundred EOs to issue in the first hundred days.

But the first step in the new Trump administration had to be immigration, in Bannon's certain view. Foreigners were the ne plus ultra mania of Trumpism. An issue often dismissed as living on the one-track-mind fringe—Jeff Sessions was one of its cranky exponents—it was Trump's firm belief that a lot of people had had it up to here with foreigners. Before Trump, Bannon had bonded with Sessions on the issue. The Trump campaign became a sudden opportunity to see if nativism really had legs. And then when they won, Bannon understood there could be no hesitation about declaring their ethnocentric heart and soul.

To boot, it was an issue that made liberals bat-shit mad.

Laxly enforced immigration laws reached to the center of the new liberal philosophy and, for Bannon, exposed its hypocrisy. In the liberal worldview, diversity was an absolute good, whereas Bannon believed any reasonable person who was not wholly blinded by the liberal light could see that waves of immigrants came with a load of problems—just look at Europe. And these were problems borne not by cosseted liberals but by the more exposed citizens at the other end of the economic scale.

It was out of some instinctive or idiot-savant-like political understanding that Trump had made this issue his own, frequently observing, *Wasn't anybody an American anymore?* In some of his earliest political outings, even before Obama's election in 2008, Trump talked with bewilderment and resentment about strict quotas on European immigration and the deluge from "Asia and other places." (This deluge, as liberals would be quick to fact-check, was, even as it had grown, still quite a modest stream.) His obsessive focus on Obama's birth certificate was in part about the scourge of non-European foreignness—a certain race-baiting. *Who were these people? Why were they here?*

The campaign sometimes shared a striking graphic. It showed a map of the country reflecting dominant immigration trends in each state from fifty years ago—here was a multitude of countries, many European. Today, the equivalent map showed that every state in the United States was now dominated by Mexican immigration. This was the daily reality of the American workingman, in Bannon's view, the ever growing presence of an alternative, discount workforce.

Bannon's entire political career, such as it was, had been in political media. It was also in Internet media—that is, media ruled by immediate response. The Breitbart formula was to so appall the liberals that the base was doubly satisfied, generating clicks in a ricochet of disgust and delight. You defined yourself by your enemy's reaction. Conflict was the media bait—hence, now, the political chum. The new politics was not the art of the compromise but the art of conflict.

The real goal was to expose the hypocrisy of the liberal view. Somehow, despite laws, rules, and customs, liberal globalists had pushed a myth of more or less open immigration. It was a double liberal hypocrisy, because, sotto voce, the Obama administration had been quite aggressive in deporting illegal aliens—except don't tell the liberals that.

"People want their countries back," said Bannon. "A simple thing."

* * *

Bannon meant his EO to strip away the liberal conceits on an already illiberal process. Rather than seeking to accomplish his goals with the least amount of upset—keeping liberal fig leaves in place—he sought the most.

*Why would you?* was the logical question of anyone who saw the higher function of government as avoiding conflict.

This included most people in office. The new appointees in place at the affected agencies and departments, among them Homeland Security and State—General John Kelly, then the director of Homeland Security, would carry a grudge about the disarray caused by the immigration EO—wanted nothing more than a moment to get their footing before they might even consider dramatic and contentious new policies. Old appointees—Obama appointees who still occupied most executive branch jobs—found it unfathomable that the new administration would go out of its way to take procedures that largely already existed and to restate them in incendiary, red-flag, and ad hominem terms, such that liberals would have to oppose them.

Bannon's mission was to puncture the global-liberal-emperor-wears-no-clothes bubble, nowhere, in his view, as ludicrously demonstrated as the refusal to see the colossally difficult and costly effects of uncontrolled immigration. He wanted to force liberals to acknowledge that even liberal governments, even the Obama government, were engaged in the real politics of slowing immigration—ever hampered by the liberal refusal to acknowledge this effort.

The EO would be drafted to remorselessly express the administration's (or Bannon's) pitiless view. The problem was, Bannon really didn't know how to do this—change rules and laws. This limitation, Bannon understood, might easily be used to thwart them. Process was their enemy. But just doing it—the hell with how—and doing it immediately, could be a powerful countermeasure.

Just doing things became a Bannon principle, the sweeping antidote to bureaucratic and establishment ennui and resistance. It was the chaos of just doing things that actually got things done. Except, even if you assumed that not knowing how to do things didn't much matter if you just did them, it was still not clear who was going to do what you wanted to do. Or, a corollary, because nobody in the Trump administration really knew how to do anything, it was therefore not clear what anyone did.

Sean Spicer, whose job was literally to explain what people did and why, often simply could not—*because nobody really had a job, because nobody could do a job.*

Priebus, as chief of staff, had to organize meetings, schedules, and the hiring of staff; he also had to oversee the individual functions of the executive office departments. But Bannon, Kushner, Conway, and the president's daughter actually had no specific responsibilities—they could make it up as they went along. They did what they wanted. They would seize the day if they could—even if they really didn't know how to do what they wanted to do.

Bannon, for instance, even driven by his imperative just to get things done, did not use a computer. *How did he do anything?* Katie Walsh wondered. But that was the difference between big visions and small. Process was bunk. Expertise was the last refuge of liberals, ever defeated by the big picture. The will to get big things done was how big things got done. "Don't sweat the small stuff" was a pretty good gist of Donald Trump's—and Steve Bannon's—worldview. "Chaos was Steve's strategy," said Walsh.

Bannon got Stephen Miller to write the immigration EO. Miller, a fifty-five-year-old trapped in a thirty-two-year-old's body, was a former Jeff Sessions staffer brought on to the Trump campaign for his political experience. Except, other than being a dedicated far-right conservative, it was unclear what particular abilities accompanied Miller's political views. He was supposed to be a speechwriter, but if so, he seemed restricted to bullet points and unable to construct sentences. He was supposed to be a policy adviser but knew little about policy. He was supposed to be the house intellectual but was militantly unread. He was supposed to be a communications specialist, but he antagonized almost everyone. Bannon, during the transition, sent him to the Internet to learn about and to try to draft the EO.

By the time he arrived in the White House, Bannon had his back-of-the-envelope executive order on immigration and his travel ban, a sweeping, Trumpian exclusion of most Muslims from the United States, only begrudgingly whittled down, in part at Priebus's urging, to what would shortly be perceived as merely draconian.

In the mania to seize the day, with an almost total lack of knowing how, the nutty inaugural crowd numbers and the wacky CIA speech were followed, without almost anybody in the federal government having seen it or even being aware of it, by an executive order overhauling U.S. immigration policy. Bypassing lawyers, regulators, and the agencies and personnel responsible for enforcing it, President Trump—with Bannon's low, intense voice behind him, offering a rush of complex information—signed what was put in front of him.

On Friday, January 27, the travel ban was signed and took immediate effect. The result was an emotional outpouring of horror and indignation from liberal media, terror in immigrant communities, tumultuous protests at major airports, confusion throughout the government, and, in the White House, an inundation of lectures, warnings, and opprobrium from friends and family. *What have you done? Do you know what you're doing? You have to undo this! You're finished before you even start! Who is in charge there?*

But Steve Bannon was satisfied. He could not have hoped to draw a more vivid line between the two Americas—Trump's and liberals'—and between his White House and the White House inhabited by those not yet ready to burn the place down.

Why did we do this on a Friday when it would hit the airports hardest and bring out the most protesters? almost the entire White House staff demanded to know.

"Errr . . . that's why," said Bannon. "So the snowflakes would show up at the airports and riot." That was the way to crush the liberals: make them crazy and drag them to the left.

# 5

# JARVANKA

On the Sunday after the immigration order was issued, Joe Scarborough and his cohost on the MSNBC show *Morning Joe*, Mika Brzezinski, came for lunch at the White House.

Scarborough is a former Republican congressman from Pensacola, Florida, and Brzezinski is the daughter of Zbigniew Brzezinski, a high-ranking aide in the Johnson White House and Jimmy Carter's National Security Advisor. *Morning Joe* had gone on the air in 2007 and developed a following among New York political and media types. Trump was a longtime devotee.

Early in the 2016 campaign, with a change of leadership at NBC News, it seemed likely that the show, its ratings falling, would be canceled. But Scarborough and Brzezinski embraced their relationship with Trump and became one of the few media outlets not only with a positive outlook on him, but that seemed to know his thinking. Trump became a frequent call-in guest and the show a way to speak more or less directly to him.

It was the kind of relationship Trump dreamed of: media people who took him seriously, talked about him often, solicited his views, provided him with gossip, and retailed the gossip he offered them. The effect was to make them all insiders together, which was exactly where Trump wanted to be. Though he branded himself as a political outsider, actually finding himself on the outside wounded him.

Trump believed that the media, which he propelled (in the case of Scarborough and Brzezinski, helping them keep their jobs), owed him something, and the media, giving him vast amounts of free coverage, believed he owed them, with Scarborough and Brzezinski seeing themselves as something like semiofficial advisers, if not the political fixers who had put him in his job.

In August, they had had a public spat, resulting in Trump's tweet: "Some day, when things calm down, I'll tell the real story of @JoeNBC and his very insecure long-time girlfriend, @morningmika. Two clowns!" But Trump's spats often ended in a tacit admission, however grudging, of mutual advantage, and in short order they were back on cordial terms again.

On their arrival at the White House, the ninth day of his presidency, Trump proudly showed them into the Oval Office and was momentarily deflated when Brzezinski said she had been there many times before with her father, beginning at age nine. Trump showed them some of the memorabilia and, eagerly, his new portrait of Andrew Jackson—the president whom Steve Bannon had made the totem figure of the new administration.

"So how do you think the first week has gone?" Trump asked the couple, in a buoyant mood, seeking flattery.

Scarborough, puzzled by Trump's jauntiness in the face of the protests spreading across the nation, demurred and then said, "Well, I love what you did with U.S. Steel and that you had the union guys come into the Oval Office." Trump had pledged to use U.S.-made steel in U.S. pipelines and, in a Trump touch, met at the White House with union representatives from building and sheet metal unions and then invited them back to the Oval Office—something Trump insisted Obama never did.

But Trump pressed his question, leaving Scarborough with the feeling that nobody had actually told Trump that he had had a very bad week. Bannon and Priebus, wandering in and out of the office, might actually have convinced him that the week had been a success, Scarborough thought.

Scarborough then ventured his opinion that the immigration order might have been handled better and that, all in all, it seemed like a rough period.

Trump, surprised, plunged into a long monologue about how well things had gone, telling Bannon and Priebus, with a gale of laughter, "Joe doesn't think we had a good week." And turning to Scarborough: "I could have invited Hannity!"

At lunch—fish, which Brzezinski doesn't eat—Jared and Ivanka joined the president and Scarborough and Brzezinski. Jared had become quite a Scarborough confidant and would continue to supply Scarborough with an inside view of the White House—that is, leaking to him. Scarborough, in turn, would become a defender of Kushner's White House position and view. But, for now, both son-in-law and daughter were subdued and deferential as Scarborough and Brzezinski chatted with the president, and the president—taking more of the air time as usual—held forth.

Trump continued to cast for positive impressions of his first week and Scarborough again reverted to his praise of Trump's handling of the steel union leadership. At which point, Jared interjected that reaching out to unions, a traditional Democratic constituency, was Bannon's doing, that this was "the Bannon way."

"Bannon?" said the president, jumping on his son-in-law. "That wasn't Bannon's idea. That was my idea. It's the Trump way, not the Bannon way."

Kushner, going concave, retreated from the discussion.

Trump, changing the topic, said to Scarborough and Brzezinski, "So what about you guys? What's going on?" He was referencing their not-so-secret secret relationship.

Scarborough and Brzezinski said it was all still complicated, and not public, officially, but it was good and everything was getting resolved.

"You guys should just get married," prodded Trump.

"I can marry you! I'm an Internet Unitarian minister," Kushner, otherwise an Orthodox Jew, said suddenly.

"What?" said the president. "What are you talking about? Why would they want *you* to marry them when *I* could marry them? When they could be married by the president! At Mar-a-Lago!"

* * *

Almost everybody advised Jared not to take the inside job. As a family member, he would command extraordinary influence from a position that no one could challenge. As an insider, a staffer, not only could his experience be challenged, but while the president himself might not yet be exposed, a family member on staff would be where enemies and critics might quite effectively start chipping from. Besides, inside Trump's West Wing, if you had a title—that is, other than son-in-law—people would surely want to take it from you.

Both Jared and Ivanka listened to this advice—from among others it came from Jared's brother, Josh, doubly making this case not only to protect his brother but also because of his antipathy to Trump—but both, balancing risk against reward, ignored it. Trump himself variously encouraged his son-in-law and his daughter in their new ambitions and, as their excitement mounted, tried to express his skepticism—while at the same time telling others that he was helpless to stop them.

For Jared and Ivanka, as really for everybody else in the new administration, quite including the president, this was a random and crazy turn of history such that how could you not seize it? It was a joint decision by the couple, and, in some sense, a joint job. Jared and Ivanka had made an earnest deal between themselves: if sometime in the future the time came, she'd be the one to run for president (or the first one of them to take the shot). The first woman president, Ivanka entertained, would not be Hillary Clinton, it would be Ivanka Trump.

Bannon, who had coined the Jarvanka conflation now in ever greater use, was horrified when the couple's deal was reported to him. "They didn't say that? Stop. Oh come on. They didn't actually say that? Please don't tell me that. Oh my god."

And the truth was that at least by then Ivanka would have more experience than almost anybody else now serving in the White House. She and Jared, or Jared, but by inference she, too, were in effect the real chief of staff—or certainly as much a chief of staff as Priebus or Bannon, all of them reporting directly to the president. Or, even more to the organizational point, Jared and Ivanka had a wholly independent standing inside the West Wing. A super status. Even as Priebus and Bannon tried, however diplomatically, to remind the couple of staff procedures and propriety, they would in turn remind the West Wing leadership of their overriding First Family prerogatives. In addition, the president had immediately handed Jared the Middle East portfolio, making him one of the significant international players in the administration—indeed, in the world. In the first weeks, this brief extended out to virtually every other international issue, about which nothing in Kushner's previous background would have prepared him for.

Kushner's most cogent reason for entering the White House was "leverage," by which he meant proximity. Quite beyond the status of being inside the family circle, anyone who had proximity to the president had leverage, the more proximity the more leverage. Trump himself you could see as a sort of Delphic oracle, sitting in place and throwing out pronouncements which had to be interpreted. Or as an energetic child, and whomever could placate or distract him became his favorite. Or as the Sun God (which is effectively how he saw himself), the absolute center of attention, dispensing favor and delegating power, which could, at any moment, be withdrawn. The added dimension was that this Sun God had little calculation. His inspiration existed in the moment, hence all the more reason to be there with him in the moment. Bannon, for one, joined Trump for dinner every night, or at least made himself available— one bachelor there for the effective other bachelor. (Priebus would observe that in the beginning everyone would try to be part of these dinners, but within a few months, they had become a torturous duty to be avoided.)

Part of Jared and Ivanka's calculation about the relative power and influence of a formal job in the West Wing versus an outside advisory role was the knowledge that influencing Trump required you to be all in. From phone call to phone call—and his day, beyond organized meetings, was almost entirely phone calls—you could lose him. The subtleties here were immense, because while he was often most influenced by the last person he spoke to, he did not actually listen to anyone. So it was not so much the force of an individual argument or petition that moved him, but rather more just someone's presence, the connection of what was going through his mind—and although he was a person of many obsessions, much of what was on his mind had no fixed view—to whomever he was with and their views.

Ultimately Trump may not be that different in his fundamental solipsism from anyone of great wealth who has lived most of his life in a highly controlled environment. But one clear difference was that he had acquired almost no formal sort of social discipline—he could not even attempt to imitate decorum. He could not really converse, for instance, not in the sense of sharing information, or of a balanced back-and-forth conversation. He neither particularly listened to what was said to him, nor particularly considered what he said in response (one reason he was so repetitive). Nor did he treat anyone with any sort of basic or reliable courtesy. If he wanted something, his focus might be sharp and attention lavish, but if someone wanted something from him, he tended to become irritable and quickly lost interest. He demanded you pay him attention, then decided you were weak for groveling. In a sense, he was like an instinctive, pampered, and hugely successful actor. Everybody was either a lackey who did his bidding or a high-ranking film functionary trying to coax out his attention and performance—and to do this without making him angry or petulant.

The payoff was his enthusiasm, quickness, spontaneity, and—if he departed for a moment from the nonstop focus on himself—an often incisive sense of the weaknesses of his opponents and a sense of their deepest desires. Politics was handicapped by incrementalism, of people knowing too much who were defeated by all the complexities and conflicting interests before they began. Trump, knowing little, might, Trumpers tried to believe, give a kooky new hope to the system.

Jared Kushner in quite a short period of time—rather less than a year—had crossed over from the standard Democratic view in which he was raised, to an acolyte of Trumpism, bewildering many friends and, as well, his own brother, whose insurance company, Oscar, funded with Kushner-family money, was destined to be shattered by a repeal of Obamacare.

This seeming conversion was partly the result of Bannon's insistent and charismatic tutoring—a kind of real-life engagement with world-bending ideas that had escaped Kushner even at Harvard. And it was helped by his own resentments toward the liberal elites whom he had tried to court with his purchase of the *New York Observer,* an effort that had backfired terribly. And it was, once he ventured onto the campaign trail, about having to convince himself that close up to the absurd everything made sense—that Trumpism was a kind of unsentimental realpolitik that would show everybody in the end. But most of all, it was that they had won. And he was determined not to look a gift horse in the mouth. And, everything that was bad about Trumpism, he had convinced himself, he could help fix.

* * *

As much as it might have surprised him—for many years, he had humored Trump more than embraced him—Kushner was in fact rather like his father-in-law. Jared's father, Charlie, bore an eerie resemblance to Donald's father, Fred. Both men used their money and power to dominate and subdue their children, and they did this so completely that their children, despite their demands, became devoted to them. In both instances, this was extreme stuff: belligerent, uncompromising, ruthless, amoral men creating long-suffering offspring who were driven to achieve their father's approval. (Trump's older brother, Freddy, failing in this effort, and, by many reports, gay, drank himself to death; he died in 1981 at age forty-three.) In business meetings, observers would be nonplussed that Charlie and Jared Kushner invariably greeted each other with a kiss and that the adult Jared called his father Daddy.

Neither Donald nor Jared, no matter their domineering fathers, went into the world with humility. Insecurity was soothed by entitlement. Both out-of-towners who were eager to prove themselves or lay rightful claim in Manhattan (Kushner from New Jersey, Trump from Queens), they were largely seen as overweening, smug, and arrogant. Each cultivated a smooth affect, which could appear more comical than graceful. Neither, by choice nor awareness, could seem to escape his privilege. "Some people who are very privileged are aware of it and put it away; Kushner not only seemed in every gesture and word to emphasize his privilege, but also not to be aware of it," said one New York media executive who dealt with Kushner. Both men were never out of their circle of privilege. The main challenge they set for themselves was to enter further into the privileged circle. Social climbing was their work.

Jared's focus was often on older men. Rupert Murdoch spent a surprising amount of time with Jared, who sought advice from the older media mogul about the media business—which the young man was determined to break into. Kushner paid long court to Ronald Perelman, the billionaire financier and takeover artist, who later would host Jared and Ivanka in his private shul on Jewish high holy days. And, of course, Kushner wooed Trump himself, who became a fan of the young man and was uncharacteristically tolerant about his daughter's conversion to Orthodox Judaism when that became a necessary next step toward marriage. Likewise, Trump as a young man had carefully cultivated a set of older mentors, including Roy Cohn, the flamboyant lawyer and fixer who had served as right-hand man to the red-baiting Senator Joe McCarthy.

And then there was the harsh fact that the world of Manhattan and particular its living voice, the media, seemed to cruelly reject them. The media long ago turned on Donald Trump as a wannabe and lightweight, and wrote him off for that ultimate sin—anyway, the ultimate sin in media terms—of trying to curry favor with the media too much. His fame, such as it was, was actually reverse fame—he was famous for being infamous. It was joke fame.

To understand the media snub, and its many levels of irony, there is no better place to look than the *New York Observer*, the Manhattan media and society weekly that Kushner bought in 2006 for $10 million—by almost every estimate $10 million more than it was worth.

\* \* \*

The *New York Observer* was, when it launched in 1987, a rich man's fancy, as much failed media often is. It was a bland weekly chronicle of the

Upper East Side, New York's wealthiest neighborhood. Its conceit was to treat this neighborhood like a small town. But nobody took any notice. Its frustrated patron, Arthur Carter, who made his money in the first generation of Wall Street consolidations, was introduced to Graydon Carter (no relation), who had started *Spy* magazine, a New York imitation of the British satirical publication *Private Eye*. *Spy* was part of a set of 1980s publications—*Manhattan, Inc.*, a relaunched *Vanity Fair*, and *New York*—obsessed with the new rich and what seemed to be a transformational moment in New York. Trump was both symbol of and punch line for this new era of excess and celebrity and the media's celebration of those things. Graydon Carter became the editor of the *New York Observer* in 1991 and not only refocused the weekly on big-money culture, but essentially made it a tip-sheet for the media writing about media culture, and for members of the big-money culture who wanted to be in the media. There may never have been such a self-conscious and self-referential publication as the *New York Observer*.

As Donald Trump, along with many others of this new-rich ilk, sought to be covered by the media—Murdoch's *New York Post* was the effective court recorder of this new publicity-hungry aristocracy—the *New York Observer* covered the process of him being covered. The story of Trump was the story of how he tried to make himself a story. He was shameless, campy, and instructive: if you were willing to risk humiliation, the world could be yours. Trump became the objective correlative for the rising appetite for fame and notoriety. Trump came to believe he understood everything about the media—who you need to know, what pretense you need to maintain, what information you could profitably trade, what lies you might tell, what lies the media expected you to tell. And the media came to believe it knew everything about Trump—his vanities, delusions, and lies, and the levels, uncharted, to which he would stoop for ever more media attention.

Graydon Carter soon used the *New York Observer* as his stepping-stone to *Vanity Fair*—where, he believed, he might have access to a higher level of celebrity than Donald Trump. Carter was followed at the *Observer* in 1994 by Peter Kaplan, an editor with a heightened sense of postmodern irony and ennui.

Trump, in Kaplan's telling, suddenly took on a new persona. Whereas he had before been the symbol of success and mocked for it, now he became, in a shift of zeitgeist (and of having to refinance a great deal of debt), a symbol of failure and mocked for it. This was a complicated reversal, not just having to do with Trump, but of how the media was now seeing itself. Donald Trump became a symbol of the media's own self-loathing: the interest in and promotion of Donald Trump was a morality tale about the media. Its ultimate end was Kaplan's pronouncement that Trump should not be covered anymore because every story about Donald Trump had become a cliché.

An important aspect of Kaplan's *New York Observer* and its self-conscious inside media baseball was that the paper became the prime school for a new generation of media reporters flooding every other publication in New York as journalism itself became ever more self-conscious and self-referential. To everyone working in media in New York, Donald Trump represented the ultimate shame of working in media in New York: you might have to write about Donald Trump. Not writing about him, or certainly not taking him at face value, became a moral stand.

In 2006, after Kaplan had edited the paper for fifteen years, Arthur Carter sold the *Observer*—which had never made a profit—to the then twenty-five-year-old Kushner, an unknown real estate heir interested in gaining stature and notoriety in the city. Kaplan was now working for someone twenty-five years his junior, a man who, ironically, was just the kind of arriviste he would otherwise have covered.

For Kushner, owning the paper soon paid off, because, with infinite ironies not necessarily apparent to him, it allowed him into the social circle where he met Donald Trump's daughter, Ivanka, whom he married in 2009. But the paper did not, irksomely for Kushner, pay off financially, which put him into increasing tension with Kaplan. Kaplan, in turn, began telling witty and devastating tales about the pretensions and callowness of his new boss, which spread, in constant retelling, among his many media protégés and hence throughout the media itself.

In 2009, Kaplan left the paper, and Kushner—making a mistake that many rich men who have bought vanity media properties are prone to making—tried to find a profit by cutting costs. In short order, the media world came to regard Kushner as the man who not only took Peter Kaplan's paper from him, but also ruined it, brutally and incompetently. And worse: in 2013, Kaplan, at fifty-nine, died of cancer. So, effectively, in the telling, Kushner had killed him, too.

Media is personal. It is a series of blood scores. The media in its often collective mind decides who is going to rise and who is going to fall, who lives and who dies. If you stay around long enough in the media eye, your fate, like that of a banana republic despot, is often an unkind one—a law Hillary Clinton was not able to circumvent. The media has the last word.

Long before he ran for president, Trump and his sidekick son-in-law Kushner had been marked not just for ignominy, but for slow torture by ridicule, contempt, and ever-more amusing persiflage. These people are nothing. They are media debris. For goodness' sake!

Trump, in a smart move, picked up his media reputation and relocated it from a hypercritical New York to a more value-free Hollywood, becoming the star of his own reality show, *The Apprentice*, and embracing a theory that would serve him well during his presidential campaign: in flyover country, there is no greater asset than celebrity. To be famous is to be loved—or at least fawned over.

The fabulous, incomprehensible irony that the Trump family had, despite the media's distaste, despite everything the media knows and understands and has said about them, risen to a level not only of ultimate consequence but even of immortality is beyond worst-case nightmare and into cosmic-joke territory. In this infuriating circumstance, Trump and his son-in-law were united, always aware and yet never quite understanding why they should be the butt of a media joke, and now the target of its stunned outrage.

\* \* \*

The fact that Trump and his son-in-law had many things in common did not mean they operated on a common playing field. Kushner, no matter how close to Trump, was yet a member of the Trump entourage, with no more ultimate control of his father-in-law than anybody else now in the business of trying to control Trump.

Still, the difficulty of controlling him had been part of Kushner's self-justification or rationalization for stepping beyond his family role and taking a senior White House job: to exercise restraint on his father-in-law and even—a considerable stretch for the inexperienced young man—to help lend him some gravitas.

If Bannon was going to pursue as his first signature White House statement the travel ban, then Kushner was going to pursue as his first leadership mark a meeting with the Mexican president, whom his father-in-law had threatened and insulted throughout the campaign.

Kushner called up the ninety-three-year-old Kissinger for advice. This was both to flatter the old man and to be able to drop his name, but it was also actually for real advice. Trump had done nothing but cause problems for the Mexican president. To bring the Mexican president to the White House would be, despite Bannon's no-pivot policy from the campaign's harshness, a truly meaningful pivot for which Kushner would be able to claim credit (although don't call it a pivot). It was what Kushner believed he should be doing: quietly following behind the president and with added nuance and subtlety clarifying the president's real intentions, if not recasting them entirely.

The negotiation to bring Mexican president Enrique Peña Nieto to the White House had begun during the transition period. Kushner saw the chance to convert the issue of the wall into a bilateral agreement addressing immigration—hence a tour de force of Trumpian politics. The negotiations surrounding the visit reached their apogee on the Wednesday after the inaugural, with a high-level Mexican delegation—the first visit by any foreign leader to the Trump White House—meeting with Kushner and Reince Priebus. Kushner's message to his father-in-law that afternoon was that Peña Nieto had signed on to a White House meeting and planning for the visit could go forward.

The next day Trump tweeted: "The U.S. has a 60 billion dollar trade deficit with Mexico. It has been a one-sided deal from the beginning of NAFTA with massive numbers..." And he continued in the next tweet... "of jobs and companies lost. If Mexico is unwilling to pay for the badly needed wall, then it would be better to cancel the upcoming meeting..."

At which point Peña Nieto did just that, leaving Kushner's negotiation and statecraft as so much scrap on the floor.

* * *

On Friday, February 3, at breakfast at the Four Seasons hotel in Georgetown, an epicenter of the swamp, Ivanka Trump, flustered, came down the stairs and entered the dining room, talking loudly on her cell phone: "Things are so messed up and I don't know how to fix it. . . ."

The week had been overwhelmed by continuing fallout from the immigration order—the administration was in court and headed to a brutal ruling against it—and more embarrassing leaks of two theoretically make-nice phone calls, one with the Mexican president ("bad hombres") and the other with the Australian prime minister ("my worst call by far"). What's more, the day before, Nordstrom had announced that it was dropping Ivanka Trump's clothing line.

The thirty-five-year-old was a harried figure, a businesswoman who had had to abruptly shift control of her business. She was also quite overwhelmed by the effort of having just moved her three children into a new house in a new city—and having to do this largely on her own. Asked how his children were adjusting to their new school several weeks after the move, Jared said that yes, they were indeed in school—but he could not immediately identify where.

Still, in another sense, Ivanka was landing on her feet. Breakfast at the Four Seasons was a natural place for her. She was among everyone who was anyone. In the restaurant that morning: House Minority Leader Nancy Pelosi; Blackstone CEO Stephen Schwarzman; Washington fixture, lobbyist, and Clinton confidant Vernon Jordan; labor secretary nominee Wilbur Ross; Bloomberg Media CEO Justin Smith; *Washington Post* national reporter Mark Berman; and a table full of women lobbyists and fixers, including the music industry's longtime representative in Washington, Hillary Rosen; Elon Musk's D.C. adviser, Juleanna Glover; Uber's political and policy executive, Niki Christoff; and Time Warner's political affairs executive, Carol Melton.

In some sense—putting aside both her father's presence in the White House and his tirades against draining the swamp, which might otherwise include most everyone here, this was the type of room Ivanka had worked hard to be in. Following the route of her father, she was crafting her name and herself into a multifaceted, multiproduct brand; she was also transitioning from her father's aspirational male golf and business types to aspirational female mom and business types. She had, well before her father's presidency could have remotely been predicted, sold a book, *Women Who Work: Rewriting the Rules for Success*, for $1 million.

In many ways, it had been an unexpected journey, requiring more discipline than you might expect from a contented, distracted, run-of-the-mill socialite. As a twenty-one-year-old, she appeared in a film made by her then boyfriend, Jamie Johnson, a Johnson & Johnson heir. It's a curious, even somewhat unsettling film, in which Johnson corrals his set of rich-kid friends into openly sharing their dissatisfactions, general lack of ambition, and contempt for their families. (One of his friends would engage in long litigation with him over the portrayal.) Ivanka, speaking with something like a Valley Girl accent—which would transform in the years ahead into something like a Disney princess voice—seems no more ambitious or even employed than anyone else, but she is notably less angry with her parents.

She treated her father with some lightness, even irony, and in at least one television interview she made fun of his comb-over. She often described the mechanics behind it to friends: an absolutely clean pate—a contained island after scalp reduction surgery—surrounded by a furry circle of hair around the sides and front, from which all ends are drawn up to meet in the center and then swept back and secured by a stiffening spray. The color, she would point out to comical effect, was from a product called Just for Men—the longer it was left on, the darker it got. Impatience resulted in Trump's orange-blond hair color.

Father and daughter got along almost peculiarly well. She was the real mini-Trump (a title that many people now seemed to aspire to). She accepted him. She was a helper not just in his business dealings, but in his marital realignments. She facilitated entrances and exits. If you have a douchebag dad, and if everyone is open about it, then maybe it becomes fun and life a romantic comedy—sort of.

Reasonably, she ought to be much angrier. She grew up not just in the middle of a troubled family but in one that was at all times immersed in bad press. But she was able to bifurcate reality and live only in the uppermost part of it, where the Trump name, no matter how often tarnished, nevertheless had come to be an affectionately tolerated presence. She resided in a bubble of other wealthy people who thrived on their relationship with one another—at first among private school and Upper East Side of Manhattan friends, then among social, fashion, and media contacts. What's more, she tended to find protection as well as status in her boyfriends' families, aggressively bonding with a series of wealthy suitors' families—including Jamie Johnson's before the Kushners—over her own.

The Ivanka-Jared relationship was shepherded by Wendi Murdoch, herself a curious social example (to nobody so much as to her then husband, Rupert). The effort among a new generation of wealthy women was to recast life as a socialite, turning a certain model of whimsy and noblesse oblige into a new status as a power woman, a kind of postfeminist socialite. In this, you worked at knowing other rich people, the best rich people, and of being an integral and valuable part of a network of the rich, and of having your name itself evoke, well . . . riches. You weren't satisfied with what you had, you wanted more. This required quite a level of indefatigability. You were marketing a product—yourself. You were your own start-up.

This was what her father had always done. This, more than real estate, was the family business.

She and Kushner then united as a power couple, consciously recasting themselves as figures of ultimate attainment, ambition, and satisfaction in the new global world and as representatives of a new eco-philanthropic-art sensibility. For Ivanka, this included her friendship with Wendi Murdoch and with Dasha Zhukova, the then wife of the Russian oligarch Roman Abramovich, a fixture in the international art world, and, just a few months before the election, attending a Deepak Chopra seminar on mediation with Kushner. She was searching for meaning—and finding it. This transformation was further expressed not just in ancillary clothing, jewelry, and footwear lines, as well as reality TV projects, but in a careful social media presence. She became a superbly coordinated everymom, who would, with her father's election, recast herself again, this time as royal family.

And yet, the larger truth was that Ivanka's relationship with her father was in no way a conventional family relationship. If it wasn't pure opportunism, it was certainly transactional. It was business. Building the brand, the presidential campaign, and now the White House—it was all business.

But what did Ivanka and Jared *really* think of their father and father-in-law? "There's great, great, great affection—you see it, you really do," replied Kellyanne Conway, somewhat avoiding the question.

"They're not fools," said Rupert Murdoch when asked the question.

"They understand him, I think truly," reflected Joe Scarborough. "And they appreciate his energy. But there's detachment." That is, Scarborough went on, they have tolerance but few illusions.

* * *

Ivanka's breakfast that Friday at the Four Seasons was with Dina Powell, the latest Goldman Sachs executive to join the White House.

In the days after the election, Ivanka and Jared had both met with a revolving door of lawyers and PR people, most of them, the couple found, leery of involvement, not least because the couple seemed less interested in bending to advice and more interested in shopping for the advice they wanted. In fact, much of the advice they were getting had the same message: surround yourself—*acquaint* yourselves—with figures of the greatest establishment credibility. In effect: you are amateurs, you need professionals.

One name that kept coming up was Powell's. A Republican operative who had gone on to high influence and compensation at Goldman Sachs, she was quite the opposite of anyone's notion of a Trump Republican. Her family emigrated from Egypt when she was a girl, and she is fluent in Arabic. She worked her way up through a series of stalwart Republicans, including Texas senator Kay Bailey Hutchison and House Speaker Dick Armey. In the Bush White House she served as chief of the personnel office and an assistant secretary of state for educational and cultural affairs. She went to Goldman in 2007 and became a partner in 2010, running its philanthropic outreach, the Goldman Sachs Foundation. Following a trend in the careers of many political operatives, she had become, as well as an über networker, a corporate public affairs and PR-type adviser—someone who knew the right people in power and had a keen sensitivity to how other people's power can be used.

The table of women lobbyists and communications professionals in the Four Seasons that morning was certainly as interested in Powell, and her presence in the new administration, as they were in the president's daughter. If Ivanka Trump was a figure more of novelty than of serious-ness, the fact that she had helped bring Powell into the White House and was now publicly conferring with her added a further dimension to the president's daughter. In a White House seeming to pursue a dead-set Trumpian way, this was a hint of an alternative course. In the assessment of the other fixers and PR women at the Four Seasons, this was a poten-tial shadow White House—Trump's own family not assaulting the power structure but expressing an obvious enthusiasm for it.

Ivanka, after a long breakfast, made her way through the room. Between issuing snappish instructions on her phone, she bestowed warm greetings and accepted business cards.

# 6

## AT HOME

Within the first weeks of his presidency a theory emerged among Trump's friends that he was not acting presidential, or, really, in any way taking into account his new status or restraining his behavior—from early morning tweets, to his refusal to follow scripted remarks, to his self-pitying calls to friends, details of which were already making it into the press—because he hadn't taken the leap that others before him had taken. Most presidents arrived in the White House from more or less ordinary political life, and could not help but be awed and reminded of their transformed circumstances by their sudden elevation to a mansion with palacelike servants and security, a plane at constant readiness, and downstairs a retinue of courtiers and advisers. But this would not have been that different from Trump's former life in Trump Tower, which was more commodious and to his taste than the White House, with servants, security, courtiers, and advisers always on the premises and a plane at the ready. The big deal of being president was not so apparent to him.

But another theory of the case was exactly opposite: he was totally off-kilter here because everything in his orderly world had been thrown on its head. In this view, the seventy-year-old Trump was a creature of habit at a level few people without despotic control of their environment could ever imagine. He had lived in the same home, a vast space in Trump

Tower, since shortly after the building was completed in 1983. Every morning since, he had made the same commute to his office a few floors down. His corner office was a time capsule from the 1980s, the same gold-lined mirrors, the same *Time* magazine covers fading on the wall; the only substantial change was the substitution of Joe Namath's football for Tom Brady's. Outside the doors to his office, everywhere he looked there were the same faces, the same retainers—servants, security, courtiers, the "yes people"—who had attended him basically always.

"Can you imagine how disruptive it would be if that's what you did every day and then suddenly you're in the White House?" marveled a longtime Trump friend, smiling broadly at this trick of fate, if not abrupt comeuppance.

Trump found the White House, an old building with only sporadic upkeep and piecemeal renovations—as well as a famous roach and rodent problem—to be vexing and even a little scary. Friends who admired his skills as a hotelier wondered why he just didn't remake the place, but he seemed cowed by the weight of the watchful eyes on him.

Kellyanne Conway, whose family had remained in New Jersey, and who had anticipated that she could commute home when the president went back to New York, was surprised that New York and Trump Tower were suddenly stricken from his schedule. Conway thought that the president, in addition to being aware of the hostility in New York, was making a conscious effort to be "part of this great house." (But, acknowledging the difficulties inherent in his change of circumstances and of adapting to presidential lifestyle, she added, "How often will he go to Camp David?"—the Spartan, woodsy presidential retreat in Catoctin Mountain Park in Maryland—"How 'bout never.")

At the White House, he retreated to his own bedroom—the first time since the Kennedy White House that a presidential couple had maintained separate rooms (although Melania was spending scant time so far in the White House). In the first days he ordered two television screens in addition to the one already there, and a lock on the door, precipitating a brief standoff with the Secret Service, who insisted they have access to the room. He reprimanded the housekeeping staff for picking up his shirt from the floor: "If my shirt is on the floor, it's because I want it on the floor." Then he imposed a set of new rules: nobody touch anything, especially not his toothbrush. (He had a longtime fear of being poisoned, one reason why he liked to eat at McDonald's—nobody knew he was coming and the food was safely premade.) Also, he would let housekeeping know when he wanted his sheets done, and he would strip his own bed.

If he was not having his six-thirty dinner with Steve Bannon, then, more to his liking, he was in bed by that time with a cheeseburger, watching his three screens and making phone calls—the phone was his true contact point with the world—to a small group of friends, among them most frequently Tom Barrack, who charted his rising and falling levels of agitation through the evening and then compared notes with one another.

\* \* \*

But after the rocky start, things started to look better—even, some argued, presidential.

On Tuesday, January 31, in an efficiently choreographed prime-time ceremony, an upbeat and confident President Trump announced the nomination of federal appellate judge Neil Gorsuch to the Supreme Court. Gorsuch was a perfect combination of impeccable conservative standing, admirable probity, and gold-standard legal and judicial credentials. The nomination not only delivered on Trump's promise to the base and to the conservative establishment, but it was a choice that seemed perfectly presidential.

Gorsuch's nomination was also a victory for a staff that had seen Trump, with this plum job and rich reward in his hand, waver again and again. Pleased by how the nomination was received, especially by how little fault the media could find with it, Trump would shortly become a Gorsuch fan. But before settling on Gorsuch, he wondered why the job wasn't going to a friend and loyalist. In the Trump view, it was rather a waste to give the job to someone he didn't even know.

At various points in the process he had run through almost all his lawyer friends—all of them unlikely, if not peculiar, choices, and, in almost every case, political nonstarters. The one unlikely, peculiar, and nonstarter choice that he kept returning to was Rudy Giuliani.

Trump owed Giuliani; not that he was so terribly focused on his debts, but this was one that was certainly unpaid. Not only was Giuliani a longtime New York friend, but when few Republicans were offering Trump their support, and almost none with a national reputation, Giuliani was there for him—and in combative, fiery, and relentless fashion. This was particularly true during the hard days following Billy Bush: when virtually everybody, including the candidate himself, Bannon, Conway, and his children, believed the campaign would implode, Giuliani barely allowed himself a break from his nonstop, passionate, and unapologetic Trump defense.

Giuliani wanted to be the secretary of state, and Trump had in so many words offered him the job. The resistance to Giuliani from the Trump circle derived from the same reason Trump was inclined to give him the job—Giuliani had Trump's ear and wouldn't let go. The staff whispered about his health and stability. Even his full-on pussygate defense now started to seem like a liability. He was offered attorney general, Department of Homeland Security, and director of national intelligence, but he turned them all down, continuing to hold out for State. Or, in what staffers took to be the ultimate presumption, or grand triangulation, the Supreme Court. Since Trump could not put someone openly pro-choice on the court without both sundering his base and risking defeat of his nominee, then, of course, he'd *have* to give Giuliani State.

When this strategy failed—Rex Tillerson got the secretary of state job—that should have been the end of it, but Trump kept returning to the idea of putting Giuliani on the court. On February 8, during the confirmation process, Gorsuch took public exception to Trump's disparagement of the courts. Trump, in a moment of pique, decided to pull his nomination and, during conversations with his after-dinner callers, went back to discussing how he should have given the nod to Rudy. He was the only loyal guy. It was Bannon and Priebus who kept having to remind him, and to endlessly repeat, that in one of the campaign's few masterful pieces of issue-defusing politics, and perfect courtship of the conservative base, it had let the Federalist Society produce a list of candidates. The campaign had promised that the nominee would come from that list—and needless to say, Giuliani wasn't on it.

Gorsuch was it. And Trump would shortly not remember when he had ever wanted anyone but Gorsuch.

* * *

On February 3, the White House hosted a carefully orchestrated meeting of one of the newly organized business councils, the president's Strategic and Policy Forum. It was a group of highly placed CEOs and weighty business types brought together by Blackstone chief Stephen Schwarzman. The planning for the event—with a precise agenda, choreographed seating and introductions, and fancy handouts—was more due to Schwarzman than to the White House. But it ended up being the kind of event that Trump did very well at and very much enjoyed. Kellyanne Conway, often referencing the Schwarzman gathering, would soon begin a frequent theme of complaint, namely that these kinds of events—Trump sitting down with serious-minded people and looking for solutions to the nation's problems—were the soul of Trump's White House and the media was giving them scant coverage.

Hosting business advisory councils was a Kushner strategy. It was an enlightened business approach, distracting Trump from what Kushner viewed as the unenlightened right-wing agenda. To an increasingly scornful Bannon, its real purpose was to allow Kushner himself to consort with CEOs.

Schwarzman reflected what to many was a surprising and sudden business and Wall Street affinity for Trump. Although few major-company CEOs had publicly supported him—with many, if not all, big companies planning for a Hillary Clinton victory and already hiring Clinton-connected public policy teams and with a pervasive media belief that a Trump victory would assure a market tailspin—there was suddenly an overnight warming. An antiregulatory White House and the promise of tax reform outweighed the prospect of disruptive tweeting and other forms of Trump chaos; besides, the market had not stopped climbing since November 9, the day after the election. What's more, in one-on-one meetings, CEOs were reporting good vibes from Trump's effusive and artful flattery—and the sudden relief of not having to deal with what some knew to be relentless Clinton-team hondling (what can you do for us today and can we use your plan?).

On the other hand, while there was a warming C-suite feeling for Trump, there was also rising concern about the consumer side of many big brands. The Trump brand was suddenly the world's biggest brand—the new Apple, except the opposite, since it was universally disdained (at least among many of the consumers who most top brands sought to court).

Hence, on inaugural morning, the employees of Uber, the ride sharing company, whose then CEO Travis Kalanick had signed on to the Schwarzman council, woke up to find people chained to the doors of their San Francisco headquarters. The charge was that Uber and Kalanick were "collaborating"—with its whiff of Vichy—a much different status than a business looking to sober forums with the president as a way to influence the government. Indeed, the protesters who believed they were seeing the company's relationship with Trump in political terms were actually seeing this in conventional brand terms and zooming in on the disconnect. Uber's customer base is strongly young, urban, and progressive, and therefore out of sync with the Trump base. Brand-conscious millennials saw this as beyond policy dickering and as part of an epic identity clash. The Trump White House stood less for government and the push-pull of competing interests and developing policies, and more, in a brand-savvy world, as a fixed and unpopular cultural symbol.

Uber's Kalanick resigned from the council. Disney CEO Bob Iger simply found that he was otherwise occupied on the occasion of the forum's first meeting.

But most of the people on the council—other than Elon Musk, the investor, inventor, and founder of Tesla (who would later resign)—were not from media or tech companies, with their liberal bent, but from old-line, when-America-was-great enterprises. They included Mary Barra, the CEO of General Motors; Ginni Rometty of IBM; Jack Welch, the former CEO of GE; Jim McNerney, the former CEO of Boeing; and Indra

Nooyi of PepsiCo. If the new right had elected Trump, it was the older Fortune 100 executives who most pleased him.

Trump attended the meeting with his full retinue—the circle that seemed always to move with him in lockstep, including Bannon, Priebus, Kushner, Stephen Miller, and National Economic Council chief Gary Cohn—but conducted it entirely himself. Each of the people at the table, taking a point of interest, spoke for five minutes, with Trump then asking follow-up questions. Though Trump appeared not to have particularly, or at all, prepared for any of the subjects being discussed, he asked engaged and interested questions, pursuing things he wanted to know more about, making the meeting quite an easy back-and-forth. One of the CEOs observed that this seemed like the way Trump preferred to get information—talking about what he was interested in and getting other people to talk about his interests.

The meeting went on for two hours. In the White House view, this was Trump at his best. He was most at home around people he respected—and these were "the most respected people in the country," according to Trump—who seemed to respect him, too.

This became a staff goal—to create situations in which he was comfortable, to construct something of a bubble, to wall him off from a mean-spirited world. Indeed, they sought to carefully replicate this formula: Trump in the Oval or in a larger West Wing ceremonial room presiding in front of a receptive audience, with a photo opportunity. Trump was often his own stage manager at these events, directing people in and out of the picture.

* * *

The media has a careful if selective filter when it comes to portraying real life in the White House. The president and First Family are not, at least not usually, subjected to the sort of paparazzi pursuit that in celebrity media results in unflattering to embarrassing to mocking photographs, or in endless speculation about their private lives. Even in the worst scandals, a businesslike suit-and-tie formality is still accorded the president. *Saturday Night Live* presidential skits are funny in part because they play on our belief that in reality, presidents are quite contained and buttoned-down figures, and their families, trotting not far behind, colorless and obedient. The joke on Nixon was that he was pitiably uptight—even at the height of Watergate, drinking heavily, he remained in his coat and tie, kneeling in prayer. Gerald Ford merely tripped coming off Air Force One, providing great hilarity in this break from formal presidential poise. Ronald Reagan, likely suffering the early effects of Alzheimer's, remained a carefully managed picture of calm and confidence. Bill Clinton, amid the greatest break in presidential decorum in modern history, was even so always portrayed as a man in control. George W. Bush, for all his disengagement, was allowed by the media to be presented as dramatically in charge. Barack Obama, perhaps to his disadvantage, was consistently presented as thoughtful, steady, and determined. This is partly a benefit of overweening image control, but it is also because the president is thought to be the ultimate executive—or because the national myth requires him to be.

That was actually the kind of image that Donald Trump had worked to project throughout most of his career. His is a 1950s businessman sort of ideal. He aspires to look like his father—or, anyway, not to displease his father. Except when he's in golf wear, it is hard to imagine him out of a suit and tie, because he almost never is. Personal dignity—that is, apparent uprightness and respectability—is one of his fixations. He is uncomfortable when the men around him are not wearing suit and ties. Formality and convention—before he became president, almost everybody without high celebrity or a billion dollars called him "Mr. Trump"—are a central part of his identity. Casualness is the enemy of pretense. And his pretense was that the Trump brand stood for power, wealth, arrival.

On the February 5, the *New York Times* published an inside-the-White-House story that had the president, two weeks into his term, stalking around in the late hours of the night in his bathrobe, unable to work the light switches. Trump fell apart. It was, the president not incorrectly saw, a way of portraying him as losing it, as Norma Desmond in the movie *Sunset Boulevard*, a faded or even senile star living in a fantasy world. (This was Bannon's interpretation of the *Times*'s image of Trump, which was quickly adopted by everyone in the White House.) And, of course, once again, it was a media thing—he was being treated in a way that no other president had ever been treated.

This was not incorrect. The *New York Times*, in its efforts to cover a presidency that it openly saw as aberrant, had added to its White House beat something of a new form of coverage. Along with highlighting White House announcements—separating the trivial from the significant—the paper would also highlight, often in front-page coverage, the sense of the absurd, the pitiable, and the all-too-human. These stories turned Trump into a figure of ridicule. The two White House reporters most consistently on this beat, Maggie Haberman and Glenn Thrush, would become part of Trump's constant refrain about the media being out to get him. Thrush would even become a fixture in *Saturday Night Live* sketches that mocked the president, his children, his press secretary Sean Spicer, and his advisers Bannon and Conway.

The president, while often a fabulist in his depiction of the world, was quite a literalist when it came to how he saw himself. Hence he rebutted this picture of him as a half-demented or seriously addled midnight stalker in the White House by insisting that he didn't own a bathrobe.

"Do I seem like a bathrobe kind of guy, really?" he demanded, not humorously, of almost every person with whom he spoke over the next forty-eight hours. "Seriously, can you see me in a bathrobe?"

Who had leaked it? For Trump, the details of his personal life suddenly became a far greater matter of concern than all the other kinds of leaks.

The *New York Times* Washington bureau, itself quite literal and worried by the possible lack of an actual bathrobe, reverse-leaked that Bannon was the source of the story.

Bannon, who styled himself as a kind of black hole of silence, had also become a sort of official black-hole voice, everybody's Deep Throat. He was witty, intense, evocative, and bubbling over, his theoretical discretion ever giving way to a constant semipublic commentary on the pretensions and fatuousness and hopeless lack of seriousness of most everyone else in the White House. By the second week of the Trump presidency, everybody in the White House seemed to be maintaining their own list of likely leakers and doing their best to leak before being leaked about.

But another likely leak source about his angst in the White House was

Trump himself. In his calls throughout the day and at night from his bed, he frequently spoke to people who had no reason to keep his confidences. He was a river of grievances—including about what a dump the White House was on close inspection—examples of which many recipients of his calls promptly spread throughout the ever attentive and merciless gossip world.

* * *

On February 6, Trump made one of his seething, self-pitying, and unsolicited phone calls without presumption of confidentiality to a passing New York media acquaintance. The call had no discernible point other than to express his bent-out-of-shape feelings about the relentless contempt of the media and the disloyalty of his staff.

The initial subject of his ire was the *New York Times* and its reporter Maggie Haberman, whom he called "a nut job." The *Times*'s Gail Collins, who had written a column unfavorably comparing Trump to Vice President Pence, was "a moron." But then, continuing under the rubric of media he hated, he veered to CNN and the deep disloyalty of its chief, Jeff Zucker. Zucker, who as the head of NBC had commissioned *The Apprentice*, had been "made by Trump," Trump said of himself in the third person. And Trump had "personally" gotten Zucker his job at CNN. "Yes, yes, I did," said Trump.

He then repeated a story that he was obsessively telling almost everyone he spoke to. He'd gone to a dinner, he didn't remember when, where he had sat next to "a gentleman named Kent"—undoubtedly Phil Kent, a former CEO of Turner Broadcasting, the Time Warner division that oversaw CNN—"and he had a list of four names." Three of them Trump had never heard of, but he knew Jeff Zucker because of *The Apprentice*. "Zucker was number four on the list, so I talked him up to number one. I probably shouldn't have because Zucker is not that smart but I like to show I can do that sort of thing." But Zucker, "a very bad guy who has done terrible with the ratings," had turned around after Trump had gotten him the job and had said, well, it's "unbelievably disgusting." This was the Russian "dossier" and the "golden shower" story—the practice CNN had accused him of being party to in the Moscow hotel suite with assorted prostitutes.

Having dispensed with Zucker, the president of the United States went on to speculate on what was involved with a golden shower. And how this was all just part of a media campaign that would never succeed in driving him from the White House. Because they were sore losers and hated him for winning, they spread total lies, 100 percent made-up things, totally untrue, for instance, the cover that week of *Time* magazine—which, Trump reminded his listeners, he had been on more than anyone in history—that showed Steve Bannon, a good guy, saying he was the real president. "How much influence do you think Steve Bannon has over me?" Trump demanded and repeated the question, and then repeated the answer: "Zero! Zero!" And that went for his son-in-law, too, who had a lot to learn.

The media was not only hurting him, he said—he was not looking for any agreement or really even any response—but hurting his negotiating capabilities, which hurt the nation. And that went for *Saturday Night Live*, too, which might think it was very funny but was actually hurting everybody in the country. And while he understood that *SNL* was there to be mean to him, they were being very, very mean. It was "fake comedy." He had reviewed the treatment of all other presidents in the media and there was nothing like this ever, even of Nixon who was treated very unfairly. "Kellyanne, who is very fair, has this all documented. You can look at it."

The point is, he said, that that very day, he had saved $700 million a year in jobs that were going to Mexico but the media was talking about him in his bathrobe, which "I don't have because I've never worn a bathrobe. And would never wear one, because I'm not that kind of guy." And what the media was doing was undermining this very dignified house, and "dignity is so important." But Murdoch, "who had never called me, never once," was now calling all the time. So that should tell people something.

The call went on for twenty-six minutes.

# 7

# RUSSIA

Even before there was reason to suspect Sally Yates, they suspected her. The transition report said Trump wouldn't like the fifty-six-year-old Atlanta-born University of Georgia career Justice Department lawyer slated to step up to acting attorney general. There was something about a particular kind of Obama person. Something about the way they walked and held themselves. *Superiority.* And about a certain kind of woman who would immediately rub Trump the wrong way—Obama women being a good tip-off, Hillary women another. Later this would be extended to "DOJ women."

Here was an elemental divide: between Trump and career government employees. He could understand politicians, but he was finding it hard to get a handle on these bureaucrat types, their temperament and motives. He couldn't grasp what they wanted. Why would they, or anyone, be a permanent government employee? "They max out at what? Two hundred grand? Tops," he said, expressing something like wonder.

Sally Yates could have been passed over for the acting AG spot—to serve in place while the attorney-general-designate, Jeff Sessions, waited for confirmation—and before long Trump would be furious about why she wasn't. But she was the sitting deputy and she'd been confirmed by the Senate, and the acting AG job needed someone with Senate confirmation. And even though she seemed to see herself as something of a prisoner held in hostile territory, Yates accepted the job.

Given this context, the curious information she presented to White House counsel Don McGahn during the administration's first week—this was before, in the second week, she refused to enforce the immigration order and was thereupon promptly fired—seemed not only unwelcome but suspect.

The newly confirmed National Security Advisor, Michael Flynn, had brushed off reports in the *Washington Post* about a conversation with Russian ambassador Sergey Kislyak. It was a simple meet and greet, he said. He assured the transition team—among others, Vice President–elect Pence—that there were no discussions of Obama administration sanctions against the Russians, an assurance Pence publicly repeated.

Yates now told the White House that Flynn's conversation with Kislyak had actually been captured as part of an "incidental collection" of authorized wiretaps. That is, a wiretap had presumably been authorized on the Russian ambassador by the secret Foreign Intelligence Surveillance Court and, incidentally, picked up Flynn.

The FISA court had achieved a moment of notoriety after the Edward Snowden revelations briefly made it a bête noire for liberals who were angry about privacy incursions. Now it was achieving another moment, but this time as the friend of liberals, who hoped to use these "incidental" wiretaps as a way to tie the Trump camp to a wide-ranging conspiracy with Russia.

In short order, McGahn, Priebus, and Bannon, each with prior doubts about Flynn's reliability and judgment—"a fuck-up," according to Bannon—conferred about the Yates message. Flynn was asked again about his call with Kislyak; he was also told that a recording might exist. Again he scoffed at any suggestion that this was a meaningful conversation about anything.

In one White House view, Yates's tattling was little more than "like she found out her girlfriend's husband flirted with somebody else and, standing on principle, had to tell on him."

Of more alarm to the White House was how, in an incidental collection wherein the names of American citizens are supposedly "masked"—with complicated procedures required to "unmask" them—had Yates so handily and conveniently picked up Flynn? Her report would also seem to confirm that the leak to the *Post* about these recordings came from the FBI, DOJ, or Obama White House sources—part of the growing river of leaks, with the *Times* and the *Post* the leakers' favored destinations.

The White House in its assessment of the Yates message ended up seeing this as less a problem with an always hard-to-handle Flynn than as a problem with Yates, even as a threat from her: the Justice Department, with its vast staff of career and Obama-inclined prosecutors, had ears on the Trump team.

* * *

"It's unfair," said Kellyanne Conway, sitting in her yet undecorated second-floor office while representing the president's hurt feelings. "It's obviously unfair. It's very unfair. They lost. They didn't win. This is so unfair. So POTUS just doesn't want to talk about it."

There was nobody in the White House who wanted to talk about—or even anyone who had been officially delegated to talk about—Russia, the story that, evident to most, even before they entered the White House, was certain to overwhelm the first year of the Trump administration at the very least. Nobody was prepared to deal with it.

"There's no reason to even talk about it," said Sean Spicer, sitting on the couch in his office, firmly crossing his arms. "There's no reason to even talk about it," he said again, stubbornly.

For his part, the president did not use, though he might have, the word "Kafkaesque." He regarded the Russia story as senseless and inexplicable and having no basis in reality. They were just being sucked in.

They had survived scandal during the campaign—the Billy Bush weekend—which virtually no one in Trump's inner circle had thought they could survive, only to be hit by the Russia scandal. Compared to Pussygate, Russia seemed like the only-desperate-thing-left-gate. What seemed unfair now was that the issue still wasn't going away, and that, incomprehensibly, people took it seriously. When at best it was . . . nothing.

*It was the media.*

The White House had quickly become accustomed to media-led scandals, but they were also used to their passing. But now this one was, frustratingly, holding on.

If there was any single piece of proof not just of media bias but of the intention of the media to do anything it could to undermine this president, it was—in the view of the Trump circle—this, the Russia story, what the *Washington Post* termed "Russia's attack on our political system." ("So terribly, terribly unfair, with no proof of one vote changed," according to Conway.) It was insidious. It was, to them, although they didn't put it this way, similar to the kind of dark Clinton-like conspiracies that Republicans were more wont to accuse liberals of—Whitewater, Benghazi, Emailgate. That is, an obsessive narrative that leads to investigations, which lead to other investigations, and to more obsessive no-escape media coverage. This was modern politics: blood-sport conspiracies that were about trying to destroy people and careers.

When the comparison to Whitewater was made to Conway, she, rather proving the point about obsessions, immediately began to argue the particulars involving Webster Hubbell, a mostly forgotten figure in the Whitewater affair, and the culpability of the Rose Law Firm in Arkansas, where Hillary Clinton was a partner. Everybody believed their side's conspiracies, while utterly, and righteously, rejecting the conspiracies leveled at them. To call something a conspiracy was to dismiss it.

As for Bannon, who had himself promoted many conspiracies, he dismissed the Russia story in textbook fashion: "It's just a conspiracy theory." And, he added, the Trump team wasn't capable of conspiring about anything.

\* \* \*

The Russia story was—just two weeks into the new presidency—a dividing line with each side viewing the other as pushing fake news.

The greater White House wholly believed that the story was an invented construct of weak if not preposterous narrative threads, with a mind-boggling thesis: *We fixed the election with the Russians, OMG!* The anti-Trump world, and especially its media—that is, *the* media—believed that there was a high, if not overwhelming, likelihood that there was *something* significant there, and a decent chance that it could be brought home.

If the media, self-righteously, saw it as the Holy Grail and silver bullet of Trump destruction, and the Trump White House saw it, with quite some self-pity, as a desperate effort to concoct a scandal, there was also a range of smart money in the middle.

The congressional Democrats had everything to gain by insisting, Benghazi-like, that where there was smoke (even if they were desperately working the bellows) there was fire, and by using investigations as a forum to promote their minority opinion (and for members to promote themselves).

For Republicans in Congress, the investigations were a card to play against Trump's vengefulness and unpredictability. Defending him—or something less than defending him and, indeed, possibly pursuing him— offered Republicans a new source of leverage in their dealings with him.

The intelligence community—with its myriad separate fiefdoms as suspicious of Trump as of any incoming president in memory—would, at will, have the threat of drip-drip-drip leaks to protect its own interests.

The FBI and DOJ would evaluate the evidence—and the opportunity— through their own lenses of righteousness and careerism. ("The DOJ is filled with women prosecutors like Yates who hate him," said a Trump aide, with a curiously gender-biased view of the growing challenge.)

If all politics is a test of your opponent's strength, acumen, and for-bearance, then this, regardless of the empirical facts, was quite a clever test, with many traps that many people might fall into. Indeed, in many ways the issue was not Russia but, in fact, strength, acumen, and forbear-ance, the qualities Trump seemed clearly to lack. The constant harping about a possible crime, even if there wasn't an actual crime—and no one was yet pointing to a specific act of criminal collusion, or in fact any other clear violation of the law—could force a cover-up which might then turn into a crime. Or turn up a perfect storm of stupidity and cupidity.

"They take everything I've ever said and exaggerate it," said the president in his first week in the White House during a late-night call. "It's all exaggerated. My exaggerations are exaggerated."

\* \* \*

Franklin Foer, the Washington-based former editor of the *New Republic*, made an early case for a Trump-Putin conspiracy on July 4, 2016, in *Slate*. His piece reflected the incredulity that had suddenly possessed the media and political intelligentsia: Trump, the unserious candidate, had, however incomprehensibly, become a more or less serious one. And somehow, because of his prior unseriousness, and his what-you-see-is-what-you-get nature, the braggart businessman, with his bankruptcies, casinos, and beauty pageants, had avoided serious vetting. For Trump students—which, over his thirty years of courting attention, many in the media had become—the New York real estate deals were dirty, the Atlantic City ventures were dirty, the Trump airline was dirty, Mar-a-Lago, the golf courses, and the hotels all dirty. No reasonable candidate could have survived a recounting of even one of these deals. But somehow a genial amount of corruption had been figured into the Trump candidacy—that, after all, was the platform he was running on. *I'll do for you what a tough businessman does for himself.*

To really see his corruption, you had to see it on a bigger stage. Foer was suggesting a fabulous one.

Assembling a detailed road map for a scandal that did not yet exist, Foer, without anything resembling smoking guns or even real evidence, pulled together in July virtually all of the circumstantial and thematic threads and many of the various characters that would play out over the next eighteen months. (Unbeknownst to the public or even most media or political insiders, Fusion GPS had by this point hired the former British spy Christopher Steele to investigate a connection between Trump and the Russian government.)

Putin was seeking a resurgence of Russian power and, as well, to block encroachments by the European Union and NATO. Trump's refusal to treat Putin as a semi-outlaw—not to mention what often seemed like a man crush on him—meant, ipso facto, that Trump was sanguine about a return of Russian power and might actually be promoting it.

Why? What could possibly be in it for an American politician to publicly embrace—sycophantically embrace—Vladimir Putin and to encourage what the West saw as Russian adventurism?

Theory 1: Trump was drawn to authoritarian strongmen. Foer

recounted Trump's longtime fascination with Russia, including being duped by a Gorbachev look-alike who visited Trump Tower in the 1980s, and his many fulsome and unnecessary "odes to Putin." This suggested a lie-down-with-dogs-wake-up-with-fleas vulnerability: consorting with or looking favorably upon politicians whose power lies partly in their toler-ance of corruption brings you closer to corruption. Likewise, Putin was drawn to populist strongmen in his own image: hence, Foer asked, "Why *wouldn't* the Russians offer him the same furtive assistance they've lavished on Le Pen, Berlusconi, and the rest?"

Theory 2: Trump was part of a less-than-blue-chip (much less) inter-national business set, feeding off the rivers of dubious wealth that had been unleashed by all the efforts to move cash, much of it from Russia and China, out of political harm's way. Such money, or rumors of such money, became an explanation—still only a circumstantial one—in try-ing to assess all the Trump business dealings that largely remained hid-den from view. (There were two contradictory theories here: he had hidden these dealings because he didn't want to admit their paucity, or he had hidden them to mask their disreputableness.) Because Trump is less than creditworthy, Foer was among many who concluded that Trump needed to turn to other sources—more or less dirty money, or money with other sorts of strings attached. (One way the process can work is, roughly speaking, as follows: an oligarch makes an investment in a more or less legitimate third-party investment fund, which, quid pro quo, makes an investment in Trump.) And while Trump would categorically deny that he had any loans or investments from Russia, one would, of course, not have dirty money on one's books.

As a subset of this theory, Trump—never very scrupulous about vet-ting his people—surrounded himself with a variety of hustlers working their own deals, and, plausibly, aiding Trump's deals. Foer identified the following characters as part of a possible Russian conspiracy:

- Tevfik Arif, a former Russian official who ran the Bayrock Group, a middleman in Trump financings with an office in Trump Tower.
- Felix Sater (sometimes spelled Satter), a Russian-born immigrant to Brighton Beach in Brooklyn, who had previously served time in

prison in connection with a fraud at a Mafia-run brokerage and who went to work for Bayrock and had a business card identifying him as senior adviser to Donald Trump. (When Sater's name later continued to surface, Trump assured Bannon he didn't know Sater at all.)

- Carter Page, a banker of uncertain portfolio who had spent time in Russia and billed himself as having advised the state-run oil company, Gazprom, and who showed up on a hastily assembled list of Trump foreign policy advisers and who, it would turn out, the FBI was closely monitoring in what it said was a Russian intelligence effort to turn him. (Trump would later deny ever meeting Page, and the FBI would say that it believed Russian intelligence had targeted Page in an effort to turn him.)

- Michael Flynn, the former head of the Defense Intelligence Agency— fired by Obama for unclear reasons—who had yet to emerge as Trump's key foreign policy counselor and future National Security Advisor, but who was accompanying him on many campaign trips and who earlier in the year had been paid a $45,000 speaking fee in Moscow and been photographed sitting at a dinner with Putin.

- Paul Manafort, whom, along with serving as Trump's campaign manager, Foer highlighted as a political operative and consultant who had generated substantial income advising Kremlin-backed Viktor Yanukovych, who successfully ran for the presidency of Ukraine in 2010, was later deposed in 2014, and had been in business with the Russian oligarch and Putin crony Oleg Deripaska.

More than a year later, each of these men would be part of the near-daily Russia-Trump news cycle.

Theory 3: The Holy Grail proposition was that Trump and the Russians—perhaps even Putin himself—had gotten together to hack the Democratic National Committee.

Theory 4: But then there was the those-that-know-him-best theory, some version of which most Trumpers would come to embrace. He was just star-fucking. He took his beauty pageant to Russia because he thought Putin was going to be his friend. But Putin couldn't have cared less, and in the end Trump found himself at the promised gala dinner seated on one side next to a guy who looked like he had never used a utensil and on the other side Jabba the Hutt in a golf shirt. In other words, Trump—however foolish his sucking-up might have been, and however suspicious it might look in hindsight—just wanted a little respect.

Theory 5: The Russians, holding damaging information about Trump, were blackmailing him. He was a Manchurian Candidate.

* * *

On January 6, 2017—nearly six months to the day after Foer's piece was published—the CIA, FBI, and NSA announced their joint conclusion that "Vladimir Putin ordered an influence campaign in 2016 aimed at the U.S. presidential election." From the Steele dossier, to the steady leaks from the U.S. intelligence community, to testimony and statements from the leadership of U.S. intelligence agencies, a firm consensus had emerged. There was a nefarious connection, perhaps an ongoing one, between Trump and his campaign and the Russian government.

Still, this could yet be seen as highly wishful thinking by Trump opponents. "The underlying premise of the case is that spies tell the truth," said the veteran intelligence community journalist Edward Jay Epstein. "Who knew?" And, indeed, the worry in the White House was not about collusion—which seemed implausible if not farcical—but what, if the unraveling began, would likely lead to the messy Trump (and Kushner) business dealings. On this subject every member of the senior staff shrugged helplessly, covering eyes, ears, and mouth.

This was the peculiar and haunting consensus—not that Trump was guilty of all that he was accused of, but that he was guilty of so much else. It was all too possible that the hardly plausible would lead to the totally credible.

* * *

On February 13, twenty-four days into the new administration, National Security Advisor Michael Flynn became the first actual link between Russia and the White House.

Flynn had really only one supporter in the Trump administration, and that was the president himself. They were best friends during the campaign—buddy movie stuff. Post-inauguration, this translated into a total-access relationship. On Flynn's part, it led to a set of misapprehensions that was common inside Trump's circle: that the president's personal endorsement indicated your status in the White House and that Trump's level of flattery was a convincing indication that you had an unbreakable bond with him and that you were, in his eyes, and in his White House, something close to omnipotent. Trump, with his love of generals, *had* even for a moment wanted to make Michael Flynn his vice president.

Intoxicated by Trump's flattery during the campaign, Flynn—a lower-tier general and quite a flaky one at that—had become something of a Trump dancing monkey. When former generals make alliances with political candidates, they customarily position themselves as providers of expertise and figures of a special maturity. But Flynn had become quite a maniacal partisan, part of the Trump traveling road show, one of the ranters and ravers opening Trump rallies. This all-in enthusiasm and loyalty had helped win him access to Trump's ear, into which he poured his anti-intelligence-community theories.

During the early part of the transition, when Bannon and Kushner had seemed joined at the hip, this was part of their bond: an effort to disintermediate Flynn and his often problematic message. A subtext in the White House estimation of Flynn, slyly insinuated by Bannon, was that Defense Secretary Mattis was a four-star general and Flynn but a three-star.

"I like Flynn, he reminds me of my uncles," said Bannon. "But that's the problem: he reminds me of my uncles."

Bannon used the general odor that had more and more attached to Flynn among everybody except the president to help secure a seat for himself on the National Security Council. This was, for many in the national security community, a signal moment in the effort by the nationalist right wing to seize power. But Bannon's presence on the council was just as much driven by the need to babysit the impetuous Flynn, prone to antagonizing almost everyone else in the national security community. (Flynn was "a colonel in a general's uniform," according to one senior intelligence figure.)

Flynn, like everyone around Trump, was besotted by the other-worldly sense of opportunity that came with, against all odds, being in the White House. And inevitably, he had been made more grandiose by it.

In 2014, Flynn had been roughly cashiered out of government, for which he blamed his many enemies in the CIA. But he had energetically set himself up in business, joining the ranks of former government officials profiting off the ever growing globalist corporate-financial-government policy and business networks. Then, after flirting with several other Republican presidential candidates, he bonded with Trump. Both Flynn and Trump were antiglobalists—or, anyway, they believed the United States was getting screwed in global transactions. Still, money was money, and Flynn, who, when he retired, had been receiving a few hundred thousand a year on his general's pension, was not turning any of it down. Various friends and advisers—including Michael Ledeen, a longtime anti-Iran and anti-CIA crony, and the coauthor of Flynn's book, whose daughter now worked for Flynn—advised Flynn that he ought not to accept fees from Russia or the larger "consulting" assignments from Turkey.

It was in fact the sort of carelessness that almost everyone in Trump's world, including the president and his family, was guilty of. They lived with parallel realities in which, while proceeding with a presidential campaign, they also had to live in a vastly more likely world—rather a certain world—in which Donald Trump would never be president. Hence, business as usual.

In early February, an Obama administration lawyer friendly with Sally Yates remarked with some relish and considerable accuracy: "It certainly is an odd circumstance if you live your life without regard for being elected and then get elected—and quite an opportunity for your enemies."

In this, there was not only the Russian cloud hanging over the administration, but a sense that the intelligence community so distrusted Flynn, and so blamed its bad blood with Trump on him, that Flynn was the target here. Within the White House there was even a feeling that a soft trade was being implicitly offered: Flynn for the goodwill of the intelligence community.

At the same time, in what some thought a direct result of the president's rage over the Russia insinuations—particularly the insinuation about the golden shower—the president seemed to bond even more strongly with Flynn, assuring his National Security Advisor over and over again that he had his back, that the Russia accusations, those related both to Flynn and to himself, were "garbage." After Flynn's dismissal, a narrative describing Trump's increasing doubts about his adviser would be offered to the press, but in fact the opposite was true: the more doubts gathered around Flynn, the more certain the president became that Flynn was his all-important ally.

\* \* \*

The final or deadliest leak during Michael Flynn's brief tenure is as likely to have come from the National Security Advisor's antagonists inside the White House as from the Justice Department.

On Wednesday, February 8, the *Washington Post*'s Karen DeYoung came to visit Flynn for what was billed as an off-the-record interview. They met not in his office but in the most ornate room in the Eisenhower Executive Office Building—the same room where Japanese diplomats waited to meet with Secretary of State Cordell Hull as he learned of the attack on Pearl Harbor.

To all outward appearances, it was an uneventful background interview, and DeYoung, Columbo-like in her affect, aroused no suspicions when she broached the de rigueur question: "My colleagues asked me to ask you this: Did you talk to the Russians about sanctions?"

Flynn declared that he had had no such conversations, absolutely no conversation, he confirmed again, and the interview, attended by senior National Security Council official and spokesman Michael Anton, ended soon thereafter.

But later that day, DeYoung called Anton and asked if she could use Flynn's denial on the record. Anton said he saw no problem—after all, the White House wanted Flynn's denial to be clear—and notified Flynn.

A few hours later, Flynn called Anton back with some worries about the statement. Anton applied an obvious test: "If you knew that there might be a tape of this conversation that could surface, would you still be a hundred percent sure?"

Flynn equivocated, and Anton, suddenly concerned, advised him that if he couldn't be sure they ought to "walk it back."

The *Post* piece, which appeared the next day under three other bylines—indicating that DeYoung's interview was hardly the point of the story—contained new leaked details of the Kislyak phone call, which the *Post* now said had indeed dealt with the issue of sanctions. The article also contained Flynn's denial—"he twice said 'no'"—as well as his walk-back: "On Thursday, Flynn, through his spokesman, backed away from the denial. The spokesman said Flynn 'indicated that while he had no recollection of discussing sanctions, he couldn't be certain that the topic never came up.'"

After the *Post* story, Priebus and Bannon questioned Flynn again. Flynn professed not to remember what he had said; if the subject of sanctions came up, he told them, it was at most glossed over. Curiously, no one seemed to have actually heard the conversation with Kislyak or seen a transcript.

Meanwhile, the vice president's people, caught unaware by the sudden Flynn controversy, were taking particular umbrage, less about Flynn's possible misrepresentations than about the fact that they had been kept out of the loop. But the president was undisturbed—or, in one version, "aggressively defensive"—and, while the greater White House looked on askance, Trump chose to take Flynn with him to Mar-a-Lago for his scheduled weekend with Shinzō Abe, the Japanese prime minister.

That Saturday night, in a bizarre spectacle, the Mar-a-Lago terrace became a public Situation Room when President Trump and Prime Minister Abe openly discussed how to respond to North Korea's launch of a missile three hundred miles into the Sea of Japan. Standing right over the president's shoulder was Michael Flynn. If Bannon, Priebus, and Kushner believed that Flynn's fate hung in the balance, the president seemed to have no such doubts.

For the senior White House staff, the underlying concern was less about getting rid of Flynn than about the president's relationship with Flynn. What had Flynn, in essence a spy in a soldier's uniform, roped the president into? What might they have got up to together?

On Monday morning, Kellyanne Conway appeared on MSNBC and offered a firm defense of the National Security Advisor. "Yes," she said, "General Flynn does enjoy the full confidence of the president." And while this seemed to many an indication that Conway was out of the loop, it was more accurately an indication that she had been talking directly to the president.

A White House meeting that morning failed to convince Trump to fire Flynn. He was concerned about what it would look like to lose his National Security Advisor after just twenty-four days. And he was adamant about not wanting to blame Flynn for talking to the Russians, even about sanctions. In Trump's view, condemning his adviser would connect him to a plot where there was no plot. His fury wasn't directed toward Flynn but to the "incidental" wiretap that had surveilled him. Making clear his confidence in his adviser, Trump insisted that Flynn come to Monday's lunch with the Canadian prime minister, Justin Trudeau.

Lunch was followed by another meeting about the furor. There were yet more details of the phone call and a growing itemization of the money Flynn had been paid by various Russian entities; there was also increasing focus on the theory that the leaks from the intel community—that is, the *whole* Russia mess—was directed at Flynn. Finally, there was a new rationale that Flynn should be fired not because of his Russian contacts, but because he had lied about them to the vice president. This was a convenient invention of a chain of command: in fact, Flynn did not report to Vice President Pence, and he was arguably a good deal more powerful than Pence.

The new rationale appealed to Trump, and he at last agreed that Flynn had to go.

Still, the president did not waiver in his belief in Flynn. Rather, Flynn's enemies were his enemies. And Russia was a gun to his head. He might, however ruefully, have had to fire Flynn, but Flynn was still his guy.

Flynn, ejected from the White House, had become the first established direct link between Trump and Russia. And depending on what he might say to whom, he was now potentially the most powerful person in Washington.

# 8

# ORG CHART

The White House, realized former naval officer Steve Bannon after a few weeks, was really a military base, a government-issue office with a mansion's façade and a few ceremonial rooms sitting on top of a secure installation under military command. The juxtaposition was striking: military hierarchy and order in the background, the chaos of the temporary civilian occupants in the fore.

You could hardly find an entity more at odds with military discipline than a Trump organization. There was no real up-and-down structure, but merely a figure at the top and then everyone else scrambling for his attention. It wasn't task-based so much as response-oriented—whatever captured the boss's attention focused everybody's attention. That was the way in Trump Tower, just as it was now the way in the Trump White House.

The Oval Office itself had been used by prior occupants as the ultimate power symbol, a ceremonial climax. But as soon as Trump arrived, he moved in a collection of battle flags to frame him sitting at his desk, and the Oval immediately became the scene of a daily Trump cluster-fuck. It's likely that more people had easy access to this president than any president before. Nearly all meetings in the Oval with the president were invariably surrounded and interrupted by a long list of retainers—indeed, everybody strove to be in every meeting. Furtive people skulked around without clear purpose: Bannon invariably found some reason to study papers in the corner and then to have a last word; Priebus kept his eye on Bannon; Kushner kept constant tabs on the whereabouts of the others. Trump liked to keep Hicks, Conway, and, often, his old *Apprentice* sidekick Omarosa Manigault—now with a confounding White House title—in constant hovering presence. As always, Trump wanted an eager audience, encouraging as many people as possible to make as many attempts as possible to be as close to him as possible. In time, however, he would take derisive notice of those who seemed most eager to suck up to him.

Good management reduces ego. But in the Trump White House, it could often seem that nothing happened, that reality simply did not exist, if it did not happen in Trump's presence. This made an upside-down kind of sense: if something happened and he wasn't present, he didn't care about it and barely recognized it. His response then was often just a blank stare. It also fed one theory of why hiring in the West Wing and through-out the executive branch was so slow—filling out the vast bureaucracy was out of his view and thus he couldn't care less. Likewise, visitors with appointments were befuddled by the West Wing's own lack of staff: after being greeted with a smart military salute by the dress marine at the West Wing door, they discovered that the West Wing often lacked a political-appointee receptionist, leaving guests to find their own way through the warren that was the Western world's pinnacle of power.

Trump, a former military academy cadet—albeit not an enthusiastic one—had touted a return to military values and expertise. In fact, he most of all sought to preserve his personal right to defy or ignore his own organization. This, too, made sense, since not really having an organization was the most efficient way to sidestep the people in your organization and to dominate them. It was just one irony of his court-ship of admired military figures like James Mattis, H. R. McMaster, and John Kelly: they found themselves working in an administration that was in every way inimical to basic command principles.

* * *

Almost from the beginning, the West Wing was run against the near-daily report that the person charged with running it, Chief of Staff Reince Priebus, was about to lose his job. Or, if he was not about to lose his job, the only reason he was keeping it was that he had not had it long enough to yet be fired from it. But no one in Trump's inner circle doubted that he would lose his job as soon as, practically speaking, his losing it would not embarrass the president too much. So, they reasoned, no one need pay any attention to him. Priebus, who, during the transition, doubted he would make it to the inauguration, and then, once in, wondered if he could endure the torture for the minimally respectable period of a year, shortly reduced his goal to six months.

The president himself, absent any organizational rigor, often acted as his own chief of staff, or, in a sense, elevated the press secretary job to the primary staff job, and then functioned as his own press secretary—reviewing press releases, dictating quotes, getting reporters on the phone—which left the actual press secretary as a mere flunky and whipping boy. Moreover, his relatives acted as ad hoc general managers of whatever areas they might choose to be general managers in. Then there was Bannon, conducting something of an alternate-universe operation, often launching far-reaching undertakings that no one else knew about. And thus Priebus, at the center of an operation that had no center, found it easy to think there was no reason for him to be there at all.

At the same time, the president seemed to like Priebus more and more quite for the reason that he seemed entirely expendable. He took Trump's verbal abuse about his height and stature affably, or anyway stoically. He was a convenient punching bag when things went wrong—and he didn't punch back, to Trump's pleasure and disgust.

"I love Reince," said the president, with the faintest praise. "Who else would do this job?"

Among the three men with effectively equal rank in the West Wing—Priebus and Bannon and Kushner—only a shared contempt kept them from ganging up on one another.

In the early days of Trump's presidency, the situation seemed clear to everybody: three men were fighting to run the White House, to be the real chief of staff and power behind the Trump throne. And of course there was Trump himself, who didn't want to relinquish power to anyone.

In these crosshairs was thirty-two-year-old Katie Walsh.

* * *

Walsh, the White House deputy chief of staff, represented, at least to herself, a certain Republican ideal: clean, brisk, orderly, efficient. A righteous
bureaucrat, pretty but with a permanently grim expression, Walsh was a
fine example of the many political professionals in whom competence
and organizational skills transcend ideology. (To wit: "I would much
rather be part of an organization that has a clear chain of command that
I disagree with than a chaotic organization that might seem to better
reflect my views.") Walsh was an inside-the-Beltway figure—a swamp
creature. Her expertise was prioritizing Beltway goals, coordinating
Beltway personnel, marshaling Beltway resources. A head-down-get-
things-done kind of person was how she saw herself. And no nonsense.

"Any time someone goes into a meeting with the president there are
like sixty-five things that have to happen first," she enumerated. "What
cabinet secretary has to be alerted about what person is going in there;
what people on the Hill should be consulted; the president needs a policy
briefing, so who's owning the brief and getting it to appropriate staff
members, oh and by the way you have to vet the guy. . . . Then you have
to give it to comms and figure out if it's a national story, a regional story
and are we doing op-eds, going on national TV . . . and that's before you
get to political affairs or public liaison. . . . And for anybody who meets
with the president, it has to be explained why other people are not meeting with him, or else they'll go out there and shit all over the last person
who was in. . . ."

Walsh was what politics is supposed to be—or what it has been. A
business supported by, tended to, and, indeed, ennobled, by a professional
political class. Politics, evident in the sameness and particular joylessness
of Washington dress, a determined anti-fashion statement, is about
procedure and temperament. Flash passes. No flash stays in the game.

From an all-girl Catholic school in St. Louis (still wearing a diamond
cross around her neck) and volunteer work on local political campaigns,
Walsh went to George Washington University—D.C. area colleges being
among the most reliable feeders of swamp talent (government is not really
an Ivy League profession). Most government and political organizations

are not run, for better or worse, by MBAs, but by young people distinguished only by their earnestness and public sector idealism and ambition. (It is an anomaly of Republican politics that young people motivated
to work in the public sector find themselves working to limit the public
sector.) Careers advance by how well you learn on the job and how well
you get along with the rest of the swamp and play its game.

In 2008, Walsh became the McCain campaign's midwest regional
finance director—having majored in marketing and finance at GW, she
was trusted to hold the checkbook. Then on to deputy finance director of
the National Republican Senatorial Committee, deputy finance director
and then finance director of the Republican National Committee, and
finally, pre–White House, chief of staff of the RNC and its chairman,
Reince Priebus.

In retrospect, the key moment in saving the Trump campaign might
be less the Mercer-led takeover and imposition of Bannon and Conway
in mid-August than the acceptance that the bare-bones and still largely
one-man organization would need to depend on the largesse of the
RNC. The RNC had the ground game and the data infrastructure; other
campaigns might not normally trust the national committee, with its
many snakes in the grass, but the Trump campaign had chosen not to
build this sort of organization or make this investment. In late August,
Bannon and Conway, with Kushner's consent, made a deal with the deep-
swamp RNC despite Trump's continued insistence that they'd gotten
this far without the RNC, so why come crawling now?

Almost right away Walsh became a key player in the campaign, a
dedicated, make-the-trains-run-on-time power centralizer—a figure
without which few organizations can run. Commuting between RNC
headquarters in Washington and Trump Tower, she was the quartermas-
ter who made national political resources available to the campaign.

If Trump himself was often a disruption in the final months of the
race and during the transition, the campaign around him, in part because
its only option was to smoothly integrate with the RNC, was a vastly
more responsive and unified organization than, say, the Hillary Clinton
campaign with its significantly greater resources. Facing catastrophe

and seeming certain humiliation, the Trump campaign pulled together—with Priebus, Bannon, and Kushner all starring in buddy-movie roles.

The camaraderie barely survived a few days in the West Wing.

* * *

To Katie Walsh, it became almost immediately clear that the common purpose of the campaign and the urgency of the transition were lost as soon as the Trump team stepped into the White House. They had gone from managing Donald Trump to the expectation of being managed by him—or at least through him and almost solely for his purposes. Yet the president, while proposing the most radical departure from governing and policy norms in several generations, had few specific ideas about how to turn his themes and vitriol into policy, nor a team that could reasonably unite behind him.

In most White Houses, policy and action flow down, with staff trying to implement what the president wants—or, at the very least, what the chief of staff says the president wants. In the Trump White House, policy making, from the very first instance of Bannon's immigration EO, flowed up. It was a process of suggesting, in throw-it-against-the-wall style, what the president might want, and hoping he might then think that he had thought of this himself (a result that was often helped along with the suggestion that he had in fact already had the thought).

Trump, observed Walsh, had a set of beliefs and impulses, much of them on his mind for many years, some of them fairly contradictory, and little of them fitting legislative or political conventions or form. Hence, she and everyone else was translating a set of desires and urges into a program, a process that required a lot of guess work. It was, said Walsh, "like trying to figure out what a child wants."

But making suggestions was deeply complicated. Here was, arguably, the central issue of the Trump presidency, informing every aspect of Trumpian policy and leadership: he didn't process information in any conventional sense—or, in a way, he didn't process it at all.

Trump didn't read. He didn't really even skim. If it was print, it might as well not exist. Some believed that for all practical purposes he was no more than semiliterate. (There was some argument about this, because he could read headlines and articles about himself, or at least headlines on articles about himself, and the gossip squibs on the *New York Post*'s Page Six.) Some thought him dyslexic; certainly his comprehension was limited. Others concluded that he didn't read because he just didn't have to, and that in fact this was one of his key attributes as a populist. He was postliterate—total television.

But not only didn't he read, he didn't listen. He preferred to be the person talking. And he trusted his own expertise—no matter how paltry or irrelevant—more than anyone else's. What's more, he had an extremely short attention span, even when he thought you were worthy of attention.

The organization therefore needed a set of internal rationalizations that would allow it to trust a man who, while he knew little, was entirely confident of his own gut instincts and reflexive opinions, however frequently they might change.

Here was a key Trump White House rationale: expertise, that liberal virtue, was overrated. After all, so often people who had worked hard to know what they knew made the wrong decisions. So maybe the gut was as good, or maybe better, at getting to the heart of the matter than the wonkish and data-driven inability to see the forest for the trees that often seemed to plague U.S. policy making. Maybe. *Hopefully.*

Of course, nobody really believed that, except the president himself.

Still, here was the basic faith, overriding his impetuousness and eccentricities and limited knowledge base: nobody became the president of the United States—that camel-through-the-eye-of-the-needle accomplishment—without unique astuteness and cunning. *Right?* In the early days of the White House, this was the fundamental hypothesis of the senior staff, shared by Walsh and everyone else: Trump must know what he was doing, his intuition must be profound.

But then there was the other aspect of his supposedly superb insight and apprehension, and it was hard to miss: he was often confident, but he was just as often paralyzed, less a savant in these instances than a figure of sputtering and dangerous insecurities, whose instinctive response was to lash out and behave as if his gut, however silent and confused, was in fact in some clear and forceful way telling him what to do.

During the campaign, he became a kind of vaunted action figure. His staff marveled at his willingness to keep moving, getting back on the plane and getting off the plane and getting back on, and doing rally after rally, with a pride in doing more events than anybody else—double Hillary's!—and ever ridiculing his opponent's slow pace. He *performed.* "This man never takes a break from being Donald Trump," noted Bannon, with a complicated sort of faint praise, a few weeks after joining the campaign full time.

It was during Trump's early intelligence briefings, held soon after he captured the nomination, that alarm signals first went off among his new campaign staff: he seemed to lack the ability to take in third-party information. Or maybe he lacked the interest; whichever, he seemed almost phobic about having formal demands on his attention. He stonewalled every written page and balked at every explanation. "He's a guy who really hated school," said Bannon. "And he's not going to start liking it now."

However alarming, Trump's way of operating also presented an opportunity to the people in closest proximity to him: by understanding him, by observing the kind of habits and reflexive responses that his business opponents had long learned to use to their advantage, they might be able to game him, to *move* him. Still, while he might be moved today, nobody underestimated the complexities of continuing to move him in the same direction tomorrow.

* * *

One of the ways to establish what Trump wanted and where he stood and what his underlying policy intentions were—or at least the intentions that you could convince him were his—came to involve an improbably close textual analysis of his largely off-the-cuff speeches, random remarks, and reflexive tweets during the campaign.

Bannon doggedly went through the Trump oeuvre highlighting possible insights and policy proscriptions. Part of Bannon's authority in the new White House was as keeper of the Trump promises, meticulously logged onto the white board in his office. Some of these promises Trump enthusiastically remembered making, others he had little memory of, but was happy to accept that he had said it. Bannon acted as disciple and promoted Trump to guru—or inscrutable God.

This devolved into a further rationalization, or Trump truth: "The president was very clear on what he wanted to deliver to the American public," said Walsh. He was "excellent in communicating this." At the same time, she acknowledged that it was not at all clear in any specific sense what he wanted. Hence, there was another rationalization: Trump was "inspirational not operational."

Kushner, understanding that Bannon's white board represented Bannon's agenda more than the president's agenda, got to wondering how much of this source text was being edited by Bannon. He made several attempts to comb through his father-in-law's words on his own before expressing frustration with the task and giving up.

Mick Mulvaney, the former South Carolina congressman now head of the Office of Management and Budget and directly charged with creating the Trump budget that would underlie the White House program, also fell back on the Trump spoken record. Bob Woodward's 1994 book, *The Agenda*, is a blow-by-blow account of the first eighteen months of the Clinton White House, most of it focused on creating the Clinton budget, with the single largest block of the president's time devoted to deep contemplation and arguments about how to allocate resources. In Trump's case, this sort of close and continuous engagement was inconceivable; budgeting was simply too small-bore for him.

"The first couple of times when I went to the White House, someone had to say, This is Mick Mulvaney, he's the budget director," said Mulvaney. And in Mulvaney's telling Trump was too scattershot to ever be of much help, tending to interrupt planning with random questions that seem to have come from someone's recent lobbying or by some burst of free association. If Trump cared about something, he usually already had a fixed view based on limited information. If he didn't care, he had no view and no information. Hence, the Trump budget team was also largely forced to return to Trump's speeches when searching for the general policy themes they could then fasten into a budget program.

* * *

Walsh, sitting within sight of the Oval Office, was located at something like the ground zero of the information flow between the president and his staff. As Trump's primary scheduler, her job was to ration the president's time and organize the flow of information to him around the priorities that the White House had set. In this, Walsh became the effective middle person among the three men working hardest to maneuver the president—Bannon, Kushner, and Priebus.

Each man saw the president as something of a blank page—or a scrambled one. And each, Walsh came to appreciate with increasing incredulity, had a radically different idea of how to fill or remake that page. Bannon was the alt-right militant. Kushner was the New York Democrat. And Priebus was the establishment Republican. "Steve wants to force a million people out of the country and repeal the nation's health law and lay on a bunch of tariffs that will completely decimate how we trade, and Jared wants to deal with human trafficking and protecting Planned Parenthood." And Priebus wanted Donald Trump to be another kind of Republican altogether.

As Walsh saw it, Steve Bannon was running the Steve Bannon White House, Jared Kushner was running the Michael Bloomberg White House, and Reince Priebus was running the Paul Ryan White House. It was a 1970s video game, the white ball pinging back and forth in the black triangle.

Priebus—who was supposed to be the weak link, thus allowing both Bannon and Kushner, variously, to be the effective chief of staff—was actually turning out to be quite a barking dog, even if a small one. In the Bannon world and in the Kushner world, Trumpism represented politics with no connection to the Republican mainstream, with Bannon reviling that mainstream and Kushner operating as a Democrat. Priebus, meanwhile, was the designated mainstream terrier.

Bannon and Kushner were therefore more than a little irritated to discover that the unimposing Priebus had an agenda of his own: heeding Senate leader Mitch McConnell's prescription that "this president will sign whatever is put in front of him," while also taking advantage of the White House's lack of political and legislative experience and outsourcing as much policy as possible to Capitol Hill.

In the early weeks of the administration, Priebus arranged for House

Speaker Paul Ryan, however much a Trumpist bête noire for much of the campaign, to come into the White House with a group of ranking committee chairmen. In the meeting, the president blithely announced that he had never had much patience for committees and so was glad someone else did. Ryan, henceforth, became another figure with unfettered access to the president—and to whom the president, entirely uninterested in legislative strategy or procedures, granted virtual carte blanche.

Almost nobody represented what Bannon opposed as well as Paul Ryan. The essence of Bannonism (and Mercerism) was a radical isolationism, a protean protectionism, and a determined Keynesianism. Bannon ascribed these principles to Trumpism, and they ran as counter to Republicanism as it was perhaps possible to get. What's more, Bannon found Ryan, in theory the House's policy whiz, to be slow-witted if not incompetent, and an easy and constant target of Bannon's under-his-breath ridicule. Still, if the president had unaccountably embraced Priebus-Ryan, he also could not do without Bannon.

Bannon's unique ability—partly through becoming more familiar with the president's own words than the president was himself, and partly through a cunning self-effacement (upended by his bursts of self-promotion)—was to egg the president on by convincing him that Bannon's own views were entirely derived from the president's views. Bannon didn't promote internal debate, provide policy rationale, or deliver Power-Point presentations; instead, he was the equivalent of Trump's personal talk radio. Trump could turn him on at any moment, and it pleased him that Bannon's pronouncements and views would consistently be fully formed and ever available, a bracing, unified-field narrative. As well, he could turn him off, and Bannon would be tactically quiet until turned on again.

Kushner had neither Bannon's policy imagination nor Priebus's institutional ties. But, of course, he had family status, carrying its own high authority. In addition, he had billionaire status. He had cultivated a wide range of New York and international money people, Trump acquaintances and cronies, and, often, people whom Trump would have wished to like him better than they did. In this, Kushner became the representative in the White House of the liberal status quo. He was something like what used to be called a Rockefeller Republican and now might more properly be a Goldman Sachs Democrat. He—and, perhaps even more, Ivanka—was at diametric odds with both Priebus, the stout-right, Sun Belt–leaning, evangelical dependent Republican, and Bannon, the alt-right, populist, anti-party disruptor.

From their separate corners each man pursued his own strategy. Bannon did all he could to roll over Priebus and Kushner in an effort to prosecute the war for Trumpism/Bannonism as quickly as possible. Priebus, already complaining about "political neophytes and the boss's relatives," subcontracted his agenda out to Ryan and the Hill. And Kushner, on one of the steepest learning curves in the history of politics (not that everyone in the White House wasn't on a steep curve, but Kushner's was perhaps the steepest), and often exhibiting a painful naïveté as he aspired to be one of the world's savviest players, was advocating doing nothing fast and everything in moderation. Each had coteries opposed to the other: Bannonites pursued their goal of breaking everything fast, Priebus's RNC faction focused on the opportunities for the Republican agenda, Kushner and his wife did their best to make their unpredictable relative look temperate and rational.

And in the middle was Trump.

\* \* \*

"The three gentlemen running things," as Walsh came to coolly characterize them, all served Trump in different ways. Walsh understood that Bannon provided the president with inspiration and purpose, while the Priebus-Ryan connection promised to do what to Trump seemed like the specialized work of government. For his part, Kushner best coordinated the rich men who spoke to Trump at night, with Kushner often urging them to caution him against both Bannon and Priebus.

The three advisers were in open conflict by the end of the second week following the immigration EO and travel ban debacle. This internal rivalry was the result of stylistic, philosophic, and temperamental differences; perhaps more important, it was the direct result of the lack of a rational org chart or chain of command. For Walsh, it was a daily process of managing an impossible task: almost as soon as she received direction from one of the three men, she would be countermanded by one or another of them.

"I take a conversation at face value and move forward with it," she defended herself. "I put what was decided on the schedule and bring in comms and build a press plan around it and bring in political affairs and office of public liaison. And then Jared says, Why did you do that. And I say, 'Because we had a meeting three days ago with you and Reince and Steve where you agreed to do this.' And he says, 'But that didn't mean I wanted it on the schedule. That's not why I had that conversation.' It almost doesn't matter what anyone says: Jared will agree, and then it will get sabotaged, and then Jared goes to the president and says, See, that was Reince's idea or Steve's idea."

Bannon concentrated on a succession of EOs that would move the new administration forward without having to wade through Congress. That focus was countermanded by Priebus, who was cultivating the Trump-Ryan romance and the Republican agenda, which in turn was countermanded by Kushner, who was concentrating on presidential bonhomie and CEO roundtables, not least because he knew how much the president liked them (and, as Bannon pointed out, because Kushner himself liked them). And instead of facing the inherent conflicts in each strategy, the three men recognized that the conflicts were largely irresolvable and avoided facing that fact by avoiding each other.

Each man had, in his own astute fashion, found his own way to appeal to the president and to communicate with him. Bannon offered a rousing fuck-you show of force; Priebus offered flattery from the congressional leadership; Kushner offered the approval of blue-chip businessmen. So strong were these particular appeals that the president typically preferred not to distinguish among them. They were all exactly what he wanted from the presidency, and he didn't understand why he couldn't have them all. He wanted to break things, he wanted a Republican Congress to give him bills to sign, and he wanted the love and respect of New York *machers* and socialites. Some inside the White House perceived that Bannon's EOs were meant to be a workaround in response to Priebus's courtship of the party, and that Kushner's CEOs were appalled by

Bannon's EOs and resistant to much of the Republican agenda. But if the president understood this, it did not particularly trouble him.

* * *

Having achieved something like executive paralysis within the first month of the new administration—each of the three gentlemen was as powerful in his allure to the president as the others and each, at times, was equally annoying to the president—Bannon, Priebus, and Kushner all built their own mechanisms to influence the president and undermine the others.

Analysis or argument or PowerPoint did not work. But who said what to Trump and when often did. If, at Bannon's prodding, Rebekah Mercer called him, that had an effect. Priebus could count on Paul Ryan's clout with him. If Kushner set up Murdoch to call, that registered. At the same time, each successive call mostly canceled the others out.

This paralysis led the three advisers to rely on the other particularly effective way to move him, which was to use the media. Hence each man became an inveterate and polished leaker. Bannon and Kushner studiously avoided press exposure; two of the most powerful people in government were, for the most part, entirely silent, eschewing almost all interviews and even the traditional political conversations on Sunday morning television. Curiously, however, both men became the background voices to virtually all media coverage of the White House. Early on, before getting down to attacking each other, Bannon and Kushner were united in their separate offensives against Priebus. Kushner's preferred outlet was Joe Scarborough and Mika Brzezinski's *Morning Joe*, one of the president's certain morning shows. Bannon's first port of call was the alt-right media ("Bannon's Breitbart shenanigans," in Walsh's view). By the end of the first month in the White House, Bannon and Kushner had each built a network of primary outlets, as well as secondary ones to deflect from the obviousness of the primary ones, creating a White House that simultaneously displayed extreme animosity toward the press and yet great willingness to leak to it. In this, at least, Trump's administration was achieving a landmark transparency.

The constant leaking was often blamed on lower minions and permanent executive branch staff, culminating in late February with an all-hands meeting of staffers called by Sean Spicer—cell phones surrendered at the door—during which the press secretary issued threats of random phone checks and admonitions about the use of encrypted texting apps. Everybody was a potential leaker; everybody was accusing everybody else of being a leaker.

Everybody *was* a leaker.

One day, when Kushner accused Walsh of leaking about him, she challenged him back: "My phone records versus yours, my email versus yours."

But most of the leaks, certainly the juiciest ones, were coming from the higher-ups—not to mention from the person occupying the topmost echelon.

The president couldn't stop talking. He was plaintive and self-pitying, and it was obvious to everyone that if he had a north star, it was just to be liked. He was ever uncomprehending about why everyone did not like him, or why it should be so difficult to get everyone to like him. He might be happy throughout the day as a parade of union steel workers or CEOs trooped into the White House, with the president praising his visitors and them praising him, but that good cheer would sour in the evening after several hours of cable television. Then he would get on the phone, and in unguarded ramblings to friends and others, conversations that would routinely last for thirty or forty minutes, and could go much longer, he would vent, largely at the media and his staff. In what was termed by some of the self-appointed Trump experts around him—and everyone was a Trump expert—he seemed intent on "poisoning the well," in which he created a loop of suspicion, disgruntlement, and blame heaped on others.

When the president got on the phone after dinner, it was often a rambling affair. In paranoid or sadistic fashion, he'd speculate on the flaws and weaknesses of each member of his staff. Bannon was disloyal (not to mention he always looks like shit). Priebus was weak (not to mention he was short—a midget). Kushner was a suck-up. Spicer was stupid (and looks terrible too). Conway was a crybaby. Jared and Ivanka should never have come to Washington.

His callers, largely because they found his conversation peculiar, alarming, or completely contrary to reason and common sense, often overrode what they might otherwise have assumed to be the confidential nature of the calls and shared the content with someone else. Hence news about the inner workings of the White House went into free circulation. Except it was not so much the inner workings of the White House— although it would often be reported as such—but the perambulations of the president's mind, which changed direction almost as fast as he could express himself. Yet there were constant tropes in his own narrative: Bannon was about to be cast out, Priebus too, and Kushner needed his protection from the other bullies.

So if Bannon, Priebus, and Kushner were now fighting a daily war with one another, it was mightily exacerbated by something of a running disinformation campaign about them that was being prosecuted by the president himself. A chronic naysayer, he viewed each member of his inner circle as a problem child whose fate he held in his hand. "We are sinners and he is God" was one view; "We serve at the president's displeasure," another.

\* \* \*

In the West Wing of every administration since at least that of Clinton and Gore, the vice president has occupied a certain independent power base in the organization. And yet Vice President Mike Pence—the fallback guy in an administration the length of whose term remained the subject of something like a national office betting pool—was a cipher, a smiling presence either resisting his own obvious power or unable to seize it.

"I do funerals and ribbon cuttings," he told a former Republican Hill colleague. In this, he was seen as either feigning an old-fashioned, what-me-worry, standard-issue veep identity lest he upset his patron or, in fact, honestly acknowledging who he was.

Katie Walsh, amid the chaos, saw the vice president's office as a point of calm in the storm. Pence's staff was not only known by people outside the White House for the alacrity with which it returned calls and for the ease with which it seemed to accomplish West Wing tasks, it also seemed to be comprised of people who liked each other and who were dedicated to a common goal: eliminating as much friction as possible around the vice president.

Pence started nearly every speech saying, "I bring greetings from our forty-fifth president of the United States, Donald J. Trump . . ."—a salutation directed more to the president than to the audience.

Pence cast himself as blandly uninteresting, sometimes barely seeming to exist in the shadow of Donald Trump. Little leaked out of the Pence side of the White House. The people who worked for the vice president, were, like Pence himself, people of few words.

In a sense, he had solved the riddle of how to serve as the junior partner to a president who could not tolerate any kind of comparisons: extreme self-effacement.

"Pence," said Walsh, "is not dumb."

Actually, well short of intelligent was exactly how others in the West Wing saw him. And because he wasn't smart, he was not able to provide any leadership ballast.

On the Jarvanka side, Pence became a point of grateful amusement. He was almost absurdly happy to be Donald Trump's vice president, happy to play the role of exactly the kind of vice president that would not ruffle Trump's feathers. The Jarvanka side credited Pence's wife, Karen, as the guiding hand behind his convenient meekness. Indeed, he took to this role so well that, later, his extreme submissiveness struck some as suspicious.

The Priebus side, where Walsh firmly sat, saw Pence as one of the few senior West Wing figures who treated Priebus as though he was truly the chief of staff. Pence often seemed like a mere staffer, the ever present note taker in so many meetings.

From the Bannon side, Pence garnered only contempt. "Pence is like the husband in *Ozzie and Harriet*, a nonevent," said one Bannonite.

Although many saw him as a vice president who might well assume the presidency someday, he was also perceived as the weakest vice president in decades and, in organizational terms, an empty suit who was useless in the daily effort to help restrain the president and stabilize the West Wing.

* * *

During that first month, Walsh's disbelief and even fear about what was happening in the White House moved her to think about quitting. Every day after that became its own countdown toward the moment she knew she wouldn't be able to take it anymore—which would finally come at the end of March. To Walsh, the proud political pro, the chaos, the rivalries, and the president's own lack of focus and lack of concern were simply incomprehensible.

In early March, Walsh confronted Kushner and demanded: "Just give me the three things the president wants to focus on. What are the three priorities of this White House?"

"Yes," said Kushner, wholly absent an answer, "we should probably have that conversation."

# 9

# CPAC

On February 23, a 75-degree day in Washington, the president woke up complaining about an overheated White House. But for once, the president's complaints were not the main concern. The excited focus in the West Wing was organizing a series of car pools out to the Conservative Political Action Conference, the annual gathering of conservative movement activists, which had outgrown the accommodations of Washington hotels and moved to the Gaylord Resort on Maryland's National Harbor waterfront. CPAC, right of right-of-center and trying to hold steady there, ambivalent about all the conservative vectors that further diverged from that point, had long had an uncomfortable relationship with Trump, viewing him as an unlikely conservative, if not a charlatan. CPAC, too, saw Bannon and Breitbart as practicing an outré conservatism. For several years Breitbart had staged a nearby competitive conference dubbed "The Uninvited."

But the Trump White House would dominate or even subsume the conference this year, and everybody wanted to turn out for this sweet moment. The president, set to speak on the second day, would, like Ronald Reagan, address the conference in his first year in office, whereas both Bushes, wary of CPAC and conservative activists, had largely snubbed the gathering.

Kellyanne Conway, a conference opener, was accompanied by her assistant, two daughters, and a babysitter. Bannon was making his first official pubic appearance of the Trump presidency, and his retinue included Rebekah Mercer, the pivotal Trump donor and Breitbart funder, her young daughter, and Allie Hanley, a Palm Beach aristocrat, conservative donor, and Mercer friend. (The imperious Hanley, who had not met Bannon before, pronounced him "dirty" looking.)

Bannon was scheduled to be interviewed in the afternoon session by CPAC chairman Matt Schlapp, a figure of strained affability who seemed to be trying to embrace the Trump takeover of his conference. A few days before, Bannon had decided to add Priebus to the interview, as both a private gesture of goodwill and a public display of unity—a sign of a budding alliance against Kushner.

In nearby Alexandria, Virginia, Richard Spencer, the president of the National Policy Institute, which is sometimes described as a "white supremacist think tank," who had, peskily for the White House, adopted the Trump presidency as a personal victory, was organizing his trip to CPAC, which would be as much a victory march for him as it was for the Trump team. Spencer—who, in 2016, he had declared, "Let's party like it's 1933," as in the year Hitler came to power—provoked an outcry with his widely covered "Heil Trump" (or "Hail Trump," which of course amounts to the same thing) salute after the election, and then achieved a kind of reverse martyrdom by taking a punch from a protester on Inauguration Day that was memorialized on YouTube.

CPAC, organized by the remnants of the conservative movement after Barry Goldwater's apocalyptic defeat in 1964, had, with stoic indefatigability, turned itself into the backbone of conservative survival and triumph. It had purged John Birchers and the racist right and embraced the philosophic conservative tenets of Russell Kirk and William F. Buckley. In time, it endorsed Reagan-era small government and antiregulatory reform, and then added the components of the cultural wars—antiabortion, anti-gay-marriage, and a tilt toward evangelicals— and married itself to conservative media, first right-wing radio and later Fox News. From this agglomeration it spun an ever more elaborate and all-embracing argument of conservative purity, synchronicity, and intellectual weight. Part of the fun of a CPAC conference, which attracted a wide assortment of conservative young people (reliably mocked as the Alex P. Keaton crowd by the growing throng of liberal press that covered the conference), was the learning of the conservative catechism.

But after a great Clinton surge in the 1990s, CPAC started to splinter during the George W. Bush years. Fox News became the emotional center of American conservativism. Bush neocons and the Iraq War were increasingly rejected by the libertarians and other suddenly breakaway factions (among them the paleocons); the family values right, meanwhile, was more and more challenged by younger conservatives. In the Obama years, the conservative movement was increasingly bewildered by Tea Party rejectionism and a new iconoclastic right-wing media, exemplified by Breitbart News, which was pointedly excluded from the CPAC conference.

In 2011, professing conservative fealty, Trump lobbied the group for a speaking slot and, with reports of a substantial cash contribution, was awarded a fifteen-minute berth. If CPAC was supposedly about honing a certain sort of conservative party line, it was also attentive to a wide variety of conservative celebrities, including, over the years, Rush Limbaugh, Ann Coulter, and various Fox News stars. The year before Obama's reelection, Trump fell into this category. But he was viewed quite differently four years later. In the winter of 2016, during the still competitive Republican primary race, Trump—now eyed as much as a Republican apostate as a Republican crowd pleaser—decided to forgo CPAC and what he feared would be less than a joyous welcome.

This year, as part of its new alignment with the Trump-Bannon White House, CPAC's personality headliner was slated to be the alt-right figure Milo Yiannopoulos, a gay British right-wing provocateur attached to Breitbart News. Yiannopoulos—whose entire position, rather more like a circa-1968 left-wing provocateur, seemed to be about flouting political correctness and social convention, resulting in left-wing hysteria and protests against him—was as confounding a conservative figure as could be imagined. Indeed, there was a subtle suggestion that CPAC had chosen Yiannopoulos precisely to hoist Bannon and the White House on the implicit connection to him—Yiannopoulos had been something of a

Bannon protégé. When, two days before CPAC opened, a conservative
blogger discovered a video of Yiannopoulos in bizarre revelry seeming
to rationalize pedophilia, the White House made it clear he had to go.

Still, the White House presence at CPAC—which included, along
with the president, Bannon, Conway, Education Secretary Betsy DeVos,
and the oddball White House foreign policy adviser and former Breitbart
writer Sebastian Gorka—seemed to push the Yiannopoulos mess to the
side. If CPAC was always looking to leaven boring politicians with star
power, Trump, and anyone connected him, were now the biggest stars.
With her family positioned out in front of a full house, Conway was
interviewed in Oprah-like style by Mercedes Schlapp (wife of Matt
Schlapp—CPAC was a family affair), a columnist for the conservative
*Washington Times* who would later join the White House communications staff. It was an intimate and inspirational view of a woman of high
achievement, the kind of interview that Conway believed she would have
been treated to on network and cable television if she were not a Trump
Republican—the type of treatment, she'd point out, that had been given
to Democratic predecessors like Valerie Jarrett.

At about the time that Conway was explaining her particular brand
of antifeminist feminism, Richard Spencer arrived at the convention center hoping to attend the breakout session "The Alt-Right Ain't Right at
All," a modest effort to reaffirm CPAC's traditional values. Spencer, who
since the Trump victory had committed himself to full-time activism and
press opportunities, had planned to position himself to get in the first
question. But almost immediately upon arriving and paying his $150 reg-
istration fee, he had attracted first one reporter and then a growing circle, a spontaneous press scrum, and he responded by giving an ad hoc
news conference. Like Yiannopoulos, and in many ways like Trump and
Bannon, Spencer helped frame the ironies of the modern conservative
movement. He was a racist but hardly a conservative—he doggedly supported single-payer health care, for instance. And the attention he received
was somehow less a credit to conservatism than another effort by the liberal media to smear conservatism. Hence, as the scrum around him
increased to as many as thirty people, the CPAC irony police stepped in.

"You're not welcome on the property," announced one of the security guards. "They want you off the property. They want you to cease. They want you off the property."

"Wow," said Spencer. "Can they?"

"Enough debate," the guard said. "This is private property and CPAC wants you off the property."

Relieved of his credentials, Spencer was ushered to the CPAC perimeter of the hotel, where, his pride not all that wounded, he turned, in the comfort of the atrium lounge area, to social media and to texting and emailing reporters on his contact list.

The point Spencer was making was that his presence here was not really so disruptive or ironic as Bannon's, or, for that matter, Trump's. He might be ejected, but in a larger historical sense it was the conservatives who were now being ejected from their own movement by the new cadre—which included Trump and Bannon—of what Spencer called the identitarians, proponents of "white interests, values, customs, and culture."

Spencer was, he believed, the true Trumper and the rest of CPAC now the outliers.

* * *

In the green room, after Bannon, Priebus, and their retinues had arrived, Bannon—in dark shirt, dark jacket, and white pants—stood off to the side talking to his aide, Alexandra Preate. Priebus sat in the makeup chair, patiently receiving a layer of foundation, powder, and lip gloss.

"Steve—" said Priebus, gesturing to the chair as he got up.

"That's okay," said Bannon. He put up his hand, making another of the continual small gestures meant, pointedly, to define himself as something other than every phony baloney in swampland politics—and something other than Reince Priebus, with his heavy powder foundation.

The significance of Bannon's first appearance in public—after days of apparent West Wing turmoil, a *Time* magazine cover story about him, nearly endless speculation about his power and true intentions, and his elevation at least in the media mind to the essential mystery of the Trump White House—could hardly be underestimated. For Bannon himself this was, in his own mind, a carefully choreographed moment. It was his victory walk. He had, he thought, prevailed in the West Wing. He had, again in his own mind, projected his superiority over both Priebus and the idiot son-in-law. And he would now dominate CPAC. But for the moment he attempted a shucks-nothing-to-it lack of self-consciousness even as, at the same time, he was unquestionably the preening man of the hour. Demurring about accepting makeup was not just a way to belittle Priebus, but also a way to say that, ever the commando, he went into battle fully exposed.

"You know what he thinks even when you don't know what he thinks," explained Alexandra Preate. "He's a bit like a good boy who everybody knows is a bad boy."

When the two men emerged onto the stage and appeared on the big-screen monitors, the contrast between them could hardly have been greater. The powder made Priebus look mannequin-like, and his suit with lapel pin, little-boyish. Bannon, the supposedly publicity-shy man, was eating up the camera. He was a country music star—he was Johnny Cash. He seized Priebus's hand in a power handshake, then relaxed in his chair as Priebus came too eagerly forward in his.

Priebus opened with traditional bromides. Bannon, taking his turn, went wryly for the dig: "I want to thank you for finally inviting me to CPAC."

"We decided to say that everybody is a part of our conservative family," said Matt Schlapp, resigned. He then welcomed "the back of the room," where the hundreds of reporters covering the event were positioned.

"Is that the opposition party?" asked Bannon, shielding his eyes.

Schlapp went to the setup question: "We read a lot about you two. Ahem . . ."

"It's all good," replied Priebus tightly.

"I'll bet not all of it's accurate," said Schlapp. "I'll bet there's things that don't get written correctly. Let me ask both of you, what's the biggest misconception about what's going on in the Donald Trump White House?"

Bannon responded with something just less than a smirk and said nothing.

Priebus offered a testimonial to the closeness of his relationship with Bannon.

Bannon, eyes dancing, lifted the microphone trumpetlike and made a joke about Priebus's commodious office—two couches and a fireplace—and his own rough-and-ready one.

Priebus hewed to the message. "It's, ahh . . . it's actually . . . something that you all have helped build, which is, when you bring together, and what this election shows, and what President Trump showed, and let's not kid ourselves, I can talk about data and ground game and Steve can talk about big ideas but the truth of the matter is Donald Trump, President Trump, brought together the party and the conservative movement, and I tell you if the party and the conservative movement are together"—Priebus knocked his fists—"similar to Steve and I, it can't be stopped. And President Trump is the one guy, he was the one person, and I can say this after overseeing sixteen people kill each other, it was Donald Trump who was able to bring this country, this party, and this movement together. And Steve and I know that and we live it every day and our job is to get the agenda of President Trump through the door and on pen and paper."

With Priebus gasping for breath, Bannon snatched the relay baton. "I think if you look at the opposition party"—throwing his hand out to the back of the room—"and how they portrayed the campaign, how they portrayed the transition, and now how they are portraying the administration, it's always wrong. I mean on the very first day that Kellyanne and I started, we reached out to Reince, Sean Spicer, Katie. . . . It's the same team, you know, that every day was grinding away at the campaign, the same team that did the transition, and if you remember, the campaign was the most chaotic, in the media's description, most chaotic, most disorganized, most unprofessional, had no earthly idea what they were doing, and then you saw 'em all crying and weeping that night on November 8."

Back in the White House, Jared Kushner, watching the proceedings casually and then more attentively, suddenly felt a rising anger. Thin-skinned, defensive, on guard, he perceived Bannon's speech as a message sent directly to him. Bannon has just credited the Trump victory to everybody else. Kushner was certain he was being taunted.

When Schlapp asked the two men to enumerate the accomplishments of the last thirty days, Priebus floundered and then seized on Judge Gorsuch and the deregulation executive orders, all things, said Priebus, "that"—he paused, struggling—"eighty percent of Americans agree with."

After a brief pause, as though waiting for the air to clear, Bannon raised the microphone: "I kind of break it down into three verticals, three buckets; the first, national security and sovereignty, and that's your intelligence, defense department, homeland security. The second line of work is what I refer to as economic nationalism, and that is Wilbur Ross at Commerce, Steve Mnuchin at Treasury, [Robert] Lighthizer at Trade, Peter Navarro, [and] Stephen Miller, who are rethinking how we are going to reconstruct our trade arrangements around the world. The third, broadly, line of work is deconstruction of the administrative state—" Bannon stopped for a moment; the phrase, which had never before been uttered in American politics, drew wild applause. "The way the progressive left runs is that if they can't get it passed they're just going to put it in some sort of regulation in an agency. That's all going to be deconstructed."

Schlapp fed another setup question, this one about the media.

Priebus grabbed it, rambled and fumphered for a while, and ended up, somehow, on a positive note: *We'll all come together.*

Lifting the microphone, once again Joshua-like, and with a sweeping wave of his hand, Bannon pronounced, "It's not only not going to get better, it's going to get worse every day"—his fundamental apocalyptic song—"and here's why—and by the way, the internal logic makes sense, corporatist, globalist media, that are adamantly opposed, adamantly opposed, to an economic nationalist agenda like Donald Trump has. And here's why it's going to get worse: because he's going to continue to press his agenda. And as economic conditions continue to get better, as more jobs get better, they're going to continue to fight. If you think they're going to give you your country back without a fight you are sadly mistaken. Every day it is going to be a fight. This is why I'm proudest of Donald Trump. All the opportunities he had to waver off this. All the people he had coming to him saying 'Oh, you got to moderate.'" Another dig at Kushner. "Every day in the Oval Office he tells Reince and me, 'I committed this to the American people. I promised this when I ran. And I'm going to deliver on this.'"

And then the final, agreed-upon-beforehand question: "Can this Trump movement be combined with what's happening at CPAC and other conservative movements for fifty years? Can this be brought together . . . and is this going to save the country?"

"Well, we have to stick together as a team," said Priebus. "It's gonna take all of us working together to make it happen."

As Bannon started into his answer, he spoke slowly, looking out at his captive and riveted audience: "I've said that there is a new political order being formed out of this and it's still being formed. If you look at the wide degree of opinions in this room, whether you are a populist, whether you're a limited-government conservative, whether you're a libertarian, whether you're an economic nationalist, we have wide and sometimes divergent opinions, but I think the center core of what we believe, that we're a nation with an economy, not an economy just in some global market place with open borders, but that we are a nation with a culture, and a reason for being. I think that's what unites us. And that's what's going to unite this movement going forward."

Bannon lowered the microphone to, after what might be interpreted as a beat of uncertainty, suddenly thunderous applause.

Watching from the White House, Kushner—who had come to believe that there was something insidious when Bannon used the words "borders," "global," "culture," and "unite," and who was more and more convinced that they were personally directed against him—was now in a rage.

*　*　*

Kellyanne Conway had increasingly been worrying about the seventy-year-old president's sleeplessness and his worn look. It was the president's indefatigability—a constant restlessness—that she believed carried the team. On the campaign trail, he would always add stops and speeches. He doubled his own campaign time. Hillary worked at half time; he worked at double time. He sucked in the energy from the crowds. Now that he was living alone in the White House, though, he had seemed to lose a step.

But today he was back. He had been under the sunlamp and lightened his hair, and when the climate-change-denying president woke up on another springlike morning, 77 degrees in the middle of winter, on the second day of CPAC, he seemed practically a different person, or anyway a noticeably younger one. At the appointed hour, to the locked-down ballroom at the Gaylord Resort, filled to capacity with all stripes of the conservative faithful—Rebekah Mercer and her daughter up front—and hundreds of media people in an SRO gallery, the president emerged onto the stage, not in an energetic television-style rush, but with a slow swagger to the low strains of "I'm Proud to Be an American." He came to the stage as a political strongman, a man occupying his moment, clapping—here he reverted to entertainer pose—as he slowly approached the podium, mouthing "Thank you," crimson tie dipping over his belt.

This would be Trump's fifth CPAC address. As much as Steve Bannon liked to see himself as the author of Donald Trump, he also seemed to find it proof of some added legitimacy—and somehow amazing in itself—that since 2011 Trump had basically come to CPAC with the same message. He wasn't a cipher, he was a messenger. The country was a "mess"—a word that had stood the Trump test of time. Its leaders were weak. Its greatness had been lost. The only thing different was that in 2011 he was still reading his speeches with only occasional ad-libs, and now he ad-libbed everything.

"My first major speech was at CPAC," the president began. "Probably five or six years ago. My first major political speech. You were there. I loved it. I loved the people. I loved the commotion. They did these polls where I went through the roof. I wasn't even running, right? But it gave me an idea! And I got a little bit concerned when I saw what was happening in the country so I said let's go to it. It was very exciting. I walked the stage at CPAC. I had very little notes and even less preparation." (In fact, he read his 2011 speech from a sheet of paper.) "So when you have practically no notes and no preparation and then you leave and everybody was thrilled. I said, I think I like this business."

This first preamble gave way to the next preamble.

"I want you all to know that we are fighting the fake news. It's phony.

Fake. A few days ago I called the fake news the enemy of the people. Because they have no sources. They just make 'em up when there are none. I saw one story recently where they said nine people have confirmed. There are no nine people. I don't believe there was one or two people. Nine people. And I said, Give me a break. I know the people. I know who they talk to. There were no nine people. But they say nine people. . . ."

A few minutes into the forty-eight-minute speech and it was already off the rails, riff sustained by repetition.

"Maybe they're just bad at polling. Or maybe they're not legit. It's one or the other. They're very smart. They're very cunning. And they're very dishonest. . . . Just to conclude"—although he would go on for thirty-seven minutes more—"it's a very sensitive topic and they get upset when we expose their false stories. They say we can't criticize their dishonest coverage because of the First Amendment. You know they always bring up"—he went into a falsetto voice—"*the First Amendment.* Now I love the First Amendment. Nobody loves it better than me. Nobody."

Each member of the Trump traveling retinue was now maintaining a careful poker face. When they did break it, it was as though on a delay, given permission by the crowd's cheering or laughter. Otherwise, they seemed not to know whether the president had in fact gotten away with his peculiar rambles.

"By the way, you folks in here, the place is packed, there are lines that go back six blocks"—there were no lines outside the crowded lobby—"I tell you that because you won't read about it. But there are lines that go back six blocks. . . .

"There is one allegiance that unites us all, to America, America. . . . We all salute with pride the same American flag . . . and we are all equal, equal in the eyes of Almighty God. . . . We're equal . . . and I want to thank, by the way, the evangelical community, the Christian community, communities of faith, rabbis and priests and pastors, ministers, because the support for me, as you know, was a record, not only numbers of people but percentages of those numbers who voted for Trump . . . an amazing outpouring and I will not disappoint you . . . as long as we have faith in each other and trust in God then there is no goal beyond our reach . . .

there is no dream too large . . . no task too great . . . we are Americans and the future belongs to us . . . America is roaring. It's going to be bigger and better and stronger than ever before. . . ."

Inside the West Wing, some had idly speculated about how long he would go on if he could command time as well as language. The consensus seemed to be forever. The sound of his own voice, his lack of inhibition, the fact that linear thought and presentation turned out not at all to be necessary, the wonder that this random approach seemed to command, and his own replenishing supply of free association—all this suggested that he was limited only by everyone else's schedule and attention span.

Trump's extemporaneous moments were always existential, but more so for his aides than for him. He spoke obliviously and happily, believing himself to be a perfect pitch raconteur and public performer, while everyone with him held their breath. If a wackadoo moment occurred on the occasions—the frequent occasions—when his remarks careened in no clear direction, his staff had to go into intense method-acting response. It took absolute discipline not to acknowledge what everyone could see.

* * *

As the president finished up his speech, Richard Spencer, who in less than four months from the Trump election was on his way to becoming the most famous neo-Nazi in America since George Lincoln Rockwell, had returned to a seat in the atrium of the Gaylord Resort to argue his affinity for Donald Trump—and, he believed, vice versa.

Spencer, curiously, was one of the few people trying to ascribe an intellectual doctrine to Trumpism. Between those taking him literally but not seriously, and those taking him seriously but not literally, there was Richard Spencer. Practically speaking, he was doing both, arguing the case that if Trump and Bannon were the pilot fish for a new conservative movement, Spencer himself—the owner of altright.com and, he believed, the purest exponent of the movement—was their pilot fish, whether they knew it or not.

As close to a real-life Nazi as most reporters had ever seen, Spencer was a kind of catnip for the liberal press crowded at CPAC. Arguably, he was offering as good an explanation of Trump's anomalous politics as anyone else.

Spencer had come up through writing gigs on conservative publications, but he was hardly recognizable in any sort of official Republican or conservative way. He was a post-right-wing provocateur but with none of the dinner party waspishness or bite of Ann Coulter or Milo Yiannopoulos. They were a stagey type of reactionary. He was a real one—a genuine racist with a good education, in his case UVA, the University of Chicago, and Duke.

It was Bannon who effectively gave Spencer flight by pronouncing Breitbart to be "the platform for the alt-right"—the movement Spencer claimed to have founded, or at least owned the domain name for.

"I don't think Bannon or Trump are identitarians or alt-rightists," Spencer explained while camped out just over CPAC's property line at the Gaylord. They were not, like Spencer, philosophic racists (itself different from a knee-jerk racist). "But they are open to these ideas. And open to the people who are open to these ideas. We're the spice in the mix."

Spencer was right. Trump and Bannon, with Sessions in the mix, too, had come closer than any major national politician since the Civil Rights movement to tolerating a race-tinged political view.

"Trump has said things that conservatives never would have thought. . . . His criticism of the Iraq War, bashing the Bush family, I couldn't believe he did that . . . but he did . . . . Fuck them . . . if at the end of the day an Anglo Wasp family produces Jeb and W then clearly that's a clear sign of denegation. . . . And now they marry Mexicans . . . Jeb's wife . . . he married his housekeeper or something.

"In Trump's 2011 CPAC address he specifically calls for a relaxation of immigration restrictions for Europeans . . . that we should re-create an America that was far more stable and more beautiful. . . . No other conservative politician would say those things . . . but on the other hand pretty much everyone thought it . . . so it's powerful to say it. . . . Clearly [there's] a normalization process going on."

"We are the Trump vanguard. The left will say Trump is a nationalist and an implicit or quasi-racialist. Conservatives, because they are just so douchey, say Oh, no, of course not, he's a constitutionalist, or whatever.

We on the alt-right will say, He is a nationalist and he is a racialist. His movement is a white movement. Duh."

Looking very satisfied with himself, Spencer paused and then said: "We give him a kind of permission."

* * *

Nearby, in the Gaylord atrium, Rebekah Mercer sat having a snack with her home-schooled daughter and her friend and fellow conservative donor Allie Hanley. Both women agreed that the president's CPAC speech showed him at his most gracious and charming.

# 10

# GOLDMAN

The Jarvanka side of the White House increasingly felt that rumors leaked by Bannon and his allies were undermining them. Jared and Ivanka, ever eager to enhance their status as the adults in the room, felt personally wounded by these backdoor attacks. Kushner, in fact, now believed Bannon would do anything to destroy them. This was personal. After months of defending Bannon against liberal media innuendo, Kushner had concluded that Bannon was an anti-Semite. That was the bottom-line issue. This was a complicated and frustrating business— and quite hard to communicate to his father-in-law—because one of Bannon's accusations against Kushner, the administration's point person on the Middle East, was that he was not nearly tough enough in his defense of Israel.

After the election, the Fox News anchor Tucker Carlson with sly jocularity privately pointed out to the president that by offhandedly giving the Israel portfolio to his son-in-law—who would, Trump said, make peace in the Middle East—he hadn't really done Kushner any favors.

"I know," replied Trump, quite enjoying the joke.

Jews and Israel were a curious Trump subtext. Trump's brutish father was an often vocal anti-Semite. In the split in New York real estate between the Jews and non-Jews, the Trumps were clearly on the lesser side. The Jews were white shoe, and Donald Trump, even more than his father, was perceived as a vulgarian—after all, he put his name on his buildings, quite a déclassé thing to do. (Ironically, this proved to be a significant advance in real estate marketing and, arguably, Trump's greatest accomplishment as a developer—branding buildings.) But Trump had grown up and built his business in New York, the world's largest Jewish city. He had made his reputation in the media, that most Jewish of industries, with some keen understanding of media tribal dynamics. His mentor, Roy Cohn, was a demimonde, semiunderworld, tough-guy Jew. He courted other figures he considered "tough-guy Jews" (one of his accolades): Carl Icahn, the billionaire hedge funder; Ike Perlmutter, the billionaire investor who had bought and sold Marvel Comics; Ronald Perelman, the billionaire Revlon chairman; Steven Roth, the New York billionaire real estate tycoon; and Sheldon Adelson, the billionaire casino magnate. Trump had adopted a sort of 1950s Jewish uncle (tough-guy variety) delivery, with assorted Yiddishisms—Hillary Clinton, he declared, had been "shlonged" in the 2008 primary—helping to give an inarticulate man an unexpected expressiveness. Now his daughter, a de facto First Lady, was, through her conversion, the first Jew in the White House.

The Trump campaign and the White House were constantly supplying off-note messages about Jews, from their equivocal regard for David Duke to their apparent desire to tinker with Holocaust history—or at least tendency to stumble over it. At one point early in the campaign, Trump's son-in-law, challenged by his own staff at the *New York Observer* and feeling pressure about his own bona fides, as well as seeking to stand by his father-in-law, wrote an impassioned defense of Trump in an attempt to prove that he was not an anti-Semite. For his efforts, Jared was rebuked by various members of his own family, who clearly seemed worried about both the direction of Trumpism and Jared's opportunism.

There was also the flirtation with European populism. Whenever possible, Trump seemed to side with and stoke Europe's rising right, with its anti-Semitic associations, piling on more portent and bad vibes. And then there was Bannon, who had allowed himself to become—through his orchestration of right-wing media themes and stoking of liberal outrage—a winking suggestion of anti-Semitism. It was certainly good right-wing business to annoy liberal Jews.

Kushner, for his part, was the prepped-out social climber who had rebuffed all entreaties in the past to support traditional Jewish organizations. When called upon, the billionaire scion had refused to contribute. Nobody was more perplexed by the sudden rise of Jared Kushner to his new position as Israel's great protector than U.S. Jewish organizations. Now, the Jewish great and the good, the venerated and the tried, the mandarins and myrmidons, had to pay court to Jared Kushner . . . who until little more than a few minutes ago had truly been a nobody.

For Trump, giving Israel to Kushner was not only a test, it was a Jewish test: the president was singling him out for being Jewish, rewarding him for being Jewish, saddling him with an impossible hurdle for being Jewish—and, too, defaulting to the stereotyping belief in the negotiating powers of Jews. "Henry Kissinger says Jared is going to be the new Henry Kissinger," Trump said more than once, rather a combined compliment and slur.

Bannon, meanwhile, did not hesitate to ding Kushner on Israel, that peculiar right-wing litmus test. Bannon could bait Jews—globalist, cosmopolitan, Davoscentric liberal Jews like Kushner—because the farther right you were, the more correct you were on Israel. Netanyahu was an old Kushner family friend, but when, in the fall, the Israeli prime minister came to New York to meet with Trump and Kushner, he made a point of seeking out Steve Bannon.

On Israel, Bannon had partnered with Sheldon Adelson, titan of Las Vegas, big-check right-wing contributor, and, in the president's mind, quite the toughest tough-guy Jew (that is, the richest). Adelson regularly disparaged Kushner's motives and abilities. The president, to Bannon's great satisfaction, kept telling his son-in-law, as he strategized on Israel, to check with Sheldon and, hence, Bannon.

Bannon's effort to grab the stronger-on-Israel label was deeply confounding to Kushner, who had been raised as an Orthodox Jew. His closest lieutenants in the White House, Avi Berkowitz and Josh Raffel, were

Orthodox Jews. On Friday afternoons, all Kushner business in the White House stopped before sunset for the Sabbath observance.

For Kushner, Bannon's right-wing defense of Israel, embraced by Trump, somehow became a jujitsu piece of anti-Semitism aimed directly at him. Bannon seemed determined to make Kushner appear weak and inadequate—a cuck, in alt-right speak.

So Kushner had struck back, bringing into the White House his own tough-guy Jews—Goldman Jews.

* * *

Kushner had pushed for the then president of Goldman Sachs, Gary Cohn, to run the National Economic Council and to be the president's chief economic adviser. Bannon's choice had been CNBC's conservative anchor and commentator Larry Kudlow. For Trump, the Goldman cachet outdrew even a television personality.

It was a Richie Rich moment. Kushner had been a summer intern at Goldman when Cohn was head of commodities trading. Cohn then became president of Goldman in 2006. Once Cohn joined Trump's team, Kushner often found occasion to mention that the president of Goldman Sachs was working for him. Bannon, depending on whom he wanted to slight, either referred to Kushner as Cohn's intern or pointed out that Cohn was now working for his intern. The president, for his part, was continually pulling Cohn into meetings, especially with foreign leaders, just to introduce him as the former president of Goldman Sachs.

Bannon had announced himself as Trump's brain, a boast that vastly irritated the president. But in Cohn, Kushner saw a better brain for the White House: not only was it much more politic for Cohn to be Kushner's brain than Trump's, but installing Cohn was the perfect countermove to Bannon's chaos management philosophy. Cohn was the only person in the West Wing who had ever managed a large organization (Goldman has thirty-five thousand employees). And, not to put too fine a point on it—though Kushner was happy to do so—Bannon had rolled out of Goldman having barely reached midlevel management status, whereas Cohn, his contemporary, had continued on to the firm's highest level, making hundreds of millions of dollars in the process. Cohn—a Democrat globalist-cosmopolitan Manhattanite who voted for Hillary Clinton and who still spoke frequently to former Goldman chief and former Democratic New Jersey senator and governor Jon Corzine— immediately became Bannon's antithesis.

For Bannon, the ideologue, Cohn was the exact inverse, a commodities trader doing what traders do—read the room and figure out which way the wind is blowing. "Getting Gary to take a position on something is like nailing butterflies to the wall," commented Katie Walsh.

Cohn started to describe a soon-to-be White House that would be business-focused and committed to advancing center-right to moderate positions. In this new configuration, Bannon would be marginalized and Cohn, who was dismissive of Priebus, would be the chief of staff in waiting. To Cohn, it seemed like easy street. Of course it would work out this way: Priebus was a lightweight and Bannon a slob who couldn't run anything.

Within weeks of Cohn's arrival on the transition team, Bannon nixed Cohn's plan to expand the National Economic Council by as many as thirty people. (Kushner, not to be denied, nixed Bannon's plan to have David Bossie build and lead his staff.) Bannon also retailed the likely not-too-far-off-the-mark view (or, anyway, a popular view inside Goldman Sachs) that Cohn, once slated to become Goldman's CEO, had been forced out for an untoward Haig-like grasping for power—in 1981 then secretary of state Alexander Haig had tried to insist he held the power after Ronald Reagan was shot—when Goldman CEO Lloyd Blankfein underwent cancer treatment. In the Bannon version, Kushner had bought damaged goods. The White House was clearly Cohn's professional lifeline—why else would he have come into the Trump administration? (Much of this was retailed to reporters by Sam Nunberg, the former Trump factotum who was now doing duty for Bannon. Nunberg was frank about his tactics: "I beat the shit out of Gary whenever possible.")

It is a measure of the power of blood (or blood by marriage), and likely the power of Goldman Sachs, too, that in the middle of a Republican-controlled Washington and a virulent, if not anti-Semitic (at least toward liberal Jews), right-wing West Wing, the Kushner-Cohn Democrats appeared to be ascendant. Part of the credit went to Kushner, who showed an unexpected tenacity. Conflict averse—in the Kushner household, his father, monopolizing all the conflict, forced everyone else to be a mollifier—confronting neither Bannon nor his father-in-law, he began to see himself in a stoic sense: he was the last man of moderation, the true figure of self-effacement, the necessary ballast of the ship. This would all be made manifest by a spectacular accomplishment. He would complete the mission his father-in-law had foisted on him, the one he was more and more seeing as his, yes, destiny. He *would* make peace in the Middle East.

"He's going to make peace in the Middle East," Bannon said often, his voice reverent and his expression deadpan, cracking up all the Bannonites.

So in one sense Kushner was a figure of heightened foolishness and ridicule. In another, he was a man, encouraged by his wife and by Cohn, who saw himself on the world stage carrying out a singular mission.

Here was yet another battle to be won or lost. Bannon regarded Kushner and Cohn (and Ivanka) as occupying an alternative reality that had little bearing on the real Trump revolution. Kushner and Cohn saw Bannon as not just destructive but self-destructive, and they were confident he would destroy himself before he destroyed them.

In the Trump White House, observed Henry Kissinger, "it is a war between the Jews and the non-Jews."

* * *

For Dina Powell, the other Goldman hire in the West Wing, the main consideration when Ivanka pitched her on coming to work at the White House was the downside assessment of being associated with a Trump presidency. Powell ran the Goldman Sachs philanthropic arm, a public relations initiative as well as a courtship of the increasingly powerful pools of philanthropic money. Representing Goldman, she had become something of a legend at Davos, a supreme networker among the world's supreme networkers. She stood at an intersection of image and fortune, in a world increasingly swayed by private wealth and personal brands.

It was a function of both her ambition and Ivanka Trump's sales talents during swift meetings in New York and Washington that Powell, swallowing her doubts, had come on board. That, and the politically risky but high-return gamble that she, aligned with Jared and Ivanka, and working closely with Cohn, her Goldman friend and ally, could take over the White House. That was the implicit plan: nothing less. Specifically, the idea was that Cohn or Powell—and quite possibly both over the course of the next four or eight years—would, as Bannon and Priebus faltered, come to hold the chief of staff job. The president's own constant grumbling about Bannon and Priebus, noted by Ivanka, encouraged this scenario.

This was no small point: a motivating force behind Powell's move was the certain belief on the part of Jared and Ivanka (a belief that Cohn and Powell found convincing) that the White House was theirs to take. For Cohn and Powell, the offer to join the Trump administration was transmuted beyond opportunity and became something like duty. It would be their job, working with Jared and Ivanka, to help manage and shape a White House that might otherwise become the opposite of the reason and moderation they could bring. They could be instrumental in saving the place—and, as well, take a quantum personal leap forward.

More immediately for Ivanka, who was focused on concerns about women in the Trump White House, Powell was an image correction to Kellyanne Conway, whom, quite apart from their war with Bannon, Ivanka and Jared disdained. Conway, who continued to hold the president's favor and to be his preferred defender on the cable news shows, had publicly declared herself the face of the administration—and for Ivanka and Jared, this was a horrifying face. The president's worst impulses seem to run through Conway without benefit of a filter. She compounded Trump's anger, impulsiveness, and miscues. Whereas a presidential adviser was supposed to buffer and interpret his gut calls, Conway expressed them, doubled down on them, made opera out of them. She took Trump's demand for loyalty too literally. In Ivanka and Jared's view, Conway was a cussed, antagonistic, self-dramatizing cable head, and Powell, they hoped, would be a deliberate, circumspect, adult guest on the Sunday morning shows.

By late February, after the first helter-skelter month in the West Wing, the campaign by Jared and Ivanka to undermine Bannon seemed to be working. The couple had created a feedback loop, which included Scarborough and Murdoch, that reinforced the president's deep annoyance with and frustration about Bannon's purported importance in the White House. For weeks after the *Time* magazine cover story featuring Bannon, there was hardly a conversation in which Trump didn't refer to it bitterly. ("He views *Time* covers as zero sum," said Roger Ailes. "If someone else gets on it, he doesn't.") Scarborough, cruelly, kept up a constant patter about President Bannon. Murdoch forcefully lectured the president about the oddness and extremism of Bannonism, linking Bannon with Ailes: "They're both crazy," he told Trump.

Kushner also pressed the view to the president—ever phobic about any age-related weakness—that the sixty-three-year-old Bannon wouldn't hold up under the strain of working in the White House. Indeed, Bannon was working sixteen- and eighteen-hour days, seven days a week, and, for fear of missing a presidential summons or afraid that someone else might grab it, he considered himself on call pretty much all night. As the weeks went by, Bannon seemed physically to deteriorate in front of everybody's eyes: his face became more puffy, his legs more swollen, his eyes more bleary, his clothes more slept in, his attention more distracted.

\* \* \*

As Trump's second month in office began, the Jared-Ivanka-Gary-Dina camp focused on the president's February 28 speech to the joint session of Congress.

"Reset," declared Kushner. "Total reset."

The occasion provided an ideal opportunity. Trump would have to deliver the speech in front of him. It was not only on the teleprompter but distributed widely beforehand. What's more, the well-mannered crowd wouldn't egg him on. His handlers were in control. And for this occasion at least, Jared-Ivanka-Gary-Dina were the handlers.

"Steve will take credit for this speech if there's even one word of his in it," Ivanka told her father. She knew well that for Trump, credit, much more than content, was the hot-button driver, and her comment ensured that Trump would keep it out of Bannon's hands.

"The Goldman speech," Bannon called it.

The inaugural, largely written by Bannon and Stephen Miller, had shocked Jared and Ivanka. But a particular peculiarity of the Trump White House, compounding its messaging problems, was its lack of a speech-writing team. There was the literate and highly verbal Bannon, who did not really do any actual writing himself; there was Stephen Miller, who did little more than produce bullet points. Beyond that, it was pretty much just catch as catch can. There was a lack of coherent message because there was nobody to write a coherent message—just one more instance of disregarding political craft.

Ivanka grabbed firm control of the joint session draft and quickly began pulling in contributions from the Jarvanka camp. In the event, the president behaved exactly as they hoped. Here was an upbeat Trump, a salesman Trump, a nothing-to-be-afraid-of Trump, a happy-warrior Trump. Jared, Ivanka, and all their allies judged it a magnificent night, agreeing that finally, amid the pageantry—*Mr. Speaker, the President of the United States*—the president really did seem presidential. And for once, even the media agreed.

The hours following the president's speech were Trump's best time in the White House. It was, for at least one news cycle, a different presidency. For a moment, there was even something like a crisis of conscience among parts of the media: Had this president been grievously misread? Had the media, the biased media, missed well-intentioned Donald Trump? Was he finally showing his better nature? The president himself spent almost two full days doing nothing but reviewing his good press. He had arrived, finally, at a balmy shore (with appreciative natives on the beach). What's more, the success of the speech confirmed the Jared and Ivanka strategy: look for common ground. It also confirmed Ivanka's understanding of her father: he just wanted to be loved. And, likewise, it confirmed Bannon's worst fear: Trump, in his true heart, was a marsh-mallow.

The Trump on view the night of the joint session was not just a new Trump, but a declaration of a new West Wing brain trust (which Ivanka was making plans to formally join in just a few weeks). Jared and Ivanka, with an assist from their Goldman Sachs advisers, were changing the message, style, and themes of the White House. "Reaching out" was the new theme.

Bannon, hardly helping his cause, cast himself as a Cassandra to anyone who would listen. He insisted that only disaster would come from trying to mollify your mortal enemies. You need to keep taking the fight to them; you're fooling yourself if you believe that compromise is possible. The virtue of Donald Trump—the virtue, anyway, of Donald Trump to Steve Bannon—was that the cosmopolitan elite was never going to accept him. He was, after all, Donald Trump, however much you shined him up.

# 11

# WIRETAP

With three screens in his White House bedroom, the president was his own best cable curator. But for print he depended on Hope Hicks. Hicks, who had been his junior aide for most of the campaign and his spokesperson (although, as he would point out, he was really his own spokesperson), had been, many thought, pushed to the sidelines in the West Wing by the Bannonites, the Goldman wing, and the Priebus-RNC professionals. To the senior staff, she seemed not only too young and too inexperienced—she was famous among campaign reporters for her hard-to-maneuver-in short skirts—but a way-too-overeager yes woman, always in fear of making a mistake, ever tremulously second-guessing herself and looking for Trump's approval. But the president kept rescuing her—"Where's Hope?"—from any oblivion others tried to assign her to. Baffling to almost everyone, Hicks remained his closest and most trusted aide, with, perhaps, the single most important job in this White House: interpreting the media for him in the most positive way it could be interpreted, and buffering him from the media that could not be positively spun.

The day after his "reset" speech before the joint session of Congress presented a certain conundrum for Hicks. Here were the first generally good notices for the administration. But in the *Post*, the *Times*, and the

*New Yorker* that day, there was also an ugly bouquet of very bad news. Fortunately the three different stories had not quite sunk into cable, so there was yet a brief respite. And at least for the better part of the day, March 1, Hicks herself did not entirely seem to grasp how bad the news actually was.

The *Washington Post*'s story was built around a leak from a Justice Department source (characterized as a "former senior American official"—hence, most likely someone from the Obama White House) saying that the new attorney general, Jeff Sessions, had, on two occasions, met with the Russian ambassador, Sergey Kislyak.

When the president was shown the story, he didn't see its significance. "So what?" he said.

Well, during his confirmation, it was explained to the president, Sessions had said he didn't.

Facing Sessions at the January 10 hearing, Al Franken, the former comedian and Democratic senator from Minnesota, appeared to be casting blindly for an elusive fish in his efforts to find a question. Stopping and starting, slogging through his sentence construction, Franken, who had been handed a question based on the just-revealed Steele dossier, got to this end:

> These documents also allegedly say, quote, "There was a continuing exchange of information during the campaign between Trump's surrogates and intermediaries for the Russian government."
>
> Now, again, I'm telling you this as it's coming out, so you know. But if it's true, it's obviously extremely serious and if there is any evidence that anyone affiliated with the Trump campaign communicated with the Russian government in the course of this campaign, what will you do?

Instead of answering Franken's circuitous question—"What will you do?"—with an easy "We will of course investigate and pursue any and all illegal actions," a confused Sessions answered a question he wasn't asked.

Senator Franken, I'm not aware of any of those activities. I have been called a surrogate at a time or two in that campaign and I didn't have—did not have communications with the Russians, and I'm unable to comment on it.

The president's immediate focus was on the question of why anyone believed that communicating with the Russians was bad. There *is* nothing wrong with that, Trump insisted. As in the past, it was hard to move him off this point and to the issue at hand: a possible lie to Congress. The *Post* story, to the extent that it registered at all, didn't worry him. Supported by Hicks, he saw it a way-long-shot effort to pin something on Sessions. And anyway, Sessions was saying he didn't meet with the Russians as *a campaign surrogate.* So? He didn't. Case closed.

"Fake news," said the president, using his now all-purpose rejoinder.

As for the bad *Times* story, as Hicks related it to the president, it appeared to him to be good news. Briefed by anonymous sources in the Obama administration (*more* anonymous Obama sources), the story revealed a new dimension to the ever growing suggestion of a connection between the Trump campaign and Russian efforts to influence the U.S. election:

American allies, including the British and the Dutch, had provided information describing meetings in European cities between Russian officials—and others close to Russia's president, Vladimir V. Putin— and associates of President-elect Trump, according to three former American officials who requested anonymity in discussing classified intelligence.

And:

Separately, American intelligence agencies had intercepted communications of Russian officials, some of them within the Kremlin, discussing contacts with Trump associates.

The story went on:

Mr. Trump has denied that his campaign had any contact with Russian officials, and at one point he openly suggested that American spy
agencies had cooked up intelligence suggesting that the Russian government had tried to meddle in the presidential election. Mr. Trump
has accused the Obama administration of hyping the Russia story
line as a way to discredit his new administration.

And then the real point:

At the Obama White House, Mr. Trump's statements stoked fears
among some that intelligence could be covered up or destroyed—or
its sources exposed—once power changed hands. What followed was
a push to preserve the intelligence that underscored the deep anxiety
with which the White House and American intelligence agencies had
come to view the threat from Moscow.

Here was more confirmation of a central Trump thesis: The previous
administration, its own candidate defeated, was not just disregarding the
democratic custom of smoothing the way for the winner of the election;
rather, in the Trump White House view, Obama's people had plotted with
the intelligence community to put land mines in the new administration's
way. Secret intelligence was, the story suggested, being widely distributed
across intelligence agencies so as to make it easier to leak, and at the same
time to protect the leakers. This intelligence, it was rumored, consisted of
spreadsheets kept by Susan Rice that listed the Trump team's Russian
contacts; borrowing a technique from WikiLeaks, the documents were
secreted on a dozen servers in different places. Before this broad distribution, when the information was held tightly, it would have been easy to
identify the small pool of leakers. But the Obama administration had significantly expanded that pool.

So this was good news, right? Wasn't this proof, the president asked,
that Obama and his people were out to get him? The *Times* story was a

leak about a plan to leak—and it provided clear evidence of the deep state.

Hope Hicks, as always, supported Trump's view. The crime was leaking and the culprit was the Obama administration. The Justice Department, the president was confident, was now going to investigate the former president and his people. Finally.

* * *

Hope Hicks also brought to the president a big piece in the *New Yorker*. The magazine had just published an article by three authors—Evan Osnos, David Remnick, and Joshua Yaffa—attributing Russian aggressiveness to a new cold war. Remnick, the editor of the *New Yorker*, had, since the Trump election, propounded an absolutist view that Trump's election imperiled Democratic norms.

This 13,500-word story—handily connecting the dots of Russia's geopolitical mortification, Putin's ambition, the country's cyber talents, Trump's own nascent authoritarianism, and the U.S. intelligence community's suspicions about Putin and Russia—codified a new narrative as coherent and as apocalyptic as the one about the old cold war. The difference was that in this one, the ultimate result was Donald Trump—he was the nuclear bomb. One of the frequently quoted sources in the article was Ben Rhodes, the Obama aide who, Trump's camp believed, was a key leaker, if not one of the architects of the Obama administration's continued effort to connect Trump and his team to Putin and Russia. Rhodes, many in the White House believed, *was* the deep state. They also believed that every time a leak was credited to "former and current officials," Rhodes was the former official who was in close touch with current officials.

While the article was largely just a dire recapitulation of fears about Putin and Trump, it did, in a parenthesis toward the end of the article— quite burying the lead—connect Jared Kushner to Kislyak, the Russian ambassador, in a meeting in Trump Tower with Michael Flynn in December.

Hicks missed this point; later, it had to be highlighted for the president by Bannon.

Three people in the Trump administration—the former National Security Advisor, the current attorney general, and the president's senior adviser and son-in-law—had now been directly connected to the Russian diplomat.

To Kushner and his wife, this was less than innocent: they would, with a sense of deepening threat, suspect Bannon of leaking the information about Kushner's meeting with Kislyak.

\* \* \*

Few jobs in the Trump administration seemed so right, fitting, and even destined to their holder as Jeff Sessions's appointment as the nation's top law enforcement officer. As he viewed his work as AG, it was his mandate to curb, circumscribe, and undo the interpretation of federal law that had for three generations undermined American culture and offended his own place in it. "This is his life's work," said Steve Bannon.

And Sessions was certainly not going to risk his job over the silly Russia business, with its growing collection of slapstick Trump figures. God knows what those characters were up to—nothing good, everybody assumed. Best to have nothing to do with it.

Without consulting the president or, ostensibly, anyone in the White House, Sessions decided to move as far as possible out of harm's way. On March 2, the day after the *Post* story, he recused himself from anything having to do with the Russia investigation.

The news of the attorney general's recusal exploded like an IED in the White House. Sessions was Trump's protection against an overly aggressive Russian investigation. The president just could not grasp the logic here. He railed to friends: Why would Sessions not want to protect him? What would Sessions gain? Did he think this stuff was real? Sessions needed to do his job!

In fact, Trump already had good reason to worry about the DOJ. The president had a private source, one of his frequent callers, who, he believed, was keeping him abreast of what was going on in the Justice Department—and, the president noted, doing a much better job of it than Sessions himself.

The Trump administration, as a consequence of the Russia story, was involved in a high-stakes bureaucratic push-pull, with the president going outside government to find out what was happening in his own government. The source, a longtime friend with his own DOJ sources— many of the president's rich and powerful friends had their own reasons to keep close tabs on what was happening at the Justice Department—fed the president a bleak picture of a Justice Department and an FBI run amok in its efforts to get him. "Treason" was a word that was being used, the president was told.

"The DOJ," the president's source told him, "was filled with women who hated him." It was an army of lawyers and investigators taking instructions from the former administration. "They want to make Water-gate look like Pissgate," the president was told. This comparison confused Trump; he thought his friend was making a reference to the Steele dossier and its tale of the golden showers.

After the attorney general's recusal, the president, whose instinctive reaction to every problem was to fire someone, right away, thought he should just get rid of Sessions. At the same time, there was little doubt in his mind about what was happening here. He knew where this Russia stuff was coming from, and if these Obama people thought they were going to get away with it they had another think coming. He would expose them all!

\* \* \*

One of Jared Kushner's many new patrons was Tony Blair, the former British prime minister, whom Kushner had gotten to know when, on the banks of the River Jordan in 2010, they both attended the baptism of Grace and Chloe Murdoch, the young daughters of Rupert Murdoch and his then wife, Wendi. Jared and Ivanka had also lived in the same Trump building on Park Avenue where the Murdochs lived (for the Murdochs it was a temporary rental apartment while their grand triplex on Fifth Avenue was renovated, but the renovation had lasted for four years), and during that period Ivanka Trump had become one of Wendi Murdoch's closest friends. Blair, godfather to Grace, would later be accused by Mur-doch of having an affair with his wife, and of being the cause of their breakup. In the divorce, Wendi got the Trumps.

But once in the White House, the president's daughter and son-in-law became the target of a renewed and eager cultivation by, with quite some irony, both Blair and Murdoch. Lacking a circle of influence in almost all of the many areas of government with which he was now involved, Kushner was both susceptible to cultivation and more than a little desperate for the advice his cultivators had to offer. Blair, now with philanthropic, private diplomatic, and varied business interests in the Middle East, was particularly intent on helping shepherd some of Jared's Middle East initiatives.

In February, Blair visited Kushner in the White House.

On this trip, the now freelance diplomat, seeking to prove his usefulness to this new White House, imparted a juicy nugget of information. There was, he suggested, the possibility that the British had had the Trump campaign staff under surveillance, monitoring its telephone calls and other communications and possibly even Trump himself. This was, as Kushner might understand, the Sabbath goy theory of intelligence. On the Sabbath, observant Jews could not turn on the lights, nor ask someone else to turn on the lights. But if they expressed the view that it would be much easier to see with light, and if a non-Jew then happened to turn them on, that would be fine. So although the Obama administration would not have asked the British to spy on the Trump campaign, the Brits would have been led to understand how helpful it might be if they did.

It was unclear whether Blair's information was rumor, informed conjecture, his own speculation, or solid stuff. But, as it churned and festered in the president's mind, Kushner and Bannon went out to CIA headquarters in Langley to meet with Mike Pompeo and his deputy director Gina Haspel to check it out. A few days later, the CIA opaquely reported back that the information was not correct; it was a "miscommunication."

\* \* \*

Politics had seemed to become, even well before the age of Trump, a mortal affair. It was now zero-sum: When one side profited, another lost. One side's victory was another's death. The old notion that politics was a trader's game, an understanding that somebody else had something you wanted—a vote, goodwill, old-fashioned patronage—and that in the end the only issue was cost, had gone out of fashion. Now it was a battle between good and evil.

Curiously, for a man who seemed to have led a movement based in anger and retribution, Trump was very much (or believed he was very much) a politician of the old stripe—a let's-work-it-out guy. You scratch my back, I'll scratch yours. He was, in his mind, the ultimate tactician, always knowing what the other guy wanted.

Steve Bannon had pressed him to invoke Andrew Jackson as his populist model, and he had loaded up on Jackson books (they remained unread). But his real beau ideal was Lyndon Johnson. LBJ was a big man who could knock heads, do deals, and bend lesser men to his will. Trade it out so in the end everyone got something, and the better dealmaker got a little more. (Trump did not, however, appreciate the irony of where Lyndon Johnson ended up—one of the first modern politicians to have found himself on the wrong end of both mortal and moral politics.)

But now, after little more than seven weeks in office, Trump saw his own predicament as unique and overwhelming. Like no other president before (though he did make some allowances for Bill Clinton), his enemies were out to get him. Worse, the system was rigged against him. The bureaucratic swamp, the intelligence agencies, the unfair courts, the lying media—they were all lined up against him. This was, for his senior staff, a reliable topic of conversation with him: the possible martyrdom of Donald Trump.

In the president's nighttime calls, he kept coming back to how unfair this was, and to what Tony Blair had said—and others, too! It all added up. There was a plot against him.

Now, it was certainly true that Trump's closest staff appreciated his volatility, and, to a person, was alarmed by it. At points on the day's spectrum of adverse political developments, he could have moments of, almost everyone would admit, irrationality. When that happened, he was alone in his anger and not approachable by anyone. His senior staff largely dealt with these dark hours by agreeing with him, no matter what he said. And if some of them occasionally tried to hedge, Hope Hicks never did. She agreed absolutely with all of it.

At Mar-a-Lago on the evening of March 3, the president watched
Bret Baier interview Paul Ryan on Fox. Baier asked the Speaker about a
report on the online news site Circa—owned by Sinclair, the conservative
broadcast group—involving allegations that Trump Tower had been surveilled during the campaign.

On March 4, Trump's early morning tweets began:

> Terrible! Just found out that Obama had my "wires tapped" in Trump
> Tower just before the victory. Nothing found. This is McCarthyism!
> (4:35 a.m.)

> Is it legal for a sitting President to be "wire tapping" a race for
> president prior to an election? Turned down by court earlier. A NEW
> LOW! (4:49 a.m.)

> How low has President Obama gone to tap my phones during the
> very sacred election process. This is Nixon/Watergate. Bad (or sick)
> guy! (5:02 a.m.)

At 6:40 he called Priebus, waking him up. "Did you see my tweet?" he
asked. "We've caught them red-handed!" Then the president held his
phone so Priebus could hear the playback of the Baier show.

He had no interest in precision, or even any ability to be precise. This
was pure public exclamation, a window into pain and frustration. With
his misspellings and his use of 1970s lingo—"wire tapping" called up an
image of FBI agents crouched in a van on Fifth Avenue—it seemed kooky
and farcical. Of the many tweets that Trump had seemed to hoist himself
by, from the point of view of the media, intelligence community, and
extremely satisfied Democrats, the wiretap tweets had pulled him highest
and most left him dangling in ignorance and embarrassment.

According to CNN, "Two former senior U.S. officials quickly dismissed
Trump's accusations out of hand. 'Just nonsense,' said one former senior
U.S. intelligence official." Inside the White House, the "just nonsense"
quote was thought to be from Ben Rhodes, offered in cat-that-swallowed-
the-canary fashion.

Ryan, for his part, told Priebus he had no idea what Baier was talking about and that he was just BSing through the interview.

But if tapping Trump's phones wasn't literally true, there was a sudden effort to find something that might be, and a frantic White House dished up a Breitbart article that linked to a piece by Louise Mensch, a former British politician who, now living in the United States, had become the Jim Garrison of the Trump-Russia connection.

There was a further effort to push aggressive incidental collection and unmasking back onto the Obama White House. But in the end, this was another—and to some quite the ultimate—example of how difficult it was for the president to function in a literal, definitional, lawyerly, cause-and-effect political world.

It was a turning point. Until now, Trump's inner circle had been mostly game to defend him. But after the wiretap tweets, everybody, save perhaps Hope Hicks, moved into a state of queasy sheepishness, if not constant incredulity.

Sean Spicer, for one, kept repeating his daily, if not hourly, mantra: "You can't make this shit up."

# 12

## REPEAL AND REPLACE

A few days after the election, Steve Bannon told the president-elect—in what Katie Walsh would characterize with a raised eyebrow as more "Breitbart shenanigans"—that they had the votes to replace Paul Ryan as Speaker of the House with Mark Meadows, the head of the Tea Party–inspired Freedom Caucus and an early Trump supporter. (Meadows's wife had a particular place of regard in the Trump camp for continuing a campaign swing across the Bible Belt over Billy Bush weekend.)

Nearly as much as winning the presidency itself, removing Ryan—indeed, humiliating him—was an ultimate expression of what Bannon sought to accomplish and of the mind-meld of Bannonism and Trumpism. From the beginning, the Breitbart campaign *against* Paul Ryan was a central part of its campaign *for* Donald Trump. Its embrace of Trump, and Bannon's personal enlistment in the campaign fourteen months after it began, was in part because Trump, throwing political sense to the wind, was willing to lead the charge against Ryan and the GOP godfathers. Still, there was a difference between the way Breitbart viewed Ryan and the way Trump viewed him.

For Breitbart, the House rebellion and transformation that had driven the former Speaker, John Boehner, from office, and which, plausibly, was set to remake the House into the center of the new radical Republicanism had been halted by Ryan's election as Speaker. Mitt Romney's running mate, and a figure who had merged a conservative fiscal wonkishness—he had been the chairman of the House Ways and Means Committee and, as well, chairman of the House Budget Committee—with an old-fashioned idea of unassailable Republican rectitude, Ryan was the official last, best hope of the Republican Party. (Bannon, typically, had turned this trope into an official Trumpist talking point: "Ryan was created in a petri dish at the Heritage Foundation.") If the Republican Party had been moved further right by the Tea Party rebellion, Ryan was part of the ballast that would prevent it from moving further, or at least at a vastly slower pace. In this he represented an adult, older-brother steadiness in contrast to the Tea Party's ADD-hyper immaturity—and a stoic, almost martyr-like resistance to the Trump movement.

Where the Republican establishment had promoted Ryan into this figure of not only maturity but sagaciousness, the Tea Party–Bannon–Breitbart wing mounted an ad hominem campaign pushing an image of Ryan as uncommitted to the cause, an inept strategist and incompetent leader. He was the Tea Party–Bannon–Breitbart punch line: the ultimate empty suit, a hee-haw sort of joke and an embarrassment.

Trump's distaste for Ryan was significantly less structural. He had no views about Ryan's political abilities, and had paid no real attention to Ryan's actual positions. His view was personal. Ryan had insulted him—again and again. Ryan had kept betting against him. Ryan had become the effective symbol of the Republican establishment's horror and disbelief about Trump. Adding insult to injury, Ryan had even achieved some moral stature by dissing Trump (and, as usual, he considered anybody's gain at his expense a double insult). By the spring of 2016, Ryan was still, and by then the only, alternative to Trump as the nominee. Say the word, many Republicans felt, and the convention would stampede to Ryan. But Ryan's seemingly smarter calculation was to let Trump win the nomination, and then to emerge as the obvious figure to lead the party after Trump's historic defeat and the inevitable purge of the Tea Party–Trump–Breitbart wing.

Instead, the election destroyed Paul Ryan, at least in Steve Bannon's eyes. Trump had not only saved the Republican Party but had given it a powerful majority. The entire Bannon dream had been realized. The Tea Party movement, with Trump as its remarkable face and voice, had come to power—something like total power. It owned the Republican Party. Publicly breaking Paul Ryan was the obvious and necessary step.

But a great deal could fall into the chasm between Bannon's structural contempt for Ryan and Trump's personal resentment. If Bannon saw Ryan as being unwilling and unable to carry out the new Bannon-Trump agenda, Trump saw a chastened Ryan as suddenly and satisfyingly abject, submissive, and useful. Bannon wanted to get rid of the entire Republican establishment; Trump was wholly satisfied that it now seemed to bend to him.

"He's quite a smart guy," Trump said after his first postelection conversation with the Speaker. "A very serious man. Everybody respects him."

Ryan, "rising to a movie-version level of flattery and sucking-up painful to witness," according to one senior Trump aide, was able to delay his execution. As Bannon pressed his case for Meadows—who was significantly less yielding than Ryan—Trump dithered and then finally decided that not only was he *not* going to push for Ryan's ouster, but Ryan was going to be his man, his partner. In an example of the odd and unpredictable effects of personal chemistry on Trump—of how easy it can be to sell the salesman—Trump would now eagerly back Ryan's agenda instead of the other way around.

"I don't think that we quite calculated that the president would give him carte blanche," reflected Katie Walsh. "The president and Paul went from such a bad place during the campaign to such a romance afterward that the president was happy to go along with whatever he wanted."

It didn't exactly surprise Bannon when Trump flipped; Bannon understood how easy it was to bullshit a bullshitter. Bannon also recognized that the Ryan rapprochement spoke to Trump's new appreciation of where he found himself. It was not just that Ryan had been willing to bow to Trump, but that Trump was willing to bow to his own fears about how little he actually knew about being president. If Ryan could be counted on to handle Congress, thought the president, well, phew, that takes care of that.

* * *

Trump had little or no interest in the central Republican goal of repealing Obamacare. An overweight seventy-year-old man with various physical phobias (for instance, he lied about his height to keep from having a
body mass index that would label him as obese), he personally found
health care and medical treatments of all kinds a distasteful subject. The
details of the contested legislation were, to him, particularly boring; his
attention would begin wandering from the first words of a policy discussion. He would have been able to enumerate few of the particulars of
Obamacare—other than expressing glee about the silly Obama pledge
that everyone could keep his or her doctor—and he certainly could not
make any kind of meaningful distinction, positive or negative, between
the health care system before Obamacare and the one after.

Prior to his presidency, he had likely never had a meaningful discussion in his life about health insurance. "No one in the country, or on
earth, has given less thought to health insurance than Donald," said Roger
Ailes. Pressed in a campaign interview about the importance of Obamacare repeal and reform, Trump was, to say the least, quite unsure of its
place on the agenda: "This is an important subject but there are a lot of
important subjects. Maybe it is in the top ten. Probably is. But there is
heavy competition. So you can't be certain. Could be twelve. Or could be
fifteen. Definitely top twenty for sure."

It was another one of his counterintuitive connections to many
voters: Obama and Hillary Clinton seemed actually to want to talk
about health care plans, whereas Trump, like most everybody else, absolutely did not.

All things considered, he probably preferred the notion of more
people having health insurance than fewer people having it. He was even,
when push came to shove, rather more for Obamacare than for repealing
Obamacare. As well, he had made a set of rash Obama-like promises,
going so far as to say that under a forthcoming Trumpcare plan (he had
to be strongly discouraged from using this kind of rebranding—political
wise men told him that this was one instance where he might not want
to claim ownership with his name), no one would lose their health

insurance, and that preexisting conditions would continue to be covered. In fact, he probably favored government-funded health care more than any other Republican. "Why can't Medicare simply cover everybody?" he had impatiently wondered aloud during one discussion with aides, all of whom were careful not to react to this heresy.

It was Bannon who held the line, insisting, sternly, that Obamacare was a litmus Republican issue, and that, holding a majority in Congress, they could not face Republican voters without having made good on the by now Republican catechism of repeal. Repeal, in Bannon's view, was the pledge, and repeal would be the most satisfying, even cathartic, result. It would also be the easiest one to achieve, since virtually every Republican was already publicly committed to voting for repeal. But Bannon, seeing health care as a weak link in Bannonism-Trumpism's appeal to the workingman, was careful to take a back seat in the debate. Later, he hardly even made an effort to rationalize how he'd washed his hands of the mess, saying just, "I hung back on health care because it's not my thing."

It was Ryan who, with "repeal and replace," obfuscated the issue and won over Trump. Repeal would satisfy the Republican bottom line, while replace would satisfy the otherwise off-the-cuff pledges that Trump had made on his own. (Pay no attention to the likelihood that what the president construed as repeal and replace might be very different from what Ryan construed as repeal and replace.) "Repeal and replace" was a useful slogan, too, in that it came to have meaning without having any actual or specific meaning.

The week after the election, Ryan, bringing Tom Price—the Georgia congressman and orthopedist who had become Ryan's resident heath care expert—traveled to Trump's Bedminster, New Jersey, estate for a repeal and replace briefing. The two men summed up for Trump—who kept wandering off topic and trying to turn the conversation to golf— seven years of Republican legislative thinking about Obamacare and the Republican alternatives. Here was a perfect example of an essential Trump paradigm: he acceded to anyone who seemed to know more about any issue he didn't care about, or simply one whose details he couldn't bring himself to focus on closely. *Great!* he would say, punctuating every statement with a similar exclamation and regularly making an effort to jump from his chair. On the spot, Trump eagerly agreed to let Ryan run the health care bill and to make Price the Health and Human Services secretary.

Kushner, largely staying silent during the health care debate, publicly seemed to accept the fact that a Republican administration had to address Obamacare, but he privately suggested that he was personally against both repeal alone and repeal and replace. He and his wife took a conventional Democratic view on Obamacare (it was better than the alternatives; its problems could be fixed in the future) and strategically believed it was best for the new administration to get some easier victories under its belt before entering a hard-to-win or no-win fight. (What's more, Kushner's brother Josh ran a health insurance company that depended on Obamacare.)

Not for the last time, then, the White House would be divided along the political spectrum, Bannon taking an absolutist base position, Priebus aligned with Ryan in support of the Republican leadership, and Kushner maintaining, and seeing no contradiction in, a moderate Democratic view. As for Trump himself, here was a man who was simply trying to get out from under something he didn't especially care about.

Ryan and Priebus's salesmanship promised to get the president out from under other issues as well. Health care reform, according to the Ryan plan, was something of a magic bullet. The reform the Speaker would push through Congress would fund the tax cuts Trump had guaranteed, which, in turn, would make all that Trump-promised infrastructure investment possible.

On this basis—this domino theory that was meant to triumphantly carry the Trump administration through to the August recess and mark it as one of the most transformational presidencies in modern times—Ryan kept his job as Speaker, rising from hated campaign symbol to the administration's man on the Hill. In effect, the president, quite aware of his and his staff's inexperience in drafting legislation (in fact, nobody on his senior staff had any experience at all), decided to outsource his agenda—and to a heretofore archenemy.

Watching Ryan steal the legislative initiative during the transition, Bannon faced an early realpolitik moment. If the president was willing to cede major initiatives, Bannon would need to run a counteroperation and be ready with more Breitbart shenanigans. Kushner, for his part, developed a certain Zen—you just had to go with the president's whims. As for the president, it was quite clear that deciding between contradictory policy approaches was not his style of leadership. He simply hoped that difficult decisions would make themselves.

\* \* \*

Bannon was not merely contemptuous of Ryan's ideology; he had no respect, either, for his craft. In Bannon's view, what the new Republican majority needed was a man like John McCormick, the Democratic Speaker of the House who had served during Bannon's teenage years and had shepherded Johnson's Great Society legislation. McCormick and other Democrats from the 1960s were Bannon's political heroes—put Tip O'Neill in that pantheon, too. An Irish Catholic working-class man was philosophically separate from aristocrats and gentry—and without aspirations to be either. Bannon venerated old-fashioned pols. He looked like one himself: liver spots, jowls, edema. And he hated modern politicians; they lacked, in addition to political talents, authenticity and soul. Ryan was an Irish Catholic altar boy who had stayed an altar boy. He had not grown up to be a thug, cop, or priest—or a true politician.

Ryan certainly wasn't a vote counter. He was a benighted figure who had no ability to see around corners. His heart was in tax reform, but as far as he could tell the only path to tax reform was through health care. But he cared so little about the issue that—just as the White House had outsourced health care to him—he outsourced the writing of the bill to insurance companies and K Street lobbyists.

In fact, Ryan had tried to act like McCormick or O'Neill, offering absolute assurances of his hold on the legislation. It was, he told the president during his several daily calls, a "done deal." Trump's trust in Ryan rose still higher, and it seemed to become in his own mind proof that he had achieved a kind of mastery over the Hill. If the president had been worried, he was worried no more. Done deal. The White House, having had to sweat hardly at all, was about to get a big victory, bragged Kushner, embracing the expected win over his dislike of the bill.

The sudden concern that the outcome might be otherwise began in early March. Katie Walsh, who Kushner now described as "demanding and petulant," began to sound the alarm. But her efforts to personally involve the president in vote collecting were blocked by Kushner in a set of increasingly tense face-offs. The unraveling had begun.

* * *

Trump still dismissively called it "the Russian thing—a whole lot of nothing." But on March 20, FBI director James Comey appeared before the House Intelligence Committee and tied the story up in a neat package:

> I have been authorized by the Department of Justice to confirm that the FBI, as part of our counterintelligence mission, is investigating the Russian government's efforts to interfere in the 2016 presidential election, and that includes investigating the nature of any links between individuals associated with the Trump campaign and the Russian government and whether there was any coordination between the campaign and Russia's efforts. As with any counter intelligence investigation, this will also include an assessment of whether any crimes were committed. Because it is an open, ongoing investigation and is classified I cannot say more about what we are doing and whose conduct we are examining.

He had, however, said quite enough. Comey converted rumor, leaks, theory, innuendo, and pundit hot air—and until this moment that was all there was, at best the hope of a scandal—into a formal pursuit of the White House. Efforts to pooh-pooh the narrative—the fake news label, the president's germaphobe defense against the golden shower accusations, the haughty dismissal of minor associates and hopeless hangers-on, the plaintive, if real, insistence that no crime had even been alleged, and the president's charge that he was the victim of an Obama wiretap—had failed. Comey himself dismissed the wiretap allegation. By the evening of Comey's appearance, it was evident to everyone that the Russia plot line, far from petering out, had a mighty and bloody life to come.

Kushner, ever mindful of his father's collision with the Justice Department, was especially agitated by Comey's increasing focus on the White House. Doing something about Comey became a Kushner theme. What can we do about him? was a constant question. And it was one he kept raising with the president.

Yet this was also—as Bannon, without too much internal success, tried to explain—a structural issue. It was an opposition move. You could express surprise at how fierce, creative, and diabolical the moves turned out to be, but you shouldn't be surprised that your enemies would try to hurt you. This was check, but far from checkmate, and you had to continue to play the game, knowing that it would be a very long one. The only way to win the game, Bannon argued, was with a disciplined strategy.

But the president, prodded here by his family, was an obsessive and not a strategist. In his mind, this was not a problem to address, this was a person to focus on: Comey. Trump eschewed abstractions and, ad hominem, zeroed in on his opponent. Comey had been a difficult puzzle for Trump: Comey had declined to have the FBI pursue charges against Clinton for her email dodge. Then, in October, Comey had single-handedly boosted Trump's fortunes with the letter reopening the Clinton email investigation.

In their personal interactions, Trump had found Comey to be a stiff—he had no banter, no game. But Trump, who invariably thought people found him irresistible, believed that Comey admired *his* banter and game. When pressed, by Bannon and others, to fire Comey as one of his early acts—an idea opposed by Kushner, and thus another bullet on Bannon's list of bad recommendations by Kushner—the president said, "Don't worry, I've got him." That is, he had no doubt that he could woo and flatter the FBI director into positive feeling for him, if not outright submission.

Some seducers are preternaturally sensitive to the signals of those they try to seduce; others indiscriminately attempt to seduce, and, by the law of averages, often succeed (this latter group of men might now be regarded as harassers). That was Trump's approach to women—pleased when he scored, unconcerned when he didn't (and, often, despite the evidence, believing that he had). And so it was with Director Comey.

In their several meetings since he took office—when Comey received a presidential hug on January 22; at their dinner on January 27, during which Comey was asked to stay on as FBI director; at their Valentine's Day chat after emptying the office of everybody else, including Sessions, Comey's titular boss—Trump was confident that he had laid on the moves. The president was all but certain that Comey, understanding that he, Trump, had his back (i.e., had let him keep his job), would have Trump's back, too.

But now this testimony. It made no sense. What *did* make sense to Trump was that Comey wanted it to be about him. He was a media whore—this Trump understood. All right, then, he, too, could play it this way.

Indeed, health care, a no-fun issue—suddenly becoming much less fun, if, as seemed increasingly possible, Ryan couldn't deliver—palled before the clarity of Comey, and the fury, enmity, and bitterness Trump, and Trump's relatives, now bore him.

Comey was the larger-than-life problem. Taking Comey down was the obvious solution. Getting Comey became the mission.

In Keystone Cops fashion, the White House enlisted House Intelligence Committee chairman Devin Nunes in a farcical effort to discredit Comey and support the wiretap theory. The scheme shortly collapsed in universal ridicule.

Bannon, taking a public hands-off with respect to both health care and Comey, began to advise reporters that the important story wasn't health care but Russia. This was cryptic advice: it was not clear whether he was trying to distract attention from the coming health care debacle, or couple it with this new dangerous variable, thus amping up the kind of chaos that he usually benefited from.

But Bannon was unequivocal about one thing. *As the Russia story unfolds*, he advised reporters, *keep your eye on Kushner.*

* * *

By mid-March, Gary Cohn had been drafted into the effort to salvage the faltering health care bill. This might have seemed like a form of hazing for Cohn, whose grasp of legislative matters was even more limited than that of most in the White House.

On Friday, March 24, the morning of the theoretical House vote for the Republican health care bill, Politico's *Playbook* characterized the chances of a vote actually coming to the floor as a "toss-up." In that morning's senior staff meeting, Cohn was asked for an assessment of where things stood and promptly said, "I think it's a toss-up."

"Really?" thought Katie Walsh. "That's what you think?"

Bannon, joining Walsh in a pitiless contempt for the White House effort, targeted Kushner, Cohn, Priebus, Price, and Ryan in a series of calls to reporters. Kushner and Cohn could, per Bannon, be counted on to run at the first sound of gunfire. (Kushner, in fact, had spent much of the week on a skiing holiday.) Priebus mouthed Ryan talking points and excuses. Price, supposedly the health care guru, was an oafish imposter; he would stand up in meetings and mumble nothing but nonsense.

These were the bad guys, setting up the administration to lose the House in 2018, thereby assuring the president's impeachment. This was vintage Bannon analysis: a certain and immediate political apocalypse that sat side by side with the potential for a half century of Bannonism-Trumpism rule.

Convinced he knew the direction of success, keenly aware of his own age and finite opportunities, and—if for no clear reason—seeing himself as a talented political infighter, Bannon sought to draw the line between believers and sell-outs, being and nothingness. For him to succeed, he needed to isolate the Ryan, Cohn, and Kushner factions.

The Bannon faction held tight on forcing a vote on the health care bill—even knowing defeat was inevitable. "I want it as a report on Ryan's job as Speaker," said Bannon. That is, a devastating report, an epic fail.

The day of the vote, Pence was sent to the Hill to make one last pitch to Meadows's Freedom Caucus. (Ryan's people believed that Bannon was secretly urging Meadows to hold out, though earlier in the week Bannon had harshly ordered the Freedom Caucus to vote for the bill—"a silly Bannon show," according to Walsh.) At three-thirty, Ryan called the president to say he was short fifteen to twenty votes and needed to pull the vote. Bannon, backed by Mulvaney, who had become the White House's Hill operative, continued to urge an immediate vote. A defeat here would be a major defeat for the Republican leadership. That suited Bannon just fine: let them fail.

But the president backed down. Faced with this singular opportunity to make the Republican leadership the issue, and to name them as the problem, Trump wobbled, provoking in Bannon a not-so-silent rage. Ryan then leaked that it was the president who had asked him to cancel the vote.

Over the weekend, Bannon called a long list of reporters and told them—off the record, but hardly—"I don't see Ryan hanging around a long time."

\* \* \*

After the bill had been pulled that Friday, Katie Walsh, feeling both angry and disgusted, told Kushner she wanted out. Outlining what she saw as the grim debacle of the Trump White House, she spoke with harsh candor about bitter rivalries joined to vast incompetence and an uncertain mission. Kushner, understanding that she needed to be discredited immediately, leaked that she had been leaking and hence had to be pushed out.

On Sunday evening, Walsh had dinner with Bannon in his Capitol Hill redoubt, the Breitbart Embassy, during which, to no avail, he implored her to stay. On Monday she sorted out the details with Priebus—she would leave to work part time for the RNC and part time for the Trump (c)(4), the outside campaign group. By Thursday she was gone.

Ten weeks into the new administration, the Trump White House had lost, after Michael Flynn, its second senior staff member—and the one whose job it was to actually get things done.

# 13

## BANNON AGONISTES

He, too, felt like a prisoner, he had told Katie Walsh when she came to tell him she was leaving.

By ten weeks in, Steve Bannon's mastery of the Trump agenda, or at least of Trump himself, appeared to have crumbled. His current misery was both Catholic in nature—the self-flagellation of a man who believed he lived on a higher moral plane than all others—and fundamentally misanthropic. As an antisocial, maladjusted, post-middle-aged man, he had to make a supreme effort to get along with others, an effort that often did not go well. Most especially, he was miserable because of Donald Trump, whose cruelties, always great even when they were casual, were unbearable when he truly turned against you.

"I hated being on the campaign, I hated the transition, I hate being here in the White House," said Bannon, sitting one evening in Reince Priebus's office, on an unseasonably warm evening in early spring, with the French doors open to the arbor-covered patio where he and Priebus, now firm friends and allies in their antipathy toward Jarvanka, had set an outdoor table.

But Bannon was, he believed, here for a reason. And it was his firm belief—a belief he was unable to keep to himself, thus continually undermining his standing with the president—that his efforts had brought everybody else here. Even more important, he was the only person showing up for work every day who was committed to the purpose of actually changing the country. Changing it quickly, radically, and truly.

The idea of a split electorate—of blue and red states, of two opposing currents of values, of globalists and nationalists, of an establishment and populist revolt—was media shorthand for cultural angst and politically roiled times, and, to a large degree, for business as usual. But Bannon believed the split was literal. The United States had become a country of two hostile peoples. One would necessarily win and the other lose. Or one would dominate while the other would become marginal.

This was modern civil war—Bannon's war. The country built on the virtue and the character and the strength of the American workingman circa 1955–65 was the ideal he meant to defend and restore: trade agreements, or *trade wars*, that supported American manufacturing; immigration policies that protected American workers (and, hence, American culture, or at least America's identity from 1955 to 1965); and an international isolation that would conserve American resources and choke off the ruling class's Davos sensibility (and also save working-class military lives). This was, in the view of almost everyone but Donald Trump and the alt-right, a crazy bit of voodoo economic and political nonsense. But it was, for Bannon, a revolutionary and religious idea.

For most others in the White House, it was Bannon's pipe dream. "Steve is . . . Steve," became the gentle term of art for tolerating him. "A lot of stuff goes on in his head," said the president, pursuing one of his reliable conversational themes, dismissing Bannon.

But it wasn't Bannon versus everybody else so much as it was Bannon Trump versus non-Bannon Trump. If Trump, in his dark, determined, and aggressive mood, could represent Bannon and his views, he could just as easily represent nothing at all—or represent solely his own need for instant gratification. That's what the non-Bannon people understood about Trump. If the boss was happy, then a normal, incremental, two-steps-forward-one-step-back approach to politics might prevail. Even a new sort of centrism, as inimical to Bannonism as it was possible to conceive, could emerge. Bannon's pronouncements about a fifty-year rule for Trumpism might then be supplanted by the rule of Jared, Ivanka, and Goldman Sachs.

By the end of March, this was the side that was winning. Bannon's efforts to use the epic health care fail as evidence that the establishment was the enemy had hopelessly backfired. Trump saw the health care failure as his own failure, but since he didn't have failures, it couldn't be a failure, and would in fact be a success—if not now, soon. So Bannon, a Cassandra on the sidelines, was the problem.

Trump rationalized his early embrace of Bannon by heaping scorn on him—and by denying that he had ever embraced him. If there was anything wrong with his White House, it was Steve Bannon. Maligning Bannon was Trump's idea of fun. When it came to Bannon, Trump rose to something like high analysis: "Steve Bannon's problem is PR. He doesn't understand it. Everybody hates him. Because . . . look at him. His bad PR rubs off on other people."

The real question, of course, was how Bannon, the fuck-the-system populist, had ever come to think that he might get along with Donald Trump, the use-the-system-to-his-own-advantage billionaire. For Bannon, Trump was the game he had to play. But in truth he hardly played it—or couldn't help undermining it. While ever proclaiming it Trump's victory, he would helplessly point out that when he had joined the campaign it was facing a polling deficit that no campaign, ten weeks from election day, had ever recovered from. Trump without Bannon, according to Bannon, was Wendell Willkie.

Bannon understood the necessity not to take what otherwise might be Trump's own spotlight; he was well aware that the president meticulously logged all claims against credit that he believed solely to be his. Both he and Kushner, the two most important figures in the White House after the president, seemed professionally mute. Still, Bannon seemed to be everywhere, and the president was convinced—rightly—that it was the result of Bannon's private press operation. More often than self-mockery could sustain, Bannon referred to himself as "President Bannon." A bitter Kellyanne Conway, regularly dissed for her own spotlight grabbing, confirmed the president's observation that Bannon stepped into as many White House photo ops as possible. (Everybody seemed to keep count of everybody else's photo bombs.) Bannon also did not much bother to disguise his innumerable blind quotes, nor to make much of an effort to temper his not-so-private slurs against Kushner, Cohn, Powell, Conway, Priebus, and even the president's daughter (often, most especially, the president's daughter).

Curiously, Bannon never expressed a sideways thought about Trump—not yet. Trump's own righteousness and soundness was perhaps too central to Bannon's construct of Trumpism. Trump was the idea you had to support. This could seem to approach the traditional idea of respecting the office. In fact, it was the inverse. The man was the vessel: there was no Bannon without Trump. However much he might stand on his unique, even magical-seeming, contributions to the Trump victory, Bannon's opportunity was wholly provided by Trump's peculiar talent. He was no more than the man behind the man—Trump's Cromwell, as he put it, even though he was perfectly aware of Cromwell's fate.

But his loyalty to the idea of Trump hardly protected him from the actual Trump's constant briefs against him. The president had assembled a wide jury to weigh Bannon's fate, putting before it, in an insulting Borscht Belt style, a long list of Bannon's annoyances: "Guy looks home-less. Take a shower, Steve. You've worn those pants for six days. He says he's made money, I don't believe it." (The president, notably, never much took issue with Bannon's policy views.) The Trump administration was hardly two months old, yet every media outlet was predicting Bannon's coming defenestration.

One particularly profitable transaction with the president was to bring him new, ever harsher criticism of his chief strategist, or reports of other people criticizing him. It was important to know not to say anything posi-tive to Trump about Bannon. Even faint praise before the "but"—"Steve is obviously smart, but . . ."—could produce a scowl and pout if you didn't hurry to the "but." (Then again, saying anyone was "smart" invariably incurred Trump's annoyance.) Kushner enlisted Scarborough and Brze-zinski in something of a regular morning television Bannon slag-a-thon.

H. R. McMaster, the three-star general who had replaced Michael Flynn as National Security Advisor, had secured the president's pledge that he could veto members of the NSC. Kushner, a supporter of McMaster's appointment, had quickly ensured that Dina Powell, a key player in the Kushner faction, would join the NSC and Bannon would be removed.

Bannonites would, with lowered voices and certain pity, ask each other how he seemed and how he was holding up; invariably they would agree about how bad he looked, the strain etching ever deeper into his already ruined face. David Bossie thought Bannon "looked like he would die."

"I now understand what it is like to be in the court of the Tudors," reflected Bannon. On the campaign trail, he recalled, Newt Gingrich "would come with all these dumb ideas. When we won he was my new best friend. Every day a hundred ideas. When"—by spring in the White House—"I got cold, when I went through my Valley of Death, I saw him one day in the lobby and he looks down, avoiding my eyes with a kind of mumbled 'Hey, Steve.' And I say, 'What are you doing here, let's get you inside,' and he says, 'No, no, I'm fine, I'm waiting for Dina Powell.'"

Having attained the unimaginable—bringing a fierce alt-right, anti-liberal ethnopopulism into a central place in the White House—Bannon found himself face to face with the untenable: undermined by and having to answer to rich, entitled Democrats.

* * *

The paradox of the Trump presidency was that it was both the most ideologically driven and the least. It represented a deeply structural assault on liberal values—Bannon's deconstruction of the administrative state meant to take with it media, academic, and not-for-profit institutions. But from the start it also was apparent that the Trump administration could just as easily turn into a country club Republican or a Wall Street Democrat regime. Or just a constant effort to keep Donald Trump happy. Trump had his collection of pet-peeve issues, test-marketed in various media rollouts and megarallies, but none seemed so significant as his greater goal of personally coming out ahead of the game.

As the drumbeat for Bannon's removal grew, the Mercers stepped in to protect their investment in radical government overthrow and the future of Steve Bannon.

In an age when all successful political candidates are surrounded by, if not at the beck and call of, difficult, even sociopathic, rich people pushing the bounds of their own power—and the richer they were, the more difficult, sociopathic, and power-mad they might be—Bob and Rebekah

Mercer were quite onto themselves. If Trump's ascent was unlikely, the Mercers' was all the more so.

Even the difficult rich—the Koch brothers and Sheldon Adelson on the right, David Geffen and George Soros on the left—are leavened and restrained by the fact that money exists in a competitive market. Obnoxiousness has its limits. The world of the rich is, in its fashion, self-regulating. Social climbing has rules.

But among the difficult and entitled rich, the Mercers remained almost wholly unsocialized, cutting a path through disbelief and incredulity. Unlike other people contributing vast sums to political candidates, they were willing not to win—ever. Their bubble was their bubble.

So when they did win, by the fluke alignment of the stars for Donald Trump, they were yet pure. Now, having found themselves—by odds that were perfect-storm outlandish—in power, they were not going to give it up because Steve Bannon had hurt feelings and wasn't getting enough sleep.

Toward the end of March, the Mercers organized a set of emergency meetings. At least one of them was with the president himself. It was exactly the kind of meeting Trump usually avoided: he had no interest in personnel problems, since they put the emphasis on other people. Suddenly he was being forced to deal with Steve Bannon, rather than the other way around. What's more, it was a problem he had in part created with his constant Bannon dissing, and now he was being asked to eat crow. Even though the president kept saying he could and should fire Bannon, he was aware of the costs—a right-wing backlash of unpredictable proportions.

Trump thought the Mercers were as odd as everybody else thought. He didn't like Bob Mercer looking at him and not saying a word; he didn't like being in the same room with Mercer or his daughter. These were superstrange bedfellows—"wackos," in his estimation. But though he refused to admit that the Mercers' decision to back him and their imposition of Bannon on the campaign in August was, likely, the event without which he would not now be in the White House, he did understand that if crossed, the Mercers and Bannon were potential world-class troublemakers.

The complexity of the Bannon-Mercer problem prompted Trump to consult two contradictory figures: Rupert Murdoch and Roger Ailes. Even as the president did so, perhaps he knew he would come up with a zero-sum answer.

Murdoch, already briefed by Kushner, said getting rid of Bannon was the only way to deal with the dysfunction in the White House. (Murdoch, of course, made the assumption that getting rid of Kushner was not an option.) It was the inevitable outcome, so do it now. Murdoch's response made perfect sense: by now, he had become an active political supporter of the Kushner-Goldman moderates, seeing them as the people who would save the world from Bannon and, indeed, from Trump as well.

Ailes, blunt and declarative as always, said, "Donald, you can't do it. You've made your bed and Steve is in it. You don't have to listen to him, you don't have to even get along with him. But you're married to him. You can't handle a divorce right now."

Jared and Ivanka were gleeful at the prospect of Bannon's ouster. His departure would return the Trump organization to pure family control—the family and its functionaries, without an internal rival for brand meaning and leadership. From the family's point of view, it would also—at least in theory—help facilitate one of the most implausible brand shifts in history: Donald Trump to respectability. The dream, long differed, of the Trump pivot, might actually happen without Bannon. Never mind that this Kushner ideal—saving Trump from himself and projecting Jared and Ivanka into the future—was nearly as far-fetched and extreme as Bannon's own fantasy of a White House dedicated to the return of a pre-1965 American mythology.

If Bannon were to go, it also might cause the ultimate split in the already fractured Republican Party. Before the election, one theory suggested that a defeated Trump would take his embittered 35 percent and make hay with a rancorous minority. Now the alarming theory was that as Kushner tried to transform his father-in-law into the kind of latter-day Rockefeller that Trump, however implausibly, had on occasion dreamed of becoming (Rockefeller Center being an inspiration for his own real estate branding), Bannon could run off with some meaningful part of that 35 percent.

This was the Breitbart threat. The Breitbart organization remained under the control of the Mercers, and it could at any moment be handed back to Steve Bannon. And now, with Bannon's overnight transformation into political genius and kingmaker, and the triumph of the alt-right, Breitbart was potentially much more powerful. Trump's victory had, in some sense, handed the Mercers the tool with which to destroy him. As push came to shove and the mainstream media and swamp bureaucracy more and more militantly organized against him, Trump was certainly going to need the Mercer-backed alt-right standing up in his defense. What, after all, was he without them?

As the pressure mounted, Bannon—until now absolutely disciplined in his regard for Donald Trump as the ideal avatar of Trumpism (and Bannonism), rigidly staying in character as aide and supporter of a maverick political talent—began to crack. Trump, as almost anyone who had ever worked for him appreciated, was, despite what you hoped he might be, Trump—and he would invariably sour on everyone around him.

But the Mercers dug in. Without Bannon, they believed the Trump presidency, at least the Trump presidency they had imagined (and helped pay for), was over. The focus became how to make Steve's life better. They made him pledge to leave the office at a reasonable time—no more waiting around for Trump to possibly need a dinner companion. (Recently, Jared and Ivanka had been heading this off anyway.) The solution included a search for a Bannon's Bannon—a chief strategist for the chief strategist.

In late March, the Mercers came to an agreed-upon truce with the president: Bannon would not be fired. While this guaranteed nothing about his influence and standing, it did buy Bannon and his allies some time. They could regroup. A presidential aide was only as good as the last good advice he gave, and in this, Bannon believed the ineptness of his rivals, Kushner and his wife, would seal their fate.

\* \* \*

Though the president agreed not to fire Bannon, he gave Kushner and his daughter something in exchange: he would enhance both their roles.

On March 27, the Office of American Innovation was created and Kushner was put in charge. Its stated mission was to reduce federal bureaucracy—that is, to reduce it by creating more of it, a committee to end committees. In addition, Kushner's new outfit would study the government's internal technology, focus on job creation, encourage and suggest policies about apprenticeships, enlist business in a partnership with government, and help with the opioid epidemic. It was, in other words, business as usual, albeit with a new burst of enthusiasm for the administrative state.

But its real import was that it gave Kushner his own internal White House staff, a team of people working not just on Kushner-supported projects—all largely antithetical to Bannon projects—but, more broadly, as Kushner explained to one staffer, "on expanding my footprint." Kushner even got his own "comms person," a dedicated spokesperson and Kushner promoter. It was a bureaucratic build-out meant not only to enhance Kushner but to diminish Steve Bannon.

Two days after the announcement about Jared's expanded power base, Ivanka was formally given a White House job, too: adviser to the president. From the beginning she had been a key adviser to her husband—and he to her. Still, it was an overnight consolidation of Trump family power in the White House. It was, quite at Steve Bannon's expense, a remarkable bureaucratic coup: a divided White House had now all but been united under the president's family.

His son-in-law and daughter hoped—they were even confident—that they could speak to DJT's better self, or at least balance Republican needs with progressive rationality, compassion, and good works. Further, they could support this moderation by routing a steady stream of like-minded CEOs through the Oval Office. And, indeed, the president seldom disagreed with and was often enthusiastic about the Jared and Ivanka program. "If they tell him the whales need to be saved, he's basically for it," noted Katie Walsh.

But Bannon, suffering in his internal exile, remained convinced that he represented what Donald Trump actually believed, or, more accurately, what the president felt. He knew Trump to be a fundamentally emotional man, and he was certain that the deepest part of him was angry and dark. However much the president wanted to support his daughter and her husband's aspirations, their worldview was not his. As Walsh saw it, "Steve believes he is Darth Vader and that Trump is called to the dark side."

Indeed, Trump's fierce efforts to deny Bannon's influence may well have been in inverse proportion to the influence Bannon actually had.

The president did not truly listen to anybody. The more you talked, the less he listened. "But Steve is careful about what he says, and there is something, a timbre in his voice and his energy and excitement, that the president can really hone in on, blocking everything else out," said Walsh.

As Jared and Ivanka were taking a victory lap, Trump signed Executive Order 13783, a change in environmental policy carefully shepherded by Bannon, which, he argued, effectively gutted the National Environmental Policy Act, the 1970 law that served as the foundation of modern environmental protections and that required all executive agencies to prepare environmental impact statements for agency actions. Among other impacts, EO 13783 removed a prior directive to consider climate change—a precursor to coming debates on the country's position regarding the Paris Climate Accord.

On April 3, Kushner unexpectedly turned up in Iraq, accompanying Gen. Joseph Dunford, chairman of the Joint Chiefs of Staff. According to the White House press office, Kushner was "traveling on behalf of the president to express the president's support and commitment to the government of Iraq and U.S. personnel currently engaged in the campaign." Kushner, otherwise a remote and clammed-up media presence, was copiously photographed throughout the trip.

Bannon, watching one of the many television screens that provided a constant background in the West Wing, glimpsed Kushner wearing a headset while flying in a helicopter over Baghdad. To no one in particular, recalling a foolish and callow George W. Bush in flight gear on the aircraft carrier USS *Abraham Lincoln* proclaiming the end of the Iraq War, he intoned, "Mission accomplished."

Gritting his teeth, Bannon saw the structure of the White House moving in the exact opposite direction from Trumpism-Bannonism. But even now, he was certain he perceived the real impulses of the administration coming his way. It was Bannon, stoic and resolute, the great if unheralded warrior, who, at least in his own mind, was destined to save the nation.

# 14

## SITUATION ROOM

Just before seven o'clock on the morning of Tuesday, April 4, the seventy-fourth day of the Trump presidency, Syrian government forces attacked the rebel-held town of Khan Sheikhoun with chemical weapons. Scores of children were killed. It was the first time a major outside event had intruded into the Trump presidency.

Most presidencies are shaped by external crises. The presidency, in its most critical role, is a reactive job. Much of the alarm about Donald Trump came from the widespread conviction that he could not be counted on to be cool or deliberate in the face of a storm. He had been lucky so far: ten weeks in, and he had not been seriously tested. In part this might have been because the crises generated from inside the White House had overshadowed all outside contenders.

Even a gruesome attack, even one on children in an already long war, might not yet be a presidential game changer of the kind that everyone knew would surely come. Still, these were chemical weapons launched by a repeat offender, Bashar al-Assad. In any other presidency, such an atrocity would command a considered and, ideally, skillful response. Obama's consideration had in fact been less than skillful in proclaiming the use of chemical weapons as a red line—and then allowing it to be crossed.

Almost nobody in the Trump administration was willing to predict how the president might react—or even whether he would react. Did he think the chemical attack important or unimportant? No one could say.

If the Trump White House was as unsettling as any in American history, the president's views of foreign policy and the world at large were among its most random, uninformed, and seemingly capricious aspects. His advisers didn't know whether he was an isolationist or a militarist, or whether he could distinguish between the two. He was enamored with generals and determined that people with military command experience take the lead in foreign policy, but he hated to be told what to do. He was against nation building, but he believed there were few situations that he couldn't personally make better. He had little to no experience in foreign policy, but he had no respect for the experts, either.

Suddenly, the question of how the president might respond to the attack in Khan Sheikhoun was a litmus test for normality and those who hoped to represent it in Trump's White House. Here was the kind of dramatic juxtaposition that might make for a vivid and efficient piece of theater: people working in the Trump White House who were trying to behave normally.

* * *

Surprisingly, perhaps, there were quite a few such people.

Acting normal, embodying normality—doing things the way a striving, achieving, rational person would do them—was how Dina Powell saw her job in the White House. At forty-three, Powell had made a career at the intersection of the corporate world and public policy; she did well (very, very well) by doing good. She had made great strides in George W. Bush's White House and then later at Goldman Sachs. Returning to the White House at a penultimate level, with at least a chance of rising to one of the country's highest unelected positions, would potentially be worth enormous sums when she returned to the corporate world.

In Trumpland, however, the exact opposite could happen. Powell's carefully cultivated reputation, her brand (and she was one of those people who thought intently about their personal brand), could become inextricably tied to the Trump brand. Worse, she could become part of what might

easily turn into historical calamity. Already, for many people who knew
Dina Powell—and everybody who was anybody knew Dina Powell—the
fact that she had taken a position in the Trump White House indicated
either recklessness or seriously bad judgment.

"How," wondered one of her longtime friends, "does she rationalize
this?" Friends, family, and neighbors asked, silently or openly, *Do you
know what you're doing? And how* could *you? And why* would *you?*

Here was the line dividing those whose reason for being in the White
House was a professed loyalty to the president from the professionals
they had needed to hire. Bannon, Conway, and Hicks—along with an
assortment of more or less peculiar ideologues that had attached themselves to Trump and, of course, his family, all people without clearly
monetizable reputations before their association with Trump—were, for
better or worse, hitched to him. (Even among dedicated Trumpers there
was always a certain amount of holding their breath and constant reex-
amination of their options.) But those within the larger circle of White
House influence, those with some stature or at least an imagined stature,
had to work through significantly more complicated contortions of personal and career justification.

Often they wore their qualms on their sleeves. Mick Mulvaney, the
OMB director, made a point of stressing the fact that he worked in the
Executive Office Building, not the West Wing. Michael Anton, holding
down Ben Rhodes's former job at the NSC, had perfected a deft eye roll
(referred to as the Anton eye roll). H. R. McMaster seemed to wear a constant grimace and have perpetual steam rising from his bald head.
("What's wrong with him?" the president often asked.)

There was, of course, a higher rationale: the White House needed
normal, sane, logical, adult professionals. To a person, these pros saw
themselves bringing positive attributes—rational minds, analytic powers, significant professional experience—to a situation sorely lacking
those things. They were doing their bit to make things more normal and,
therefore, more stable. They were bulwarks, or saw themselves that way,
against chaos, impulsiveness, and stupidity. They were less Trump supporters than an antidote to Trump.

"If it all starts going south—more south than it is already going—I

have no doubt that Joe Hagin would himself take personal responsibility, and do what needed to be done," said a senior Republican figure in
Washington, in an effort at self-reassurance, about the former Bush staffer
who now served as Trump's deputy chief of staff for operations.

But this sense of duty and virtue involved a complicated calculation
about your positive effect on the White House versus its negative effect
on you. In April, an email originally copied to more than a dozen people
went into far wider circulation when it was forwarded and reforwarded.
Purporting to represent the views of Gary Cohn and quite succinctly
summarizing the appalled sense in much of the White House, the email
read:

> It's worse than you can imagine. An idiot surrounded by clowns.
> Trump won't read anything—not one-page memos, not the brief
> policy papers; nothing. He gets up halfway through meetings with
> world leaders because he is bored. And his staff is no better. Kushner
> is an entitled baby who knows nothing. Bannon is an arrogant prick
> who thinks he's smarter than he is. Trump is less a person than a col-
> lection of terrible traits. No one will survive the first year but his
> family. I hate the work, but feel I need to stay because I'm the only
> person there with a clue what he's doing. The reason so few jobs have
> been filled is that they only accept people who pass ridiculous purity
> tests, even for midlevel policy-making jobs where the people will never
> see the light of day. I am in a constant state of shock and horror.

Still, the mess that might do serious damage to the nation, and, by
association, to your own brand, might be transcended if you were seen as
the person, by dint of competence and professional behavior, taking control of it.

Powell, who had come into the White House as an adviser to Ivanka
Trump, rose, in weeks, to a position on the National Security Council,
and was then, suddenly, along with Cohn, her Goldman colleague, a con-
tender for some of the highest posts in the administration.

At the same time, both she and Cohn were spending a good deal of time with their ad hoc outside advisers on which way they might jump out of the White House. Powell could eye seven-figure comms jobs at various Fortune 100 companies, or a C-suite future at a tech company— Facebook's Sheryl Sandberg, after all, had a background in corporate phi- lanthropy and in the Obama administration. Cohn, on his part, already a centamillionaire, was thinking about the World Bank or the Fed.

Ivanka Trump—dealing with some of the same personal and career considerations as Powell, except without a viable escape strategy—was quite in her own corner. Inexpressive and even botlike in public but, among friends, discursive and strategic, Ivanka had become both more defensive about her father and more alarmed by where his White House was heading. She and her husband blamed this on Bannon and his let-Trump-be-Trump philosophy (often interpreted as let Trump be Ban- non). The couple had come to regard him as more diabolical than Raspu- tin. Hence it was their job to keep Bannon and the ideologues from the president, who, they believed, was, in his heart, a practical-minded person (at least in his better moods), swayed only by people preying on his short attention span.

In mutually codependent fashion, Ivanka relied on Dina to suggest management tactics that would help her handle her father and the White House, while Dina relied on Ivanka to offer regular assurances that not everyone named Trump was completely crazy. This link meant that within the greater West Wing population, Powell was seen as part of the much tighter family circle, which, while it conferred influence, also made her the target of ever sharper attacks. "She will expose herself as being totally incompetent," said a bitter Katie Walsh, seeing Powell as less a nor- malizing influence than another aspect of the abnormal Trump family power play.

And indeed, both Powell and Cohn had privately concluded that the job they both had their eye on—chief of staff, that singularly necessary White House management position—would always be impossible to per- form if the president's daughter and son-in-law, no matter how much they were allied to them, were in de facto command whenever they wanted to exert it.

Dina and Ivanka were themselves spearheading an initiative that, otherwise, would have been a fundamental responsibility of the chief of staff: controlling the president's information flow.

* * *

The unique problem here was partly how to get information to someone who did not (or could not or would not) read, and who at best listened only selectively. But the other part of the problem was how best to qualify the information that he liked to get. Hope Hicks, after more than a year at this side, had honed her instincts for the kind of information—the clips—that would please him. Bannon, in his intense and confiding voice, could insinuate himself into the president's mind. Kellyanne Conway brought him the latest outrages against him. There were his after-dinner calls—the billionaire chorus. And then cable, itself programmed to reach him—to court him or enrage him.

The information he did not get was formal information. The data. The details. The options. The analysis. He didn't do PowerPoint. For anything that smacked of a classroom or of being lectured to—"professor" was one of his bad words, and he was proud of never going to class, never buying a textbook, never taking a note—he got up and left the room.

This was a problem in multiple respects—indeed, in almost all the prescribed functions of the presidency. But perhaps most of all, it was a problem in the evaluation of strategic military options.

The president liked generals. The more fruit salad they wore, the better. The president was very pleased with the compliments he got for appointing generals who commanded the respect that Mattis and Kelly and McMaster were accorded (pay no attention to Michael Flynn). What the president did not like was *listening* to generals, who, for the most part, were skilled in the new army jargon of PowerPoint, data dumps, and McKinsey-like presentations. One of the things that endeared Flynn to the president was that Flynn, quite the conspiracist and drama queen, had a vivid storytelling sense.

By the time of the Syrian attack on Khan Sheikhoun, McMaster had been Trump's National Security Advisor for only about six weeks. Yet his efforts to inform the president had already become an exercise in trying to tutor a recalcitrant and resentful student. Recently Trump's meetings with McMaster had ended up in near acrimony, and now the president was telling several friends that his new National Security Advisor was too boring and that he was going to fire him.

McMaster had been the default choice, a fact that Trump kept returning to: Why had he hired him? He blamed his son-in-law.

After the president fired Flynn in February, he had spent two days at Mar-a-Lago interviewing replacements, badly taxing his patience.

John Bolton, the former U.S. ambassador to the United Nations and Bannon's consistent choice, made his aggressive light-up-the-world, go-to-war pitch.

Then Lt. Gen. Robert L. Caslen Jr., superintendent of the United States Military Academy at West Point, presented himself with what Trump viewed positively as old-fashioned military decorum. *Yes, sir. No, sir. That's correct, sir. Well, I think we know China has some problems, sir.* And in short order it seemed that Trump was selling Caslen on the job.

"That's the guy I want," said Trump. "He's got the look."

But Caslen demurred. He had never really had a staff job. Kushner thought he might not be ready.

"Yeah, but I liked that guy," pressed Trump.

Then McMaster, wearing a uniform with his silver star, came in and immediately launched into a wide-ranging lecture on global strategy. Trump was soon, and obviously, distracted, and as the lecture continued he began sulking.

"That guy bores the shit out of me," announced Trump after McMaster left the room. But Kushner pushed him to take another meeting with McMaster, who the next day showed up without his uniform and in a baggy suit.

"He looks like a beer salesman," Trump said, announcing that he would hire McMaster but didn't want to have another meeting with him.

Shortly after his appointment, McMaster appeared on *Morning Joe.* Trump saw the show and noted admiringly, "The guy sure gets good press."

The president decided he had made a good hire.

* * *

By midmorning on April 4, a full briefing had been assembled at the White House for the president about the chemical attacks. Along with his daughter and Powell, most members of the president's inner national security circle saw the bombing of Khan Sheikhoun as a straightforward opportunity to register an absolute moral objection. The circumstance was unequivocal: Bashar al-Assad's government, once again defying international law, had used chemical weapons. There was video documenting the attack and substantial agreement among intelligence agencies about Assad's responsibility. The politics were right: Barack Obama failed to act when confronted with a Syrian chemical attack, and now Trump could. The downside was small; it would be a contained response. And it had the added advantage of seeming to stand up to the Russians, Assad's effective partners in Syria, which would score a political point at home.

Bannon, at perhaps his lowest moment of influence in the White House—many still felt that his departure was imminent—was the only voice arguing against a military response. It was a purist's rationale: keep the United States out of intractable problems, and certainly don't increase our involvement in them. He was holding the line against the rising business-as-usual faction, making decisions based on the same set of assumptions, Bannon believed, that had resulted in the Middle East quagmire. It was time to break the standard-response pattern of behavior, represented by the Jarvanka-Powell-Cohn-McMaster alliance. Forget normal—in fact, to Bannon, normal was precisely the problem.

The president had already agreed to McMaster's demand that Bannon be removed from the National Security Council, though the change wouldn't be announced until the following day. But Trump was also drawn to Bannon's strategic view: Why do anything, if you don't have to? Or, why would you do something that doesn't actually get you anything? Since taking office, the president had been developing an intuitive national security view: keep as many despots who might otherwise screw you as happy as possible. A self-styled strongman, he was also a fundamental appeaser. In this instance, then, why cross the Russians?

By the afternoon, the national security team was experiencing a sense of rising panic: the president, in their view, didn't seem to be quite registering the situation. Bannon wasn't helping. His hyperrationalist approach obviously appealed to the not-always-rational president. A chemical attack didn't change the circumstances on the ground, Bannon argued; besides, there had been far worse attacks with far more casualties than this one. If you were looking for broken children, you could find them anywhere. Why these broken children?

The president was not a debater—well, not in any Socratic sense. Nor was he in any conventional sense a decision maker. And certainly he was not a student of foreign policy views and options. But this was nevertheless turning into a genuine philosophical face-off.

"Do nothing" had long been viewed as an unacceptable position of helplessness by American foreign policy experts. The instinct to do something was driven by the desire to prove you were not limited to nothing. You couldn't do nothing and show strength. But Bannon's approach was very much "A pox on all your houses," it was not our mess, and judging by all recent evidence, no good would come of trying to help clean it up. That effort would cost military lives with no military reward. Bannon, believing in the need for a radical shift in foreign policy, was proposing a new doctrine: Fuck 'em. This iron-fisted isolationism appealed to the president's transactional self: What was in it for us (or for him)?

Hence the urgency to get Bannon off the National Security Council. The curious thing is that in the beginning he was thought to be much more reasonable than Michael Flynn, with his fixation on Iran as the source of all evil. Bannon was supposed to babysit Flynn. But Bannon, quite to Kushner's shock, had not just an isolationist worldview but an apocalyptic one. Much of the world would burn and there was nothing you could do about it.

The announcement of Bannon's removal was made the day after the attack. That in itself was a rather remarkable accomplishment on the part of the moderates. In little more than two months, Trump's radical, if not screwball, national security leadership had been replaced by so-called reasonable people.

The job was now to bring the president into this circle of reason.

* * *

As the day wore on, both Ivanka Trump and Dina Powell were united in their determination to persuade the president to react . . . normally. At the very minimum, an absolute condemnation of the use of chemical weapons, a set of sanctions, and, ideally, a military response—although not a big one. None of this was in any way exceptional. Which was sort of the point: it was critical not to respond in a radical, destabilizing way—including a radical nonresponse.

Kushner was by now complaining to his wife that her father just didn't get it. It had even been difficult to get a consensus on releasing a firm statement about the unacceptability of the use of chemical weapons at the noon press briefing. To both Kushner and McMaster it seemed obvious that the president was more annoyed about having to think about the attack than by the attack itself.

Finally, Ivanka told Dina they needed to show the president a different kind of presentation. Ivanka had long ago figured out how to make successful pitches to her father. You had to push his enthusiasm buttons. He may be a businessman, but numbers didn't do it for him. He was not a spreadsheet jockey—his numbers guys dealt with spreadsheets. He liked big names. He liked the big picture—he liked *literal* big pictures. He liked to see it. He liked "impact."

But in one sense, the military, the intelligence community, and the White House's national security team remained behind the times. Theirs was a data world rather than a picture world. As it happened, the attack on Khan Sheikhoun had produced a wealth of visual evidence. Bannon might be right that this attack was no more mortal than countless others, but by focusing on this one and curating the visual proof, this atrocity became singular.

Late that afternoon, Ivanka and Dina created a presentation that Bannon, in disgust, characterized as pictures of kids foaming at the mouth.

When the two women showed the presentation to the president, he went through it several times. He seemed mesmerized.

Watching the president's response, Bannon saw Trumpism melting before his eyes. Trump—despite his visceral resistance to the establishment ass-covering and standard-issue foreign policy expertise that had pulled the country into hopeless wars—was suddenly putty. After seeing all the horrifying photos, he immediately adopted a completely conventional point of view: it seemed inconceivable to him that we couldn't do something.

That evening, the president described the pictures in a call to a friend—the foam, all that foam. *These are just kids.* He usually displayed a consistent contempt for anything but overwhelming military response; now he expressed a sudden, wide-eyed interest in all kinds of other military options.

On Wednesday, April 5, Trump received a briefing that outlined multiple options for how to respond. But again McMaster burdened him with detail. He quickly became frustrated, feeling that he was being manipulated.

The following day, the president and several of his top aides flew to Florida for a meeting with the Chinese president, Xi Jinping—a meeting organized by Kushner with the help of Henry Kissinger. While aboard Air Force One, he held a tightly choreographed meeting of the National Security Council, tying into the staff on the ground. By this point, the decision about how to respond to the chemical attack had already been made: the military would launch a Tomahawk cruise missile strike at Al Shayrat airfield. After a final round of discussion, while on board, the president, almost ceremonially, ordered the strike for the next day.

With the meeting over and the decision made, Trump, in a buoyant mood, came back to chat with reporters traveling with him on Air Force One. In a teasing fashion, he declined to say what he planned to do about Syria. An hour later, Air Force One landed and the president was hustled to Mar-a-Lago.

The Chinese president and his wife arrived for dinner shortly after five o'clock and were greeted by a military guard on the Mar-a-Lago driveway. With Ivanka supervising arrangements, virtually the entire White House senior staff attended.

During a dinner of Dover sole, haricots verts, and thumbelina carrots—Kushner seated with the Chinese first couple, Bannon at the end of the table—the attack on Al Shayrat airfield was launched.

Shortly before ten, the president, reading straight off the teleprompter, announced that the mission had been completed. Dina Powell arranged a for-posterity photo of the president with his advisers and national security team in the makeshift situation room at Mar-a-Lago. She was the only woman in the room. Steve Bannon glowered from his seat at the table, revolted by the stagecraft and the "phoniness of the fucking thing."

It was a cheerful and relieved Trump who mingled with his guests among the palm trees and mangroves. "That was a big one," he confided to a friend. His national security staff were even more relieved. The unpredictable president seemed almost predictable. The unmanageable president, manageable.

# 15

# MEDIA

On April 19, Bill O'Reilly, the Fox anchor and the biggest star in cable news, was pushed out by the Murdoch family over charges of sexual harassment. This was a continuation of the purge at the network that had begun nine months before with the firing of its chief, Roger Ailes. Fox achieved its ultimate political influence with the election of Donald Trump, yet now the future of the network seemed held in a peculiar Murdoch family limbo between conservative father and liberal sons.

A few hours after the O'Reilly announcement, Ailes, from his new oceanfront home in Palm Beach—precluded by his separation agreement with Fox from any efforts to compete with it for eighteen months—sent an emissary into the West Wing with a question for Steve Bannon: *O'Reilly and Hannity are in, what about you?* Ailes, in secret, had been plotting his comeback with a new conservative network. Currently in internal exile inside the White House, Bannon—"the next Ailes"—was all ears.

This was not just the plotting of ambitious men, seeking both opportunity and revenge; the idea for a new network was also driven by an urgent sense that the Trump phenomenon was about, as much as anything else, right-wing media. For twenty years, Fox had honed its populist message: liberals were stealing and ruining the country. Then, just at the moment that many liberals—including Rupert Murdoch's sons, who were increasingly in control of their father's company—had begun to believe that the Fox audience was beginning to age out, with its anti-gay-marriage, anti-abortion, anti-immigrant social message, which seemed too hoary for younger Republicans, along came Breitbart News. Breitbart not only spoke to a much younger right-wing audience—here Bannon felt he was as much in tune with this audience as Ailes was with his—but it had turned this audience into a huge army of digital activists (or social media trolls).

As right-wing media had fiercely coalesced around Trump—readily excusing all the ways he might contradict the traditional conservative ethos—mainstream media had become as fiercely resistant. The country was divided as much by media as by politics. Media was the avatar of politics. A sidelined Ailes was eager to get back in the game. This was his natural playing field: (1) Trump's election proved the power of a significantly smaller but more dedicated electoral base—just as, in cable television terms, a smaller hardcore base was more valuable than a bigger, less committed one; (2) this meant an inverse dedication by an equally small circle of passionate enemies; (3) hence, there would be blood.

If Bannon was as finished as he appeared in the White House, this was his opportunity, too. Indeed, the problem with Bannon's $1.5 million a year Internetcentric Breitbart News was that it couldn't be monetized or scaled up in a big way, but with O'Reilly and Hannity on board, there could be television riches fueled by, into the foreseeable future, a new Trump-inspired era of right-wing passion and hegemony.

Ailes's message to his would-be protégé was plain: Not just the rise of Trump, but the fall of Fox could be Bannon's moment.

In reply, Bannon let Ailes know that for now, he was trying to hold on to his position in the White House. But yes, the opportunity was obvious.

\* \* \*

Even as O'Reilly's fate was being debated by the Murdochs, Trump, understanding O'Reilly's power and knowing how much O'Reilly's audience overlapped with his own base, had expressed his support and approval—"I don't think Bill did anything wrong. . . . He is a good person," he told the *New York Times*.

But in fact a paradox of the new strength of conservative media was Trump himself. During the campaign, when it suited him, he had turned on Fox. If there were other media opportunities, he took them. (In the recent past, Republicans, particularly in the primary season, paid careful obeisance to Fox over other media outlets.) Trump kept insisting that he was bigger than just conservative media.

In the past month, Ailes, a frequent Trump caller and after-dinner adviser, had all but stopped speaking to the president, piqued by the constant reports that Trump was bad-mouthing him as he praised a newly attentive Murdoch, who had, before the election, only ever ridiculed Trump.

"Men who demand the most loyalty tend to be the least loyal pricks," noted a sardonic Ailes (a man who himself demanded lots of loyalty).

The conundrum was that conservative media saw Trump as its creature, while Trump saw himself as a star, a vaunted and valued product of all media, one climbing ever higher. It was a cult of personality, and he was the personality. He was the most famous man in the world. Everybody loved him—or ought to.

On Trump's part this was, arguably, something of a large misunderstanding about the nature of conservative media. He clearly did not understand that what conservative media elevated, liberal media would necessarily take down. Trump, goaded by Bannon, would continue to do the things that would delight conservative media and incur the wrath of liberal media. That was the program. The more your supporters loved you, the more your antagonists hated you. That's how it was supposed to work. And that's how it was working.

But Trump himself was desperately wounded by his treatment in the mainstream media. He obsessed on every slight until it was overtaken by the next slight. Slights were singled out and replayed again and again, his mood worsening with each replay (he was always rerunning the DVR). Much of the president's daily conversation was a repetitive rundown of what various anchors and hosts had said about him. And he was upset not only when he was attacked, but when the people around him were attacked. But he did not credit their loyalty, or blame himself or the nature of liberal media for the indignities heaped on his staffers; he blamed them and their inability to get good press.

Mainstream media's self-righteousness and contempt for Trump helped provide a tsunami of clicks for right-wing media. But an often raging, self-pitying, tormented president had not gotten this memo, or had failed to comprehend it. He was looking for media love everywhere. In this, Trump quite profoundly seemed unable to distinguish between his political advantage and his personal needs—he thought emotionally, not strategically.

The great value of being president, in his view, was that you're the most famous man in the world, and fame is always venerated and adored by the media. Isn't it? But, confusingly, Trump was president in large part because of his particular talent, conscious or reflexive, to alienate the media, which then turned him into a figure reviled by the media. This was not a dialectical space that was comfortable for an insecure man.

"For Trump," noted Ailes, "the media represented power, much more so than politics, and he wanted the attention and respect of its most powerful men. Donald and I were really quite good friends for more than 25 years, but he would have preferred to be friends with Murdoch, who thought he was a moron—at least until he became president."

* * *

The White House Correspondents' Dinner was set for April 29, the one hundredth day of the Trump administration. The annual dinner, once an insiders' event, had become an opportunity for media organizations to promote themselves by recruiting celebrities—most of whom had nothing to do with journalism or politics—to sit at their tables. This had resulted in a notable Trump humiliation when, in 2011, Barack Obama singled out Trump for particular mockery. In Trump lore, this was the insult that pushed him to make the 2016 run.

Not long after the Trump team's arrival in the White House, the Correspondents' Dinner became a cause for worry. On a winter afternoon in Kellyanne Conway's upstairs West Wing office, Conway and Hope Hicks engaged in a pained discussion about what to do.

The central problem was that the president was neither inclined to make fun of himself, nor particularly funny himself—at least not, in Conway's description, "in that kind of humorous way."

George W. Bush had famously resisted the Correspondents' Dinner and suffered greatly at it, but he had prepped extensively, and every year he pulled out an acceptable performance. But neither woman, confiding their concerns around the small table in Conway's office to a journalist they regarded as sympathetic, thought Trump had a realistic chance of making the dinner anything like a success.

"He doesn't appreciate cruel humor," said Conway.

"His style is more old-fashioned," said Hicks.

Both women, clearly seeing the Correspondents' Dinner as an intractable problem, kept characterizing the event as "unfair," which, more generally, is how they characterized the media's view of Trump. "He's unfairly portrayed." "They don't give him the benefit of the doubt." "He's just not treated the way other presidents have been treated."

The burden here for Conway and Hicks was their understanding that the president did not see the media's lack of regard for him as part of a political divide on which he stood on a particular side. Instead, he perceived it as a deep personal attack on him: for entirely unfair reasons, ad hominem reasons, the media just did not like him. Ridiculed him. Cruelly. Why?

The journalist, trying to offer some comfort, told the two women there was a rumor going around that Graydon Carter—the editor of *Vanity Fair* and host of one of the most important parties of the Correspondents' Dinner weekend, and, for decades, one of Trump's key tormentors in the media—was shortly going to be pushed out of the magazine.

"Really?" said Hicks, jumping up. "Oh my God, can I tell him? Would that be okay? He'll want to know this." She headed quickly downstairs to the Oval Office.

* * *

Curiously, Conway and Hicks each portrayed a side of the president's alter ego media problem. Conway was the bitter antagonist, the mud-in-your-eye messenger who reliably sent the media into paroxysms of outrage against the president. Hicks was the confidante ever trying to get the president a break and some good ink in the only media he really cared about—the media that most hated him. But as different as they were in their media functions and temperament, both women had achieved remarkable influence in the administration by serving as the key lieutenants responsible for addressing the president's most pressing concern, his media reputation.

While Trump was in most ways a conventional misogynist, in the workplace he was much closer to women than to men. The former he confided in, the latter he held at arm's length. He liked and needed his office wives, and he trusted them with his most important personal issues. Women, according to Trump, were simply more loyal and trustworthy than men. Men might be more forceful and competent, but they were also more likely to have their own agendas. Women, by their nature, or Trump's version of their nature, were more likely to focus their purpose on a man. A man like Trump.

It wasn't happenstance or just casting balance that his *Apprentice* sidekick was a woman, nor that his daughter Ivanka had become one of his closest confidants. He felt women understood him. Or, the kind of women he liked—positive-outlook, can-do, loyal women, who also looked good—understood him. Everybody who successfully worked for him understood that there was always a subtext of his needs and personal tics that had to be scrupulously attended to; in this, he was not all that different from other highly successful figures, just more so. It would be hard to imagine someone who expected a greater awareness of and more catering to his peculiar whims, rhythms, prejudices, and often inchoate desires. He needed special—extra special—handling. Women, he explained to one friend with something like self-awareness, generally got this more precisely than men. In particular, women who self-selected themselves as tolerant of or oblivious to or amused by or steeled against his casual misogyny and constant sexual subtext—which was somehow, incongruously and often jarringly, matched with paternal regard—got this.

\* \* \*

Kellyanne Conway first met Donald Trump at a meeting of the condo board for the Trump International Hotel, which was directly across the street from the UN and was where, in the early 2000s, she lived with her husband and children. Conway's husband, George, a graduate of Harvard College and Yale Law School, was a partner at the premier corporate mergers and acquisitions firm Wachtell, Lipton, Rosen & Katz. (Though Wachtell was a Democratic-leaning firm, George had played a behind-the-scenes role on the team that represented Paula Jones in her pursuit of Bill Clinton.) In its professional and domestic balance, the Conway family was organized around George's career. Kellyanne's career was a sidelight.

Kellyanne, who in the Trump campaign would use her working-class biography to good effect, grew up in central New Jersey, the daughter of a trucker, raised by a single mother (and, always in her narrative, her grandmother and two unmarried aunts). She went to George Washington law school and afterward interned for Reagan's pollster, Richard Wirthlin. Then she became the assistant to Frank Luntz, a curious figure in the Republican Party, known as much for his television deals and toupee as for his polling acumen. Conway herself began to make appearances on cable TV while working for Luntz.

One virtue of the research and polling business she started in 1995 was that it could adapt to her husband's career. But she never much rose above a midrank presence in Republican political circles, nor did she become more than the also-ran behind Ann Coulter and Laura Ingraham on cable television—which is where Trump first saw her and why he singled her out at the condo board meeting.

In a real sense, however, her advantage was not meeting Trump but being taken up by the Mercers. They recruited Conway in 2015 to work on the Cruz campaign, when Trump was still far from the conservative ideal, and then, in August 2016, inserted her into the Trump campaign.

She understood her role. "I will only ever call you Mr. Trump," she told the candidate with perfect-pitch solemnity when he interviewed her for the job. It was a trope she would repeat in interview after interview— Conway was a catalog of learned lines—a message repeated as much for Trump as for others.

Her title was campaign manager, but that was a misnomer. Bannon was the real manager, and she was the senior pollster. But Bannon shortly replaced her in that role and she was left in what Trump saw as the vastly more important role of cable spokesperson.

Conway seemed to have a convenient On-Off toggle. In private, in the Off position, she seemed to regard Trump as a figure of exhausting exaggeration or even absurdity—or, at least, if you regarded him that way, she seemed to suggest that she might, too. She illustrated her opinion of her boss with a whole series of facial expressions: eyes rolling, mouth agape, head snapping back. But in the On position, she metamorphosed into believer, protector, defender, and handler. Conway is an antifeminist (or, actually, in a complicated ideological somersault, she sees feminists as being antifeminists), ascribing her methods and temperament to her being a wife and mother. She's instinctive and reactive. Hence her role as the ultimate Trump defender: she verbally threw herself in front of any bullet coming his way.

Trump loved her defend-at-all-costs shtick. Conway's appearances were on his schedule to watch live. His was often the first call she got after coming off the air. She channeled Trump: she said exactly the kind of Trump stuff that would otherwise make her put a finger-gun to her head.

After the election—Trump's victory setting off a domestic reordering in the Conway household, and a scramble to get her husband an administration job—Trump assumed she would be his press secretary. "He and my mother," Conway said, "because they both watch a lot of television, thought this was one of the most important jobs." In Conway's version, she turned Trump down or demurred. She kept proposing alternatives in which she would be the key spokesperson but would be more as well. In fact, almost everyone else was maneuvering Trump around his desire to appoint Conway.

Loyalty was Trump's most valued attribute, and in Conway's view her kamikaze-like media defense of the president had earned her a position of utmost primacy in the White House. But in her public persona, she had pushed the boundaries of loyalty too far; she was so hyperbolic that even Trump loyalists found her behavior extreme and were repelled. None were more put off than Jared and Ivanka, who, appalled at the shamelessness of her television appearances, extended this into a larger critique of Conway's vulgarity. When referring to her, they were particularly partial to using the shorthand "nails," a reference to her Cruella de Vil–length manicure treatments.

By mid-February she was already the subject of leaks—many coming from Jared and Ivanka—about how she had been sidelined. She vociferously defended herself, producing a list of television appearances still on her schedule, albeit lesser ones. But she also had a teary scene with Trump in the Oval Office, offering to resign if the president had lost faith in her. Almost invariably, when confronted with self-abnegation, Trump offered copious reassurances. "You will always have a place in my administration," he told her. "You will be here for eight years."

But she had indeed been sidelined, reduced to second-rate media, to being a designated emissary to right-wing groups, and left out of any meaningful decision making. This she blamed on the media, a scourge that further united her in self-pity with Donald Trump. In fact, her relationship with the president deepened as they bonded over their media wounds.

* * *

Hope Hicks, then age twenty-six, was the campaign's first hire. She knew the president vastly better than Conway did, and she understood that her most important media function was not to be in the media.

Hicks grew up in Greenwich, Connecticut. Her father was a PR executive who now worked for the Glover Park Group, the Democratic-leaning communications and political consulting firm; her mother was a former staffer for a democratic congressman. An indifferent student, Hicks went to Southern Methodist University and then did some modeling before getting a PR job. She first went to work for Matthew Hiltzik, who ran a small New York–based PR firm and was noted for his ability to work with high-maintenance clients, including the movie producer Harvey Weinstein (later pilloried for years of sexual harassment and abuse—accusations that Hiltzik and his staff had long helped protect him from) and the television personality Katie Couric. Hiltzik, an active Democrat who had worked for Hillary Clinton, also represented Ivanka Trump's fashion line; Hicks started to do some work for the account and then joined Ivanka's company full time. In 2015, Ivanka seconded her to her father's campaign; as the campaign progressed, moving from novelty project to political factor to juggernaut, Hicks's family increasingly, and incredulously, viewed her as rather having been taken captive. (Following the Trump victory and her move into the White House, her friends and intimates talked with great concern about what kind of therapies and recuperation she would need after her tenure was finally over.)

Over the eighteen months of the campaign, the traveling group usually consisted of the candidate, Hicks, and the campaign manager, Corey Lewandowski. In time, she became—in addition to an inadvertent participant in history, about which she was quite as astonished as anyone—a kind of Stepford factotum, as absolutely dedicated to and tolerant of Mr. Trump as anyone who had ever worked for him.

Shortly after Lewandowski, with whom Hicks had an on-and-off romantic relationship, was fired in June 2016 for clashing with Trump family members, Hicks sat in Trump Tower with Trump and his sons, worrying about Lewandowski's treatment in the press and wondering aloud how she might help him. Trump, who otherwise seemed to treat Hicks in a protective and even paternal way, looked up and said, "Why? You've already done enough for him. You're the best piece of tail he'll ever have," sending Hicks running from the room.

As new layers began to form around Trump, first as nominee and then as president-elect, Hicks continued playing the role of his personal PR woman. She would remain his constant shadow and the person with the best access to him. "Have you spoken to Hope?" were among the words most frequently uttered in the West Wing.

Hicks, sponsored by Ivanka and ever loyal to her, was in fact thought of as Trump's real daughter, while Ivanka was thought of as his real wife. More functionally, but as elementally, Hicks was the president's chief media handler. She worked by the president's side, wholly separate from the White House's forty-person-strong communications office. The president's personal message and image were entrusted to her—or, more accurately, she was the president's agent in retailing that message and image, which he trusted to no one but himself. Together they formed something of a freelance operation.

Without any particular politics of her own, and, with her New York PR background, quite looking down on the right-wing press, she was the president's official liaison to the mainstream media. The president had charged her with the ultimate job: a good write-up in the *New York Times*.

That, in the president's estimation, had yet failed to happen, "but Hope tries and tries," the president said.

On more than one occasion, after a day—one of the countless days—of particularly bad notices, the president greeted her, affectionately, with "You must be the world's worst PR person."

* * *

In the early days of the transition, with Conway out of the running for the press secretary job, Trump became determined to find a "star." The conservative radio host Laura Ingraham, who had spoken at the convention, was on the list, as was Ann Coulter. Fox Business's Maria Bartiromo was also under consideration. (This was television, the president-elect said, and it ought to be a good-looking woman.) When none of those ideas panned out, the job was offered to Fox News's Tucker Carlson, who turned it down.

But there was a counterview: the press secretary ought to be the opposite of a star. In fact, the entire press operation ought to be downgraded. If the press was the enemy, why pander to it, why give it more visibility? This was fundamental Bannonism: stop thinking you can somehow get along with your enemies.

As the debate went on, Priebus pushed for one of his deputies at the Republican National Committee, Sean Spicer, a well-liked forty-five-year-old Washington political professional with a string of posts on the Hill in the George W. Bush years as well as with the RNC. Spicer, hesitant to take the job, kept anxiously posing the question to colleagues in the Washington swamp: "If I do this, will I ever be able to work again?"

There were conflicting answers.

During the transition, many members of Trump's team came to agree with Bannon that their approach to White House press management ought to be to push it off—and the longer the arm's length the better. For the press, this initiative, or rumors of it, became another sign of the incoming administration's antipress stance and its systematic efforts to cut off the information supply. In truth, the suggestions about moving the briefing room away from the White House, or curtailing the briefing schedule, or limiting broadcast windows or press pool access, were variously discussed by other incoming administrations. In her husband's White House, Hillary Clinton had been a proponent of limiting press access.

It was Donald Trump who was not able to relinquish this proximity to the press and the stage in his own house. He regularly berated Spicer for his ham-handed performances, often giving his full attention to them. His response to Spicer's briefings was part of his continuing belief that nobody could work the media like he could, that somehow he had been stuck with an F-Troop communications team that was absent charisma, magnetism, and proper media connections.

Trump's pressure on Spicer—a constant stream of directorial castigation and instruction that reliably rattled the press secretary—helped turn the briefings into a can't-miss train wreck. Meanwhile, the real press operation had more or less devolved into a set of competing press organizations within the White House.

There was Hope Hicks and the president, living in what other West Wingers characterized as an alternative universe in which the mainstream media would yet discover the charm and wisdom of Donald Trump. Where past presidents might have spent portions of their day talking about the needs, desires, and points of leverage among various members of Congress, the president and Hicks spent a great deal of time talking about a fixed cast of media personalities, trying to second-guess the real agendas and weak spots among cable anchors and producers and *Times* and *Post* reporters.

Often the focus of this otherworldly ambition was directed at *Times* reporter Maggie Haberman. Haberman's front-page beat at the paper, which might be called the "weirdness of Donald Trump" beat, involved producing vivid tales of eccentricities, questionable behavior, and shit the president says, told in a knowing, deadpan style. Beyond acknowledging that Trump was a boy from Queens yet in awe of the *Times*, nobody in the West Wing could explain why he and Hicks would so often turn to Haberman for what would so reliably be a mocking and hurtful portrayal. There was some feeling that Trump was returning to scenes of past success: the *Times* might be against him, but Haberman had worked at the *New York Post* for many years. "She's very professional," Conway said, speaking in defense of the president and trying to justify Haberman's extraordinary access. But however intent he remained on getting good ink in the *Times*, the president saw Haberman as "mean and horrible." And yet, on a near-weekly basis, he and Hicks plotted when next to have the *Times* come in.

* * *

Kushner had his personal press operation and Bannon had his. The leaking culture had become so open and overt—most of the time everybody could identify everybody else's leaks—that it was now formally staffed.

Kushner's Office of American Innovation employed, as its spokesperson, Josh Raffel, who, like Hicks, came out of Matthew Hiltzik's PR shop. Raffel, a Democrat who had been working in Hollywood, acted as Kushner and his wife's personal rep—not least of all because the couple felt that Spicer, owing his allegiance to Priebus, was not aggressively representing them. This was explicit. "Josh is Jared's Hope," was his internal West Wing job description.

Raffel coordinated all of Kushner and Ivanka's personal press, though there was more of this for Ivanka than for Kushner. But, more importantly, Raffel coordinated all of Kushner's substantial leaking, or, as it were, his off-the-record briefings and guidance—no small part of it against Bannon. Kushner, who with great conviction asserted that he never leaked, in part justified his press operation as a defense against Bannon's press operation.

Bannon's "person," Alexandra Preate—a witty conservative socialite partial to champagne—had previously represented Breitbart News and other conservative figures like CNBC's Larry Kudlow, and was close friends with Rebekah Mercer. In a relationship that nobody seemed quite able to explain, she handled all of Bannon's press "outreach" but was not employed by the White House, although she maintained an office, or at least an officelike presence, there. The point was clear: her client was Bannon and not the Trump administration.

Bannon, to Jared and Ivanka's continued alarm, had unique access to Breitbart's significant abilities to change the right-wing mood and focus. Bannon insisted he had cut his ties to his former colleagues at Breitbart, but that strained everybody's credulity—and everybody figured nobody was supposed to believe it. Rather, everybody was supposed to fear it.

There was, curiously, general agreement in the West Wing that Donald Trump, the media president, had one of the most dysfunctional communication operations in modern White House history. Mike Dubke, a Republican PR operative who was hired as White House communications director, was, by all estimations, from the first day on his way out the door. In the end he lasted only three months.

* * *

The White House Correspondents' Dinner rose, as much as any other challenge for the new president and his team, as a test of his abilities. He wanted to do it. He was certain that the power of his charm was greater than the rancor that he bore this audience—or that they bore him.

He recalled his 2015 *Saturday Night Live* appearance—which, in his view, was entirely successful. In fact, he had refused to prepare, had kept saying he would "improvise," no problem. Comedians don't actually improvise, he was told; it's all scripted and rehearsed. But this counsel had only marginal effect.

Almost nobody except the president himself thought he could pull off the Correspondents' Dinner. His staff was terrified that he would die up there in front of a seething and contemptuous audience. Though he could dish it out, often very harshly, no one thought he could take it. Still, the president seemed eager to appear at the event, if casual about it, too—with Hicks, ordinarily encouraging his every impulse, trying not to.

Bannon pressed the symbolic point: the president should not be seen currying the favor of his enemies, or trying to entertain them. The media was a much better whipping boy than it was a partner in crime. The Bannon principle, the steel stake in the ground, remained: don't bend, don't accommodate, don't meet halfway. And in the end, rather than implying that Trump did not have the talent and wit to move this crowd, that was a much better way to persuade the president that he should not appear at the dinner.

When Trump finally agreed to forgo the event, Conway, Hicks, and virtually everybody else in the West Wing breathed a lot easier.

* * *

Shortly after five o'clock on the one hundredth day of his presidency—a particularly muggy one—while twenty-five hundred or so members of news organizations and their friends gathered at the Washington Hilton for the White House Correspondents' Dinner, the president left the West Wing for Marine One, which was soon en route to Andrews Air Force Base. Accompanying him were Steve Bannon, Stephen Miller, Reince Priebus, Hope Hicks, and Kellyanne Conway. Vice President Pence and his wife joined the group at Andrews for the brief flight on Air Force One to Harrisburg, Pennsylvania, where the president would give a speech. During the flight, crab cakes were served, and *Face the Nation*'s John Dickerson was granted a special hundredth-day interview.

The first Harrisburg event was held at a factory that manufactured landscaping and gardening tools, where the president closely inspected a line of colorful wheelbarrows. The next event, where the speech would be delivered, was at a rodeo arena in the Farm Show Complex and Expo Center.

And that was the point of this little trip. It had been designed both to remind the rest of the country that the president was not just another phony baloney in a tux like those at the White House Correspondents' Dinner (this somehow presupposed that the president's base cared about or was even aware of the event) and to keep the president's mind off the fact that he was missing the dinner.

But the president kept asking for updates on the jokes.

# 16

## COMEY

"It's impossible to make him understand you can't stop these investigations," said Roger Ailes in early May, a frustrated voice in the Trump kitchen cabinet. "In the old days, you could say leave it alone. Now you say leave it alone and you're the one who gets investigated. He can't get this through his head."

In fact, as various members of the billionaires' cabinet tried to calm down the president during their evening phone calls, they were largely egging him on by expressing deep concern about his DOJ and FBI peril. Many of Trump's wealthy friends saw themselves as having particular DOJ expertise. In their own careers, they had had enough issues with the Justice Department to prompt them to develop DOJ relationships and sources, and now they were always up on DOJ gossip. Flynn was going to throw him in the soup. Manafort was going to roll. And it wasn't just Russia. It was Atlantic City. And Mar-a-Lago. And Trump SoHo.

Both Chris Christie and Rudy Giuliani—each a self-styled expert on the DOJ and the FBI, and ever assuring Trump of their inside sources— encouraged him to take the view that the DOJ was resolved against him; it was all part of a holdover Obama plot.

Even more urgent was Charlie Kushner's fear, channeled through his son and daughter-in-law, that the Kushner family's dealings were getting wrapped up in the pursuit of Trump. Leaks in January had put the kibosh on the Kushners' deal with the Chinese financial colossus Anbang Insurance Group to refinance the family's large debt in one of its major real estate holdings, 666 Fifth Avenue. At the end of April, the *New York Times*, supplied with leaks from the DOJ, linked the Kushner business in a front-page article to Beny Steinmetz—an Israeli diamond, mining, and real estate billionaire with Russian ties who was under chronic investigation around the world. (The Kushner position was not helped by the fact that the president had been gleefully telling multiple people that Jared could solve the Middle East problem because the Kushners knew all the crooks in Israel.) During the first week of May, the *Times* and the *Washington Post* covered the Kushner family's efforts to attract Chinese investors with the promise of U.S. visas.

"The kids"—Jared and Ivanka—exhibited an increasingly panicked sense that the FBI and DOJ were moving beyond Russian election interference and into family finances. "Ivanka is terrified," said a satisfied Bannon.

Trump turned to suggesting to his billionaire chorus that he fire FBI director Comey. He had raised this idea many times before, but always, seemingly, at the same time and in the same context that he brought up the possibility of firing everybody. *Should I fire Bannon? Should I fire Reince? Should I fire McMaster? Should I fire Spicer? Should I fire Tillerson?* This ritual was, everyone understood, more a pretext to a discussion of the power he held than it was, strictly, about personnel decisions. Still, in Trump's poison-the-well fashion, the should-I-fire-so-and-so question, and any consideration of it by any of the billionaires, was translated into agreement, as in: *Carl Icahn thinks I should fire Comey (or Bannon, or Priebus, or McMaster, or Tillerson).*

His daughter and son-in-law, their urgency compounded by Charlie Kushner's panic, encouraged him, arguing that the once possibly charmable Comey was now a dangerous and uncontrollable player whose profit would inevitably be their loss. When Trump got wound up about something, Bannon noted, someone was usually winding him up. The family focus of discussion—insistent, almost frenzied—became wholly about Comey's ambition. He would rise by damaging them. And the drumbeat grew.

"That son of a bitch is going to try to fire the head of the FBI," said Ailes.

During the first week of May, the president had a ranting meeting with Sessions and his deputy Rod Rosenstein. It was a humiliating meeting for both men, with Trump insisting they couldn't control their own people and pushing them to find a reason to fire Comey—in effect, he blamed them for not having come up with that reason months ago. (It was their fault, he implied, that Comey hadn't been fired right off the bat.)

Also that week, there was a meeting that included the president, Jared and Ivanka, Bannon, Priebus, and White House counsel Don McGahn. It was a closed-door meeting—widely noted because it was unusual for the Oval Office door ever to be closed.

*All the Democrats hate Comey*, said the president, expressing his certain and self-justifying view. *All the FBI agents hate him, too—75 percent of them can't stand him*. (This was a number that Kushner had somehow alighted on, and Trump had taken it up.) *Firing Comey will be a huge fundraising advantage*, declared the president, a man who almost never talked about fundraising.

McGahn tried to explain that in fact Comey himself was not running the Russia investigation, that without Comey the investigation would proceed anyway. McGahn, the lawyer whose job was necessarily to issue cautions, was a frequent target of Trump rages. Typically these would begin as a kind of exaggeration or acting and then devolve into the real thing: uncontrollable, vein-popping, ugly-face, tantrum stuff. It got primal. Now the president's denunciations focused in a vicious fury on McGahn and his cautions about Comey.

"Comey was a rat," repeated Trump. There were rats everywhere and you had to get rid of them. *John Dean, John Dean*, he repeated. "Do you know what John Dean did to Nixon?"

Trump, who saw history through personalities—people he might have liked or disliked—was a John Dean freak. He went bananas when a now gray and much aged Dean appeared on talk shows to compare the Trump-Russia investigation to Watergate. That would bring the president to instant attention and launch an inevitable talk-back monologue to the screen about loyalty and what people would do for media attention. It might also be accompanied by several revisionist theories Trump had about Watergate and how Nixon had been framed. And always there were rats. A rat was someone who would take you down for his own advantage. If you had a rat, you needed to kill it. And there were rats all around.

(Later, it was Bannon who had to take the president aside and tell him that John Dean had been the White House counsel in the Nixon administration, so maybe it would be a good idea to lighten up on McGahn.)

As the meeting went on, Bannon, from the doghouse and now, in their mutual antipathy to Jarvanka, allied with Priebus, seized the opportunity to make an impassioned case opposing any move against Comey—which was also, as much, an effort to make the case against Jared and Ivanka and their allies, "the geniuses." ("The geniuses" was one of Trump's terms of derision for anybody who might annoy him or think they were smarter than him, and Bannon now appropriated the term and applied it to Trump's family.) Offering forceful and dire warnings, Bannon told the president: "This Russian story is a third-tier story, but you fire Comey and it'll be the biggest story in the world."

By the time the meeting ended, Bannon and Priebus believed they had prevailed. But that weekend, at Bedminster, the president, again listening to the deep dismay of his daughter and son-in-law, built up another head of steam. With Jared and Ivanka, Stephen Miller was also along for the weekend. The weather was bad and the president missed his golf game, dwelling, with Jared, on his Comey fury. It was Jared, in the version told by those outside the Jarvanka circle, that pushed for action, once more winding up his father-in-law. With the president's assent, Kushner, in this version, gave Miller notes on why the FBI director should be fired and asked him to draft a letter that could set out the basis for immediate dismissal. Miller—less than a deft drafting hand—recruited Hicks to help, another person without clearly relevant abilities. (Miller would later be admonished by Bannon for letting himself get tied up, and potentially implicated, in the Comey mess.)

The letter, in the panicky draft assembled by Miller and Hicks, either from Kushner's directions or on instructions directly coming from the president, was an off-the-wall mishmash containing the talking points— Comey's handling of the Hillary Clinton investigation; the assertion (from Kushner) that the FBI itself had turned against Comey; and, the president's key obsession, the fact that Comey wouldn't publicly acknowledge that the president wasn't under investigation—that would form the Trump family's case for firing Comey. That is, everything but the fact that Comey's FBI was investigating the president.

The Kushner side, for its part, bitterly fought back against any characterization of Kushner as the prime mover or mastermind, in effect putting the entire Bedminster letter effort—as well as the determination to get rid of Comey—entirely on the president's head and casting Kushner as passive bystander. (The Kushner side's position was articulated as follows: "Did he [Kushner] support the decision? Yes. Was he told this was happening? Yes. Did he encourage it? No. Was he fighting for it [Comey's ouster] for weeks and months? No. Did he fight [the ouster]? No. Did he say it would go badly? No.")

Horrified, McGahn quashed sending it. Nevertheless, it was passed to Sessions and Rosenstein, who quickly began drafting their own version of what Kushner and the president obviously wanted.

"I knew when he got back he might blow at any moment," said Bannon after the president returned from his Bedminster weekend.

* * *

On Monday morning, May 8, in a meeting in the Oval Office, the president told Priebus and Bannon that he had made his decision: he would fire Director Comey. Both men again made heated pleas against the move, arguing for, at the very least, more discussion. Here was a key technique for managing the president: delay. Rolling something forward likely meant that something else—an equal or greater fiasco—would come along to preempt whatever fiasco was currently at hand. What's more, delay worked advantageously with Trump's attention span; whatever the issue of the moment, he would shortly be on to something else. When the meeting ended, Priebus and Bannon thought they had bought some breathing room.

Later that day, Sally Yates and former director of National Intelligence James Clapper appeared before the Senate Judiciary Committee's Crime and Terrorism subcommittee—and were greeted by a series of furious tweets from the president.

Here was, Bannon saw again, the essential Trump problem. He hopelessly personalized everything. He saw the world in commercial and show business terms: someone else was always trying to one-up you, someone else was always trying to take the limelight. The battle was between you and someone else who wanted what you had. For Bannon, reducing the political world to face-offs and spats belittled the place in history Trump and his administration had achieved. But it also belied the real powers they were up against. Not people—institutions.

To Trump, he was just up against Sally Yates, who was, he steamed, "such a cunt."

Since her firing on January 30, Yates had remained suspiciously quiet. When journalists approached her, she, or her intermediaries, explained that per her lawyers she was shut down on all media. The president believed she was merely lying in wait. In phone calls to friends, he worried about her "plan" and "strategy," and he continued to press his after-dinner sources for what they thought she and Ben Rhodes, Trump's favorite Obama plotter, had "up their sleeves."

For each of his enemies—and, actually, for each of his friends—the issue for him came down, in many ways, to their personal press plan. The media was the battlefield. Trump assumed everybody wanted his or her fifteen minutes and that everybody had a press strategy for when they got them. If you couldn't get press directly for yourself, you became a leaker. There was no happenstance news, in Trump's view. All news was manipulated and designed, planned and planted. All news was to some extent fake—he understood that very well, because he himself had faked it so many times in his career. This was why he had so naturally cottoned to the "fake news" label. "I've made stuff up forever, and they always print it," he bragged.

The return of Sally Yates, with her appointment before the Senate Judiciary Committee, marked the beginning, Trump believed, of a sustained and well-organized media rollout for her. (His press view was confirmed later in May by a lavish, hagiographic profile of Yates in the *New Yorker*.

"How long do you think she was planning this?" he asked, rhetorically. "You know she was. It's her payday.") "Yates is only famous because of me," the president complained bitterly. "Otherwise, who is she? Nobody."

In front of Congress that Monday morning, Yates delivered a cinematic performance—cool, temperate, detailed, selfless—compounding Trump's fury and agitation.

* * *

On the morning of Tuesday, May 9, with the president still fixated on Comey, and with Kushner and his daughter behind him, Priebus again moved to delay: "There's a right way to do this and a wrong way to do this," he told the president. "We don't want him learning about this on television. I'm going to say this one last time: this is not the right way to do this. If you want to do this, the right way is to have him in and have a conversation. This is the decent way and the professional way." Once more, the president seemed to calm down and become more focused on the necessary process.

But that was a false flag. In fact, the president, in order to avoid embracing conventional process—or, for that matter, any real sense of cause and effect—merely eliminated everybody else from *his* process. For most of the day, almost no one would know that he had decided to take matters into his own hands. In presidential annals, the firing of FBI director James Comey may be the most consequential move ever made by a modern president acting entirely on his own.

As it happened, the Justice Department—Attorney General Sessions and Deputy Attorney General Rod Rosenstein—were, independent of the president's own course, preparing their case against Comey. They would take the Bedminster line and blame Comey for errors of his handling of the Clinton email mess—a problematic charge, because if that was truly the issue, why wasn't Comey dismissed on that basis as soon as the Trump administration took office? But in fact, quite regardless of the Sessions and Rosenstein case, the president had determined to act on his own.

Jared and Ivanka were urging the president on, but even they did not know that the axe would shortly fall. Hope Hicks, Trump's steadfast shadow, who otherwise knew everything the president thought—not least because he was helpless not to express it out loud—didn't know. Steve Bannon, however much he worried that the president might blow, didn't know. His chief of staff didn't know. And his press secretary didn't know. The president, on the verge of starting a war with the FBI, the DOJ, and many in Congress, was going rogue.

At some point that afternoon Trump told his daughter and son-in-law about his plan. They immediately became coconspirators and firmly shut out any competing advice.

Eerily, it was a notably on-time and unruffled day in the West Wing. Mark Halperin, the political reporter and campaign chronicler, was waiting in the reception area for Hope Hicks, who fetched him a bit before 5:00 p.m. Fox's Howard Kurtz was there, too, waiting for his appointment with Sean Spicer. And Reince Priebus's assistant had just been out to tell his five o'clock appointment it would be only a few more minutes.

Just before five, in fact, the president, having not too long before notified McGahn of his intention, pulled the trigger. Trump's personal security guard, Keith Schiller, delivered the termination letter to Comey's office at the FBI just after five o'clock. The letter's second sentence included the words "You are hereby terminated and removed from office, effective immediately."

Shortly thereafter, most of the West Wing staff, courtesy of an erroneous report from Fox News, was for a brief moment under the impression that Comey had resigned. Then, in a series of information synapses throughout the offices of the West Wing, it became clear what had actually happened.

"So next it's a special prosecutor!" said Priebus in disbelief, to no one in particular, when he learned shortly before five o'clock what was happening.

Spicer, who would later be blamed for not figuring out how to positively spin the Comey firing, had only minutes to process it.

Not only had the decision been made by the president with almost no consultation except that of his inner family circle, but the response, and explanation, and even legal justifications, were also almost exclusively managed by him and his family. Rosenstein and Sessions's parallel rationale for the firing was shoehorned in at the last minute, at which point, at Kushner's direction, the initial explanation of Comey's firing became that the president had acted solely on their recommendation. Spicer was forced to deliver this unlikely rationale, as was the vice president. But this pretense unraveled almost immediately, not least because most everyone in the West Wing, wanting nothing to do with the decision to fire Comey, was helping to unravel it.

The president, along with his family, stood on one side of the White House divide, while the staff—mouths agape, disbelieving and speechless—stood on the other.

But the president seemed also to want it known that he, aroused and dangerous, personally took down Comey. Forget Rosenstein and Sessions, it *was* personal. It was a powerful president and a vengeful one, in every way galled and affronted by those in pursuit of him, and determined to protect his family, who were in turn determined to have him protect them.

"The daughter will take down the father," said Bannon, in a Shakespearian mood.

Within the West Wing there was much replaying of alternative scenarios. If you wanted to get rid of Comey, there were surely politic ways of doing it—which had in fact been suggested to Trump. (A curious one— an idea that later would seem ironic—was to get rid of General Kelly at Homeland Security and move Comey into that job.) But the point really was that Trump had wanted to confront and humiliate the FBI director. Cruelty was a Trump attribute.

The firing had been carried out publicly and in front of his family—catching Comey entirely off guard as he gave a speech in California. Then the president had further personalized the blow with an ad hominem attack on the director, suggesting that the FBI itself was on Trump's side and that it, too, had only contempt for Comey.

The next day, as though to further emphasize and delight in both the insult and his personal impunity, the president met with Russian bigwigs in the Oval Office, including Russia's Ambassador Kislyak, the very focus of much of the Trump-Russia investigation. To the Russians he said: "I just fired the head of the FBI. He was crazy, a real nut job. I faced great pressure because of Russia. That's taken off." Then, to boot, he revealed information supplied to the United States by Israel from its agent in place in Syria about ISIS using laptops to smuggle bombs onto airlines— revealing enough information to compromise the Israeli agent. (This incident did not help Trump's reputation in intelligence circles, since, in spycraft, human sources are to be protected above all other secrets.)

"It's Trump," said Bannon. "He thinks he can fire the FBI."

* * *

Trump believed that firing Comey would make him a hero. Over the next forty-eight hours he spun his side to various friends. It was simple: he had stood up to the FBI. He proved that he was willing to take on the state power. The outsider against the insiders. After all, that's why he was elected.

At some level he had a point. One reason presidents don't fire the director of the FBI is that they fear the consequences. It's the Hoover syndrome: any president can be hostage to what the FBI knows, and a president who treats the FBI with something less than deference does so at his own peril. But this president had stood up to the feds. One man against the unaccountable power that the left had long railed against— and that more recently the right had taken as a Holy Grail issue, too. "Everybody should be rooting for me," the president said to friends, more and more plaintively.

Here was another peculiar Trump attribute: an inability to see his actions the way most others saw them. Or to fully appreciate how people expected him to behave. The notion of the presidency as an institutional and political concept, with an emphasis on ritual and propriety and semiotic messaging—statesmanship—was quite beyond him.

Inside the government, the response to Comey's firing was a kind of bureaucratic revulsion. Bannon had tried to explain to Trump the essential nature of career government officials, people whose comfort zone was in their association with hegemonic organizations and a sense of a higher cause—they were different, very different, from those who sought individual distinction. Whatever else Comey might be, he was first and foremost a bureaucrat. Casting him ignominiously out was yet another Trump insult to the bureaucracy.

Rod Rosenstein, the author of the letter that ostensibly provided the justification for firing Comey, now stood in the line of fire. The fifty-two-year-old Rosenstein, who, in rimless glasses, seemed to style himself as a bureaucrat's bureaucrat, was the longest-serving U.S. attorney in the country. He lived within the system, all by the book, his highest goal seeming to be to have people say he did things by the book. He was a straight shooter—and he wanted everyone to know it.

All this was undermined by Trump—trashed, even. The brow-beating and snarling president had hectored the country's two top law enforcement officials into an ill-considered or, at the very least, an ill-timed indictment of the director of the FBI. Rosenstein was already feeling used and abused. And then he was shown to have been tricked, too. He was a dupe.

The president had forced Rosenstein and Sessions to construct a legal rationale, yet then he could not even maintain the bureaucratic pretense of following it. Having enlisted Rosenstein and Sessions in his plot, Trump now exposed their efforts to present a reasonable and aboveboard case as a sham—and, arguably, a plan to obstruct justice. The president made it perfectly clear that he hadn't fired the director of the FBI because he did Hillary wrong; he fired Comey because the FBI was too aggressively investigating him and his administration.

Hyper-by-the-book Rod Rosenstein—heretofore the quintessential apolitical player—immediately became, in Washington eyes, a hopeless Trump tool. But Rosenstein's revenge was deft, swift, overwhelming, and (of course) by the book.

Given the decision of the attorney general to recuse himself from the Russia investigation, it fell under the authority of the deputy attorney general to determine whether a conflict existed—that is, whether the deputy attorney general, because of self-interest, might not be able to act objectively—and if, in his sole discretion, he judged a conflict to exist, to appoint an outside special counsel with wide powers and responsibilities to conduct an investigation and, potentially, a prosecution.

On May 17, twelve days after FBI director Comey was fired, without consulting the White House or the attorney general, Rosenstein appointed former FBI director Robert Mueller to oversee the investigation of Trump's, his campaign's, and his staff's ties to Russia. If Michael Flynn had recently become the most powerful man in Washington for what he might reveal about the president, now Mueller arguably assumed that position because he had the power to make Flynn, and all other assorted Trump cronies and flunkies, squeal.

Rosenstein, of course, perhaps with some satisfaction, understood that he had delivered what could be a mortal blow to the Trump presidency.

Bannon, shaking his head in wonder about Trump, commented drily: "He doesn't necessarily see what's coming."

# 17

# ABROAD AND AT HOME

On May 12, Roger Ailes was scheduled to return to New York from Palm Beach to meet with Peter Thiel, an early and lonely Trump supporter in Silicon Valley who had become increasingly astonished by Trump's unpredictability. Ailes and Thiel, both worried that Trump could bring Trumpism down, were set to discuss the funding and launch of a new cable news network. Thiel would pay for it and Ailes would bring O'Reilly, Hannity, himself, and maybe Bannon to it.

But two days before the meeting, Ailes fell in his bathroom and hit his head. Before slipping into a coma, he told his wife not to reschedule the meeting with Thiel. A week later, Ailes, that singular figure in the march from Nixon's silent majority to Reagan's Democrats to Trump's passionate base, was dead.

His funeral in Palm Beach on May 20 was quite a study in the currents of right-wing ambivalence and even mortification. Right-wing professionals remained passionate in their outward defense of Trump but were rattled, if not abashed, among one another. At the funeral, Rush Limbaugh and Laura Ingraham struggled to parse support for Trumpism even as they distanced themselves from Trump himself.

The president had surely become the right wing's meal ticket. He was the ultimate antiliberal: an authoritarian who was the living embodiment of resistance to authority. He was the exuberant inverse of everything the right wing found patronizing and gullible and sanctimonious about the left. And yet, obviously, Trump was Trump—careless, capricious, disloyal, far beyond any sort of control. Nobody knew that as well as the people who knew him best.

Ailes's wife, Beth, had militantly invited only Ailes loyalists to the funeral. Anyone who had wavered in her husband's defense since his firing or had decided that a better future lay with the Murdoch family was excluded. This put Trump, still enthralled by his new standing with Murdoch, on the other side of the line. Hours and then days—carefully tracked by Beth Ailes—ticked off without a condolence call from the president.

The morning of the funeral, Sean Hannity's private plane took off for Palm Beach from Republic Airport in Farmingdale, Long Island. Accompanying Hannity was a small group of current and former Fox employees, all Ailes and Trump partisans. But each felt some open angst, or even incredulity, about Trump being Trump: first there was the difficulty of grasping the Comey rationale, and now his failure to give even a nod to his late friend Ailes.

"He's an idiot, obviously," said the former Fox correspondent Liz Trotta.

Fox anchor Kimberly Guilfoyle spent much of the flight debating Trump's entreaties to have her replace Sean Spicer at the White House. "There are a lot of issues, including personal survival."

As for Hannity himself, his view of the right-wing world was shifting from Foxcentric to Trumpcentric. He did not think much more than a year would pass before he, too, would be pushed from the network, or find it too inhospitable to stay on. And yet he was pained by Trump's slavish attentions to Murdoch, who had not only ousted Ailes but whose conservatism was at best utilitarian. "He was for Hillary!" said Hannity.

Ruminating out loud, Hannity said he would leave the network and go work full time for Trump, because nothing was more important than that Trump succeed—"in spite of himself," Hannity added, laughing.

But he was pissed off that Trump hadn't called Beth. "Mueller," he concluded, drawing deeply on an electronic cigarette, had distracted him.

Trump may be a Frankenstein creation, but he was the right wing's creation, the first, true, right-wing original. Hannity could look past the Comey disaster. And Jared. And the mess in the White House.

Still, he hadn't called Beth.

"What the fuck is wrong with him?" asked Hannity.

* * *

Trump believed he was one win away from turning everything around. Or, perhaps more to the point, one win away from good press that would turn everything around. The fact that he had largely squandered his first hundred days—whose victories should have been the currency of the next hundred days—was immaterial. You could be down in the media one day and then the next have a hit that made you a success.

"Big things, we need big things," he said, angrily and often. "This isn't big. I need big. Bring me big. Do you even know what big is?"

Repeal and replace, infrastructure, true tax reform—the rollout Trump had promised and then depended on Paul Ryan to deliver—was effectively in tatters. Every senior staff member was now maintaining that they shouldn't have done health care, the precursor to the legislative rollout, in the first place. Whose idea was that, anyway?

The natural default might be to do smaller things, incremental versions of the program. But Trump showed little interest in the small stuff. He became listless and irritable.

So, okay, it would have to be peace in the Middle East.

For Trump, as for many showmen or press release entrepreneurs, the enemy of everything is complexity and red tape, and the solution for everything is cutting corners. Bypass or ignore the difficulties; just move in a straight line to the vision, which, if it's bold enough, or grandiose enough, will sell itself. In this formula, there is always a series of middlemen who will promise to help you cut the corners, as well as partners who will be happy to piggyback on your grandiosity.

Enter the Crown Prince of the House of Saud, Mohammed bin Salman bin Abdulaziz Al Saud, age thirty-one. Aka MBS.

The fortuitous circumstance was that the king of Saudi Arabia,

MBS's father, was losing it. The consensus in the Saudi royal family about a need to modernize was growing stronger (somewhat). MBS—an inveterate player of video games—was a new sort of personality in the Saudi leadership. He was voluble, open, and expansive, a charmer and an international player, a canny salesman rather than a remote, taciturn grandee. He had seized the economic portfolio and was pursuing a vision—quite a Trumpian vision—to out-Dubai Dubai and diversify the economy. His would be a new, modern—well, a bit more modern— kingdom (yes, women would soon be allowed to drive—so thank God self-driving cars were coming!). Saudi leadership was marked by age, traditionalism, relative anonymity, and careful consensus thinking. The Saudi royal family, on the other hand, whence the leadership class comes, was often marked by excess, flash, and the partaking of the joys of modernity in foreign ports. MBS, a man in a hurry, was trying to bridge the Saudi royal selves.

Global liberal leadership had been all but paralyzed by the election of Donald Trump—indeed, by the very *existence* of Donald Trump. But it was an inverted universe in the Middle East. The Obama truculence and hyperrationalization and micromanaging, preceded by the Bush moral militarism and ensuing disruptions, preceded by Clinton deal making, quid pro quo, and backstabbing, had opened the way for Trump's version of realpolitik. He had no patience with the our-hands-are-tied ennui of the post–cold war order, that sense of the chess board locked in place, of incremental movement being the best-case scenario— the alternative being only war. His was a much simpler view: Who's got the power? Give me his number.

And, just as basically: The enemy of my enemy is my friend. If Trump had one fixed point of reference in the Middle East, it was—mostly courtesy of Michael Flynn's tutoring—that Iran was the bad guy. Hence everybody opposed to Iran was a pretty good guy.

After the election, MBS had reached out to Kushner. In the confusion of the Trump transition, nobody with foreign policy stature and an international network had been put in place—even the new secretary of state designate, Rex Tillerson, had no real experience in foreign policy. To bewildered foreign secretaries, it seemed logical to see the president-elect's son-in-law as a figure of stability. Whatever happened, he would be there. And for certain regimes, especially the familycentric Saudis, Kushner, the son-in-law, was much more reassuring than a policy person. He wasn't in his job because of his ideas.

Of the many Trump gashes in modern major-power governing, you could certainly drive a Trojan horse through his lack of foreign policy particulars and relationships. This presented a do-over opportunity for the world in its relationship with the United States—or it did if you were willing to speak the new Trump language, whatever that was. There wasn't much of a road map here, just pure opportunism, a new transactional openness. Or, even more, a chance to use the powers of charm and seduction to which Trump responded as enthusiastically as he did to offers of advantageous new deals.

It was Kissingeresque realpolitik. Kissinger himself, long familiar with Trump by way of the New York social world and now taking Kushner under his wing, was successfully reinserting himself, helping to organize meetings with the Chinese and the Russians.

Most of America's usual partners, and even many antagonists, were unsettled if not horrified. Still, some saw opportunity. The Russians could see a free pass on the Ukraine and Georgia, as well as a lifting of sanctions, in return for giving up on Iran and Syria. Early in the transition, a high-ranking official in the Turkish government reached out in genuine confusion to a prominent U.S. business figure to inquire whether Turkey would have better leverage by putting pressure on the U.S. military presence in Turkey or by offering the new president an enviable hotel site on the Bosporus.

There was something curiously aligned between the Trump family and MBS. Like the entire Saudi leadership, MBS had, practically speaking, no education. In the past, this had worked to limit the Saudi options—nobody was equipped to confidently explore new intellectual possibilities. As a consequence, everybody was wary of trying to get them to imagine change. But MBS and Trump were on pretty much equal footing. Knowing little made them oddly comfortable with each other. When MBS offered himself to Kushner as his guy in the Saudi kingdom, that was "like meeting someone nice at your first day of boarding school," said Kushner's friend.

Casting aside, in very quick order, previously held assumptions—in fact, not really aware of those assumptions—the new Trump thinking about the Middle East became the following: There are basically four players (or at least we can forget everybody else)—Israel, Egypt, Saudi Arabia, and Iran. The first three can be united against the fourth. And Egypt and Saudi Arabia, given what they want with respect to Iran—and anything else that does not interfere with the United States' interests—will pressure the Palestinians to make a deal. Voilà.

This represented a queasy-making mishmash of thought. Bannon's isolationism (a pox on all your houses—and keep us out of it); Flynn's anti-Iranism (of all the world's perfidy and toxicity, there is none like that of the mullahs); and Kushner's Kissingerism (not so much Kissingerism as, having no point of view himself, a dutiful attempt to follow the ninety-four-year-old's advice).

But the fundamental point was that the last three administrations had gotten the Middle East wrong. It was impossible to overstate how much contempt the Trump people felt for the business-as-usual thinking that had gotten it so wrong. Hence, the new operating principle was simple: do the opposite of what they (Obama, but the Bush neocons, too) would do. Their behavior, their conceits, their ideas—in some sense even their backgrounds, education, and class—were all suspect. And, what's more, you don't really have to know all that much yourself; you just do it differently than it was done before.

The old foreign policy was based on the idea of nuance: facing an infinitely complex multilateral algebra of threats, interests, incentives, deals, and ever evolving relationships, we strain to reach a balanced future. In practice, the new foreign policy, an effective Trump doctrine, was to reduce the board to three elements: powers we can work with, powers we cannot work with, and those without enough power whom we can functionally disregard or sacrifice. It was cold war stuff. And, indeed, in the larger Trump view, it was during the cold war that time and circumstance gave the United States its greatest global advantage. That was when America was great.

* * *

Kushner was the driver of the Trump doctrine. His test cases were China, Mexico, Canada, and Saudi Arabia. He offered each country the opportunity to make his father-in-law happy.

In the first days of the administration, Mexico blew its chance. In transcripts of conversations between Trump and Mexican president Enrique Peña Nieto that would later become public, it was vividly clear that Mexico did not understand or was unwilling to play the new game. The Mexican president refused to construct a pretense for paying for the wall, a pretense that might have redounded to his vast advantage (without his having to actually pay for the wall).

Not long after, Canada's new prime minister, Justin Trudeau, a forty-five-year-old globalist in the style of Clinton and Blair, came to Washington and repeatedly smiled and bit his tongue. And that did the trick: Canada quickly became Trump's new best friend.

The Chinese, who Trump had oft maligned during the campaign, came to Mar-a-Lago for a summit advanced by Kushner and Kissinger. (This required some tutoring for Trump, who referred to the Chinese leader as "Mr. X-i"; the president was told to think of him as a woman and call him "she.") They were in an agreeable mood, evidently willing to humor Trump. And they quickly figured out that if you flatter him, he flatters you.

But it was the Saudis, also often maligned during the campaign, who, with their intuitive understanding of family, ceremony, and ritual and propriety, truly scored.

The foreign policy establishment had a long and well-honed relationship with MBS's rival, the crown prince, Mohammed bin Nayef (MBN). Key NSA and State Department figures were alarmed that Kushner's discussions and fast-advancing relationship with MBS would send a dangerous message to MBN. And of course it did. The foreign policy people believed Kushner was being duped by an opportunist whose real views were entirely untested. The Kushner view was either, naïvely, that he wasn't being duped, or, with the confidence of a thirty-six-year-old assuming the new prerogatives of the man in charge, that he didn't care: let's embrace anybody who will embrace us.

The Kushner/MBS plan that emerged was straightforward in a way that foreign policy usually isn't: If you give us what we want, we'll give you what you want. On MBS's assurance that he would deliver some seriously good news, he was invited to visit the White House in March. (The Saudis arrived with a big delegation, but they were received at the White House by only the president's small circle—and the Saudis took particular note that Trump ordered Priebus to jump up and fetch him things during the meeting.) The two large men, the older Trump and much younger MBS—both charmers, flatterers, and country club jokers, each in their way—grandly hit it off.

It was an aggressive bit of diplomacy. MBS was using this Trump embrace as part of his own power play in the kingdom. And the Trump White House, ever denying this was the case, let him. In return, MBS offered a basket of deals and announcements that would coincide with a scheduled presidential visit to Saudi Arabia—Trump's first trip abroad. Trump would get a "win."

Planned before the Comey firing and Mueller hiring, the trip had State Department professionals alarmed. The itinerary—May 19 to May 27—was too long for any president, particularly such an untested and untutored one. (Trump himself, full of phobias about travel and unfamiliar locations, had been grumbling about the burdens of the trip.) But coming immediately after Comey and Mueller it was a get-out-of-Dodge godsend. There couldn't have been a better time to be making headlines far from Washington. A road trip could transform everything.

Almost the entire West Wing, along with State Department and National Security staff, was on board for the trip: Melania Trump, Ivanka Trump, Jared Kushner, Reince Priebus, Stephen Bannon, Gary Cohn, Dina Powell, Hope Hicks, Sean Spicer, Stephen Miller, Joe Hagin, Rex Tillerson, and Michael Anton. Also included were Sarah Huckabee Sanders, the deputy press secretary; Dan Scavino, the administration's social media director; Keith Schiller, the president's personal security adviser; and Wilbur Ross, the commerce secretary. (Ross was widely ridiculed for never missing an Air Force One opportunity—as Bannon put it, "Wilbur is Zelig, every time you turn around he's in a picture.") This trip and the robust American delegation was the antidote, and alternate universe to the Mueller appointment.

The president and his son-in-law could barely contain their confidence and enthusiasm. They felt certain that they had set out on the road to peace in the Middle East—and in this, they were much like a number of other administrations that had come before them.

Trump was effusive in his praise for Kushner. "Jared's gotten the Arabs totally on our side. Done deal," he assured one of his after-dinner callers before leaving on the trip. "It's going to be beautiful."

"He believed," said the caller, "that this trip could pull it out, like a twist in a bad movie."

* * *

On the empty roads of Riyadh, the presidential motorcade passed billboards with pictures of Trump and the Saudi king (MBS's eighty-one-year-old father) with the legend TOGETHER WE PREVAIL.

In part, the president's enthusiasm seemed to be born out of—or perhaps had caused—a substantial exaggeration of what had actually been agreed to during the negotiations ahead of the trip. In the days before his departure, he was telling people that the Saudis were going to finance an entirely new military presence in the kingdom, supplanting and even replacing the U.S. command headquarters in Qatar. And there would be "the biggest breakthrough in Israel-Palestine negotiations ever." It would be "*the* game changer, major like has never been seen."

In truth, his version of what would be accomplished was a quantum leap beyond what was actually agreed, but that did not seem to alter his feelings of zeal and delight.

The Saudis would immediately buy $110 billion's worth of American arms, and a total of $350 billion over ten years. "Hundreds of billions of dollars of investments into the United States and jobs, jobs, jobs," declared the president. Plus, the Americans and the Saudis would together "counter violent extremist messaging, disrupt financing of terrorism, and advance defense cooperation." And they would establish a center in Riyadh to fight extremism. And if this was not exactly peace in the Middle East, the president, according to the secretary of state, "feels like there's a moment in time here. The president's going to talk with Netanyahu about the process going forward. He's going to be talking to President Abbas about what he feels is necessary for the Palestinians to be successful."

It was all a Trumpian big deal. Meanwhile, the First Family—POTUS, FLOTUS, and Jared and Ivanka—were ferried around in gold golf carts, and the Saudis threw a $75 million party in Trump's honor, with Trump getting to sit on a thronelike chair. (The president, while receiving an honor from the Saudi king, appeared in a photograph to have bowed, arousing some right-wing ire.)

Fifty Arab and Muslim nations were summoned by the Saudis to pay the president court. The president called home to tell his friends how natural and easy this was, and how, inexplicably and suspiciously, Obama had messed it all up. There "has been a little strain, but there won't be strain with this administration," the president assured Hamad bin Isa Al Khalifa, the king of Bahrain.

Abdel Fattah el-Sisi, the Egyptian strongman, ably stroked the president and said, "You are a unique personality that is capable of doing the impossible." (To Sisi, Trump replied, "Love your shoes. Boy, those shoes. Man. . . .")

It was, in dramatic ways, a shift in foreign policy attitude and strategy—and its effects were almost immediate. The president, ignoring if not defying foreign policy advice, gave a nod to the Saudis' plan to bully Qatar. Trump's view was that Qatar was providing financial support to terror groups—pay no attention to a similar Saudi history. (Only *some* members of the Saudi royal family had provided such support, went the new reasoning.) Within weeks of the trip, MBS, detaining MBN quite in the dead of night, would force him to relinquish the Crown Prince title, which MBS would then assume for himself. Trump would tell friends that he and Jared had engineered a Saudi coup: "We've put our man on top!"

From Riyadh, the presidential party went on to Jerusalem, where the president met with Netanyahu and, in Bethlehem, with Abbas, expressing ever greater certainty that, in his third-person guise, "Trump will make peace." Then to Rome to meet the pope. Then to Brussels, where, in character, he meaningfully drew the line between Western-alliance-based foreign policy, which had been firmly in place since World War II, and the new America First ethos.

In Trump's view, all this should have been presidency-shaping stuff. He couldn't believe his dramatic accomplishments weren't getting bigger play. He was simply in denial, Bannon, Priebus, and others noted, about the continuing and competing Comey and Mueller headlines.

One of Trump's deficiencies—a constant in the campaign and, so far, in the presidency—was his uncertain grasp of cause and effect. Until now, whatever problems he might have caused in the past had reliably been supplanted by new events, giving him the confidence that one bad story can always be replaced by a better, more dramatic story. He could always change the conversation. The Saudi trip and his bold campaign to upend the old foreign policy world order should have accomplished exactly that. But the president continued to find himself trapped, incredulously on his part, by Comey and Mueller. Nothing seemed to move on from those two events.

After the Saudi leg of the trip, Bannon and Priebus, both exhausted by the trip's intense proximity to the president and his family, peeled off and headed back to Washington. It was now their job to deal with what had become, in the White House staff's absence, the actual, even ultimate, presidency-shaping crisis.

* * *

What did the people around Trump actually think of Trump? This was not just a reasonable question, it was the question those around Trump most asked themselves. They constantly struggled to figure out what they themselves actually thought and what they thought everybody else was truly thinking.

Mostly they kept their answers to themselves, but in the instance of Comey and Mueller, beyond all the usual dodging and weaving rationalizations, there really wasn't anybody, other than the president's family, who didn't very pointedly blame Trump himself.

This was the point at which an emperors-new-clothes threshold was crossed. Now you could, out loud, rather freely doubt his judgment, acumen, and, most of all, the advice he was getting.

"He's not only crazy," declared Tom Barrack to a friend, "he's stupid."

But Bannon, along with Priebus, had strongly opposed the Comey firing, while Ivanka and Jared had not only supported it, but insisted on it. This seismic event prompted a new theme from Bannon, repeated by him widely, which was that every piece of advice from the couple was bad advice.

Nobody now believed that firing Comey was a good idea; even the president seemed sheepish. Hence, Bannon saw his new role as saving Trump—and Trump would always need saving. He might be a brilliant actor but he could not manage his own career.

And for Bannon, this new challenge brought a clear benefit: when Trump's fortune sank, Bannon's rose.

On the trip to the Middle East, Bannon went to work. He became focused on the figure of Lanny Davis, one of the Clinton impeachment lawyers who, for the better part of two years, became a near round-the-clock spokesperson and public defender of the Clinton White House. Bannon judged Comey-Mueller to be as threatening to the Trump White House as Monica Lewinsky and Ken Starr were to the Clinton White House, and he saw the model for escaping a mortal fate in the Clinton response.

"What the Clintons did was to go to the mattresses with amazing discipline," he explained. "They set up an outside shop and then Bill and Hillary never mentioned it again. They ground through it. Starr had them dead to rights and they got through it."

Bannon knew exactly what needed to be done: seal off the West Wing and build a separate legal and communications staff to defend the president. In this construct, the president would occupy a parallel reality, removed from and uninvolved with what would become an obvious partisan blood sport—as it had in the Clinton model. Politics would be relegated to its nasty corner, and Trump would conduct himself as the president and as the commander in chief.

"So we're going to do it," insisted Bannon, with *joie de guerre* and manic energy, "the way they did it. Separate war room, separate lawyers, separate spokespeople. It's keeping that fight over there so we can wage this other fight over here. Everybody gets this. Well, maybe not Trump so much. Not clear. Maybe a little. Not what he imagined."

Bannon, in great excitement, and Priebus, grateful for an excuse to leave the president's side, rushed back to the West Wing to begin to cordon it off.

It did not escape Priebus's notice that Bannon had in mind to create a rear guard of defenders—David Bossie, Corey Lewandowski, and Jason Miller, all of whom would be outside spokespeople—that would largely be loyal to him. Most of all, it did not escape Priebus that Bannon was asking the president to play a role entirely out of character: the cool, steady, long-suffering chief executive.

And it certainly didn't help that they were unable to hire a law firm with a top-notch white-collar government practice. By the time Bannon and Priebus were back in Washington, three blue-chip firms had said no. All of them were afraid they would face a rebellion among the younger staff if they represented Trump, afraid Trump would publicly humiliate them if the going got tough, and afraid Trump would stiff them for the bill.

In the end, nine top firms turned them down.

# 18

## BANNON REDUX

Bannon was back, according to the Bannon faction. According to Bannon himself: "I'm good. I'm *good*. I'm back. I said don't do it. You don't fire the director of the FBI. The geniuses around here thought otherwise."

*Was Bannon back?* asked the worried other side of the house—Jared and Ivanka, Dina Powell, Gary Cohn, Hope Hicks, H. R. McMaster.

If he was back, that meant he had successfully defied the organizational premise of the Trump White House: the family would always prevail. Steve Bannon had, even in his internal exile, not stopped his running public verbal assault on Jared and Ivanka. Off the record became Bannon's effective on the record. These were bitter, sometimes hilarious, denunciations of the couple's acumen, intelligence, and motives: "They think they're defending him, but they are always defending themselves."

Now he declared they were finished as a power center—destroyed. And if not, they would destroy the president with their terrible and self-serving advice. Even worse than Jared was Ivanka. "She was a nonevent on the campaign. She became a White House staffer and that's when people suddenly realized she's dumb as a brick. A little marketing savvy and has a look, but as far as understanding actually how the world works and what politics is and what it means—nothing. Once you expose that, you lose such credibility. Jared just kind of flits in and does the Arab stuff."

The folks on the Jarvanka side seemed more and more genuinely afraid of what might happen if they crossed the Bannon side. Because the Bannonites, they truly seemed to fear, were assassins.

On the flight to Riyadh, Dina Powell approached Bannon about a leak involving her to a right-wing news site. She told him she knew the leak had come from Julia Hahn, one of Bannon's people and a former Breitbart writer.

"You should take it up with her," said an amused Bannon. "But she's a beast. And she will come at you. Let me know how it works out."

Among Bannon's many regular targets, Powell had become a favorite. She was often billed as Deputy National Security Advisor; that was her sometime designation even in the *New York Times*. Actually, she was Deputy National Security Advisor *for Strategy*—the difference, Bannon pointed out, between the COO of a hotel chain and the concierge.

Coming back from the overseas trip, Powell began to talk in earnest to friends about her timetable to get out of the White House and back into a private-sector job. Sheryl Sandberg, she said, was her model.

"Oh my fucking god," said Bannon.

On May 26, the day before the presidential party returned from the overseas trip, the *Washington Post* reported that during the transition, Kushner and Sergey Kislyak, the Russian ambassador, had, at Kushner's instigation, discussed the possibility of having the Russians set up a private communications channel between the transition team and the Kremlin. The *Post* cited "U.S. officials briefed on intelligence reports." The Jarvanka side believed that Bannon was the source.

Part of the by now deep enmity between the First Family couple and their allies and Bannon and his team was the Jarvanka conviction that Bannon had played a part in many of the reports of Kushner's interactions with the Russians. This was not, in other words, merely an internal policy war; it was a death match. For Bannon to live, Kushner would have to be wholly discredited—pilloried, investigated, possibly even jailed.

Bannon, assured by everyone that there was no winning against the

Trump family, hardly tried to hide his satisfied belief that he was going to outplay them. In the Oval Office, in front of her father, Bannon openly attacked her. "You," he said, pointing at her as the president watched, "are a fucking liar." Ivanka's bitter complaints to her father, which in the past had diminished Bannon, were now met by a hands-off Trump: "I told you this is a tough town, baby."

* * *

But if Bannon was back, it was far from clear what being back meant. Trump being Trump, was this true rehabilitation, or did he feel an even deeper rancor toward Bannon for having survived his initial intention to kill him? Nobody really thought Trump forgot—instead, he dwelled and ruminated and chewed. "One of the worst things is when he believes you've succeeded at his expense," explained Sam Nunberg, once on the inside of the Trump circle, then cast to the outside. "If your win is in any way perceived as his loss, phew."

For his part, Bannon believed he was back because, at a pivotal moment, his advice had proved vastly better than that of the "geniuses." Firing Comey, the solve-all-problems Jarvanka solution, had indeed unleashed a set of terrible consequences.

The Jarvanka side believed that Bannon was in essence blackmailing the president. As Bannon went, so went the virulence of right-wing digital media. Despite his apparent obsession with the "fake news" put out by the *New York Times*, the *Washington Post*, and CNN, for the president the threat of fake news was actually greater on the right. Though he would never call out fake news on Fox, Breitbart, and the others, these outlets—which could conceivably spew a catchall of conspiracies in which a weak Trump sold out to a powerful establishment—were potentially far more dangerous than their counterparts on the left.

Bannon, too, was seen to be rectifying an earlier bureaucratic mistake. Where initially he had been content to be the brains of the operation—confident that he was vastly smarter than everybody else (and, indeed, few tried to challenge him for that title)—and not staff up, now he was putting his organization and loyalists firmly in place. His off-balance-sheet communications staff—Bossie, Lewandowski, Jason

Miller, Sam Nunberg (even though he had long fallen out with Trump himself), and Alexandra Preate—formed quite a private army of leakers and defenders. What's more, whatever breach there had been between Bannon and Priebus came smoothly together over their mutual loathing of Jared and Ivanka. The professional White House was united against the amateur family White House.

Adding to Bannon's new bureaucratic advantage, he had maximum influence on the staffing of the new firewall team, the lawyers and comm staff who would collectively become the Lanny Davis of the Trump defense. Unable to hire prestige talent, Bannon turned to one of the president's longtime hit-man lawyers, Marc Kasowitz. Bannon had previously bonded with Kasowitz when the attorney had handled a series of near-death problems on the campaign, including dealing with a vast number of allegations and legal threats from an ever growing list of women accusing Trump of molesting and harassing them.

On May 31, the Bannon firewall plan went into effect. Henceforth, all discussion related to Russia, the Mueller and congressional investigations, and other personal legal issues would be entirely handled by the Kasowitz team. The president, as Bannon described the plan in private and as he urged his boss, would no longer be addressing any of these areas. Among the many, many efforts to force Trump into presidential mode, this was the latest.

Bannon then installed Mark Corallo, a former Karl Rove communications staffer, as the firewall spokesperson. He was also planning to put in Bossie and Lewandowski as part of the crisis management team. And at Bannon's prompting, Kasowitz attempted to further insulate the president by giving his client a central piece of advice: send the kids home.

Bannon was indeed back. It was his team. It was his wall around the president—one that he hoped would keep Jarvanka out.

Bannon's formal moment of being back was marked by a major milestone. On June 1, after a long and bitter internal debate, the president announced that he had decided to withdraw from the Paris Climate Agreement. For Bannon, it was a deeply satisfying slap in the face of liberal rectitude—Elon Musk and Bob Iger immediately resigned from

Trump's business council—and confirmation of Trump's true Bannonite instincts.

It was, likewise, the move that Ivanka Trump had campaigned hardest against in the White House.

"Score," said Bannon. "The bitch is dead."

* * *

There are few modern political variables more disruptive than a dedicated prosecutor. It's the ultimate wild card.

A prosecutor means that the issue under investigation—or, invariably, cascading issues—will be a constant media focus. Setting their own public stage, prosecutors are certain leakers.

It means that everybody in a widening circle has to hire a lawyer. Even tangential involvement can cost six figures; central involvement quickly rises into the millions.

By early summer, there was already an intense seller's market in Washington for top criminal legal talent. As the Mueller investigation got under way, White House staffers made a panicky rush to get the best firm before someone else got there first and created a conflict.

"Can't talk about Russia, nothing, can't go there," said Katie Walsh, now three months removed from the White House, on advice of her new counsel.

Any interviews or depositions given to investigators risked putting you in jeopardy. What's more, every day in the White House brought new dangers: any random meeting you might find yourself in exposed you more.

Bannon kept insisting on the absolute importance of this point— and for him the strategic importance. If you didn't want to find yourself getting wrung out in front of Congress, your career and your net worth in jeopardy, be careful who you spoke to. More to the point: you must not under any circumstances speak to Jared and Ivanka, who were now Russia toxic. It was Bannon's widely advertised virtue and advantage: "I've never been to Russia. I don't know anybody from Russia. I've never spoken to any Russians. And I'd just as well not speak to anyone who has."

Bannon observed a hapless Pence in a lot of "wrong meetings," and helped to bring in the Republican operative Nick Ayers as Pence's chief of staff, and to get "our fallback guy" out of the White House and "running around the world and looking like a vice president."

And beyond the immediate fears and disruption, there was the virtually certain outcome that a special prosecutor delegated to find a crime would find one—likely many. Everybody became a potential agent of implicating others. Dominos would fall. Targets would flip.

Paul Manafort, making a good living in international financial gray areas, his risk calculation based on the long-shot odds that an under-the-radar privateer would ever receive close scrutiny, would now be subjected to microscopic review. His nemesis, Oleg Deripaska—still pursuing his $17 million claim against Manafort and himself looking for favorable treatment from federal authorities who had restricted his travel to the United States—was said to be offering U.S. prosecutors fruits of his own deep investigation into Manafort's Russian and Ukrainian business affairs.

Tom Barrack, privy to the president's stream of consciousness as well as his financial history, was suddenly taking stock of his own exposure. Indeed, all the billionaire friends with whom Trump got on the phone and gossiped and rambled were potential witnesses.

In the past, administrations forced to deal with a special prosecutor appointed to investigate and prosecute matters with which the president might have been involved usually became consumed by the effort to cope. Their tenure broke into "before" and "after" periods—with the "after" period hopelessly bogged down in the soap opera of G-man pursuit. Now it looked like the "after" period would be almost the entirety of the Trump administration.

The idea of formal collusion and artful conspiracy—as media and Democrats more or less breathlessly believed or hoped had happened between Trump and the Russians—seemed unlikely to everybody in the White House. (Bannon's comment that the Trump campaign was not organized enough to collude with its own state organizations became everybody's favorite talking point—not least because it was true.) But nobody was vouching for the side deals and freelance operations and otherwise nothing-burger stuff that was a prosecutor's daily bread and the likely detritus of the Trump hangers-on. And everybody believed that if the investigation moved into the long chain of Trump financial transactions, it would almost certainly reach the Trump family and the Trump White House.

And then there was the president's insistent claim that he could do something. *I can fire him*, he would say. Indeed, it was another of his repetitive loops: I can fire him. I *can* fire him. Mueller. The idea of a showdown in which the stronger, more determined, more intransigent, more damn-the-consequences man prevails was central to Trump's own personal mythology. He lived in a mano a mano world, one in which if your own respectability and sense of personal dignity were not a paramount issue—if you weren't weak in the sense of needing to seem like a reasonable and respectable person—you had a terrific advantage. And if you made it personal, if you believed that when the fight really mattered that it was kill or be killed, you were unlikely to meet someone willing to make it as personal as you were.

This was Bannon's fundamental insight about Trump: he made *everything* personal, and he was helpless not to.

* * *

Dissuaded by everyone from focusing his anger on Mueller (at least for now), the president focused on Sessions.

Sessions—"Beauregard"—was a close Bannon ally, and in May and June the president's almost daily digs against the attorney general—beyond even his loyalty and resolve, Trump issued scathing criticism of his stature, voice, and dress—provided a sudden bit of good news for the anti-Bannon side of the house. Bannon, they reasoned, couldn't really be on top if his key proxy was now being blamed for everything bad in Trump's life. As always, Trump's regard or scorn was infectious. If you were in favor, then whatever and whomever he associated with you was also in favor. If you weren't, then everything associated with you was poisonous.

The brutality of Trump's dissatisfaction kept increasing. A small man with a Mr. Magoo stature and an old-fashioned Southern accent, Sessions was bitterly mocked by the president, who drew a corrosive portrait of physical and mental weakness. Insult trauma radiated out of the Oval Office. You could hear it when passing by.

Bannon's efforts to talk the president down—reminding Trump of the difficulties they would encounter during another attorney general confirmation, the importance of Sessions to the hard conservative base, the loyalty that Sessions had shown during the Trump campaign—backfired. To the anti-Bannon side's satisfaction, they resulted in another round of Trump's dissing Bannon.

The attack on Sessions now became, at least in the president's mind, the opening salvo in an active effort to replace Sessions as attorney general. But there were only two candidates to run the Justice Department from whom Trump believed he could extract absolute loyalty, Chris Christie and Rudy Giuliani. He believed they would both perform kamikaze acts for him—just as everyone else knew they would almost certainly never be confirmed.

\* \* \*

As James Comey's testimony before the Senate Intelligence Committee approached—it would take place on June 8, twelve days after the presidential traveling party returned home from the long trip to the Middle East and Europe—there began among senior staffers an almost open inquiry into Trump's motives and state of mind.

This seemed spurred by an obvious question: Why hadn't he fired Comey during his first days of office, when it would likely have been seen as a natural changing of the guard with no clear connection to the Russian investigation? There were many equivocal answers: general disorganization, the fast pace of events, and a genuine sense of innocence and naïveté about the Russian charges. But now there seemed to be a new understanding: Donald Trump believed he had vastly more power, authority, and control than in fact he had, and he believed his talent for manipulating people and bending and dominating them was vastly greater than it was. Pushing this line of reasoning just a little further: senior staff believed the president had a problem with reality, and reality was now overwhelming him.

If true, this notion directly contravened the basic premise of the support for Trump among his staff. In some sense, not too closely questioned, they believed he had almost magical powers. Since his success was not explainable, he must have talents beyond what they could fathom. His instincts. Or his salesman's gifts. Or his energy. Or just the fact that he was the opposite of what he was supposed to be. This was out-of-the-ordinary politics—shock-to-the-system politics—but it could work.

But what if it didn't? What if they were all profoundly wrong?

Comey's firing and the Mueller investigation prompted a delayed reckoning that ended months of willing suspension of disbelief. These sudden doubts and considerations—at the highest level of government—did not quite yet go to the president's ability to adequately function in his job. But they did, arguably for the first time in open discussions, go to the view that he was hopelessly prone to self-sabotaging his ability to function in the job. This insight, scary as it was, at least left open the possibility that if all the elements of self-sabotage were carefully controlled—his information, his contacts, his public remarks, and the sense of danger and threat to him—he might yet be able to pull it together and successfully perform.

Quite suddenly, this became the prevailing view of the Trump presidency and the opportunity that still beckoned: you can be saved by those around you or brought down by them.

Bannon believed the Trump presidency would fail in some more or less apocalyptic fashion if Kushner and his wife remained Trump's most influential advisers. Their lack of political or real-world experience had already hobbled the presidency, but since the Comey disaster it was getting worse: as Bannon saw it, they were now acting out of personal panic.

The Kushner side believed that Bannon or Bannonism had pushed the president into a harshness that undermined his natural salesman's abilities to charm and reach out. Bannon and his ilk had made him the monster he more and more seemed to be.

Meanwhile, virtually everybody believed that a large measure of the fault lay in Reince Priebus, who had failed to create a White House that could protect the president from himself—or from Bannon or from his own children. At the same time, believing that the fundamental problem lay in Priebus was easy scapegoating, not to mention little short of risible:

with so little power, the chief of staff simply wasn't capable of directing either Trump or those around him. Priebus himself could, not too help-fully, argue only that no one had any idea how much worse all this would have been without his long-suffering mediation among the president's relatives, his Svengali, and Trump's own terrible instincts. There might be two or three debacles a day, but without Priebus's stoic resolve, and the Trump blows that he absorbed, there might have been a dozen more.

* * *

On June 8, from a little after ten in the morning to nearly one in the after-noon, James Comey testified in public before the Senate Intelligence Committee. The former FBI director's testimony, quite a tour de force of directness, moral standing, personal honor, and damning details, left the country with a simple message: the president was likely a fool and cer-tainly a liar. In the age of modern media politesse, few presidents had been so directly challenged and impugned before Congress.

Here it was, stark in Comey's telling: the president regarded the FBI director as working directly for him, of owing his job to him, and now he wanted something back. "My common sense," said Comey, "again, I could be wrong, but my common sense told me what's going on here is he's looking to get something in exchange for granting my request to stay in the job."

In Comey's telling, the president wanted the FBI to lay off Michael Flynn. And he wanted to stop the FBI from pursuing its Russia-related investigation. The point could hardly have been clearer: if the president was pressuring the director because he feared that an investigation of Michael Flynn would damage him, then this was an obstruction of justice.

The contrast between the two men, Comey and Trump, was in essence the contrast between good government and Trump himself. Comey came across as precise, compartmentalized, scrupulous in his presentation of the details of what transpired and the nature of his responsibility—he was as by-the-book as it gets. Trump, in the portrait offered by Comey, was shady, shoot-from-the-hip, heedless or even unaware of the rules, deceptive, and in it for himself.

After the hearing ended, the president told everybody he had not watched it, but everybody knew he had. To the extent that this was, as Trump saw it, a contest between the two men, it was as direct a juxtaposition as might be imagined. The entire point of the Comey testimony was to recast and contradict what the president had said in his angry and defensive tweets and statements, and to cast suspicion on his actions and motives—and to suggest that the president's intention was to suborn the director of the FBI.

Even among Trump loyalists who believed, as Trump did, that Comey was a phony and this was all a put-up job, the nearly universal feeling was that in this mortal game, Trump was quite defenseless.

* * *

Five days later, on June 13, it was Jeff Sessions's turn to testify before the Senate Intelligence Committee. His task was to try to explain the contacts he had had with the Russian ambassador, contacts that had later caused him to recuse himself—and made him the president's punching bag. Unlike Comey, who had been invited to the Senate to show off his virtue—and had seized the opportunity—Sessions had been invited to defend his equivocation, deception, or stupidity.

In an often testy exchange, the attorney general provided a squirrelly view of executive privilege. Though the president had not in fact evoked executive privilege, Sessions deemed it appropriate to try to protect it anyway.

Bannon, watching the testimony from the West Wing, quickly became frustrated. "Come on, Beauregard," he said.

Unshaven, Bannon sat at the head of the long wooden conference table in the chief of staff's office and focused intently on the flat-screen monitor across the room.

"They thought the cosmopolitans would like it if we fired Comey," he said, with "they" being Jared and Ivanka. "The cosmopolitans would be cheering for us for taking down the man who took Hillary down." Where the president saw Sessions as the cause of the Comey fiasco, Bannon saw Sessions as a victim of it.

A sylphlike Kushner, wearing a skinny gray suit and skinny black tie, slipped into the room. (Recently making the rounds was a joke about

Kushner being the best-dressed man in Washington, which is quite the opposite of a compliment.) On occasion the power struggle between Bannon and Kushner seemed to take physical form. Bannon's demeanor rarely changed, but Kushner could be petulant, condescending, and dismissive—or, as he was now, hesitating, abashed, and respectful.

Bannon ignored Kushner until the younger man cleared his throat. "How's it going?"

Bannon indicated the television set: as in, *Watch for yourself.*

Finally Bannon spoke. "They don't realize this is about institutions, not people."

"They" would appear to be the Jarvanka side—or an even broader construct referring to all those who mindlessly stood with Trump.

"This town is about institutions," Bannon continued. "We fire the FBI director and we fire the whole FBI. Trump is a man against institutions, and the institutions know it. How do you think that goes down?"

This was shorthand for a favorite Bannon riff: In the course of the campaign, Donald Trump had threatened virtually every institution in American political life. He was a clown-prince version of Jimmy Stewart in *Mr. Smith Goes to Washington.* Trump believed, offering catnip to deep American ire and resentment, that one man could be bigger than the system. This analysis presupposed that the institutions of political life were as responsive as those in the commercial life that Trump was from—and that they yearned to meet the market and find the Zeitgeist. But what if these institutions—the media, the judiciary, the intelligence community, the greater executive branch itself, and the "swamp" with its law firms, consultants, influence peddlers, and leakers—were in no way eager to adapt? If, by their nature, they were determined to endure, then this accidental president was up against it.

Kushner seemed unpersuaded. "I wouldn't put it like that," he said.

"I think that's the lesson of the first hundred days that some people around here have learned," said Bannon, ignoring Kushner. "It's not going to get better. This is what it's like."

"I don't know," said Kushner.

"Know it," said Bannon.

"I think Sessions is doing okay," said Kushner. "Don't you?"

# 19

## MIKA WHO?

The media had unlocked the value of Donald Trump, but few in the media had unlocked it more directly and personally than Joe Scarborough and Mika Brzezinski. Their MSNBC breakfast show was an ongoing soap-opera-ish or possibly Oprahesque drama about their relationship with Trump—how he had disappointed them, how far they had come from their original regard for him, and how much and how pathetically he regularly embarrassed himself. The bond he once had with them, forged through mutual celebrity and a shared proprietary sense of politics (Scarborough, the former congressman, seemed to feel that he ought reasonably to be president as much as Donald Trump felt he should be), had distinguished the show during the campaign; now its public fraying became part of the daily news cycle. Scarborough and Brzezinski lectured him, channeled the concerns of his friends and family, upbraided him, and openly worried about him—that he was getting the wrong advice (Bannon) and, too, that his mental powers were slipping. They also staked a claim at representing the reasonable center-right alternative to the president, and indeed were quite a good barometer of both the center-right's efforts to deal with him and its day-to-day difficulties of living with him.

Trump, believing he had been used and abused by Scarborough and Brzezinski, claimed he'd stopped watching the show. But Hope Hicks, every morning, quaking, had to recount it for him.

*Morning Joe* was a ground-zero study in the way the media had over-invested in Trump. He was the whale against which media emotions, self-regard, ego, *joie de guerre*, career advancement, and desire to be at the center of the story, too, all churned in nearly ecstatic obsession. In reverse regard, the media was the same whale, serving the same function, for Trump.

To this Trump added another tic, a lifelong sense that people were constantly taking unfair advantage of him. This perhaps came from his father's cheapness and lack of generosity, or from his own overawareness of being a rich kid (and, no doubt, his insecurities about this), or from a negotiator's profound understanding that it is never win-win, that where there is profit there is loss. Trump simply could not abide the knowledge that somebody was getting a leg up at his expense. His was a zero-sum ecosystem. In the world of Trump, anything that he deemed of value either accrued to him or had been robbed from him.

Scarborough and Brzezinski had taken their relationship with Trump and amply monetized it, while putting no percentage in his pocket—and in this instance, he judged his commission should be slavishly favorable treatment. To say this drove him mad would be an understatement. He dwelled and fixated on the perceived injustice. *Don't mention Joe or Mika to him* was a standing proscription.

His wounded feelings and incomprehension at the failure of people whose embrace he sought to, in return, embrace him was "deep, crazy deep," said his former aide Sam Nunberg, who had run afoul of his need for 100 percent approbation and his bitter suspicion of being profited from.

\* \* \*

Out of this accumulated rage came his June 29 tweet about Mika Brzezinski.

It was classic Trump: there was no mediation between off-the-record language and the public statement. Referring to "low I.Q. Crazy Mika" in one tweet, he wrote in another that she was "bleeding badly from a face-lift" when she and Scarborough visited Trump at Mar-a-Lago on the previous New Year's Eve. Many of his tweets were not, as they might seem, spontaneous utterances, but constant ones. Trump's rifts often began as insult comedy and solidified as bitter accusations and then, in an uncontainable moment, became an official proclamation.

The next step, in his tweet paradigm, was universal liberal opprobrium. Almost a week of social media fury, cable breast-beating, and front-page condemnation followed his tweet about Brzezinski. That was accompanied by the other part of the Trump tweet dynamic: by unifying liberal opinion against him, he unified its opposite for him.

In truth, he was often neither fully aware of the nature of what he had said nor fully cognizant of why there should be such a passionate reaction to it. As often as not, he surprised himself. "What did I say?" he would ask after getting severe blowback.

He wasn't serving up these insults for effect—well, not entirely. And his behavior wasn't carefully calculated; it was tit for tat, and he likely would have said what he'd said even if no one was left standing with him. (This very lack of calculation, this inability to be political, was part of his political charm.) It was just his good luck that the Trumpian 35 percent—that standing percentage of people who, according to most polls, seemed to support him no matter what (who would, in his estimation, let him get away with shooting someone on Fifth Avenue)—was largely unfazed and maybe even buoyed by every new expression of Trumpness.

Now, having expressed himself and gotten in the last word, Trump was cheery again.

"Mika and Joe totally love this. It's big ratings for them," said the president, with certain satisfaction and obvious truth.

\* \* \*

Ten days later, a large table of Bannonites was having dinner at the Bombay Club, a high-end Indian restaurant two blocks from the White House. One of the group—Arthur Schwartz, a PR consultant—asked a question about the Mika and Joe affair.

Perhaps it was the noise, but it was also a fitting measure of the speed of events in the Trump era: Bannon lieutenant Alexandra Preate replied, with genuine fogginess, "Who?"

The operetta of the Mika tweets—the uncouthness and verbal abuse demonstrated by the president, his serious lack of control and judgment, and the worldwide censure heaped upon him for it—had already far receded, wholly overshadowed by more Trump eruptions and controversy.

But before moving on to the next episode of ohmygodness, it is worth considering the possibility that this constant, daily, often more than once-a-day, pileup of events—each one canceling out the one before—is the true aberration and novelty at the heart of the Trump presidency.

Perhaps never before in history—not through world wars, the overthrow of empires, periods of extraordinary social transformation, or episodes of government-shaking scandal—have real-life events unfolded with such emotional and plot-thickening impact. In the fashion of binge-watching a television show, one's real life became quite secondary to the public drama. It was not unreasonable to say *Whoa, wait just a minute: public life doesn't happen like this.* Public life in fact lacks coherence and drama. (History, by contrast, attains coherence and drama only in hindsight.)

The process of accomplishing the smallest set of tasks within the sprawling and resistant executive branch is a turtle process. The burden of the White House is the boredom of bureaucracy. All White Houses struggle to rise above that, and they succeed only on occasion. In the age of hypermedia, this has not gotten easier for the White House, it's gotten harder.

It's a distracted nation, fragmented and preoccupied. It was, arguably, the peculiar tragedy of Barack Obama that even as a transformational figure—and inspirational communicator—he couldn't really command much interest. As well, it might be a central tragedy of the news media that its old-fashioned and even benighted civic-minded belief that politics is the highest form of news has helped transform it from a mass business to a narrow-cast one. Alas, politics itself has more and more become a discrete business. Its appeal is B-to-B—business-to-business. The real swamp is the swamp of insular, inbred, incestuous interests. This isn't corruption so much as overspecialization. It's a wonk's life. Politics has gone one way, the culture another. The left-right junkies might pretend otherwise, but the great middle doesn't put political concerns at the top of their minds.

And yet, contravening all cultural and media logic, Donald Trump produced on a daily basis an astonishing, can't-stop-following-it narrative. And this was not even because he was changing or upsetting the fundamentals of American life. In six months as president, failing to master almost any aspect of the bureaucratic process, he had, beyond placing his nominee on the Supreme Court, accomplished, practically speaking, nothing. And yet, *OMG!!!* There almost was no other story in America— and in much of the world. That was the radical and transformational nature of the Trump presidency: it held everybody's attention.

Inside the White House, the daily brouhaha and world's fascination was no cause for joy. It was, in the White House staff's bitter view, the media that turned every day into a climactic, dastardly moment. And, in a sense, this was correct: every development cannot be climactic. The fact that yesterday's climax would soon, compared to the next climax, be piddling, rather bore out the disproportion. The media was failing to judge the relative importance of Trump events: most Trump events came to naught (arguably all of them did), and yet all were greeted with equal shock and horror. The White House staff believed that the media's Trump coverage lacked "context"—by this, they meant that people ought to realize that Trump was mostly just huffing and puffing.

At the same time, few in the White House did not assign blame to Trump for this as well. He seemed to lack the most basic understanding that a president's words and actions would, necessarily, be magnified to the nth power. In some convenient sense, he failed to understand this because he wanted the attention, no matter how often it disappointed him. But he also wanted it because again and again the response surprised him—and, as though every time was the first time, he could not modify his behavior.

Sean Spicer caught the brunt of the daily drama, turning this otherwise reasonable, mild-mannered, process-oriented professional into a joke figure standing at the White House door. In his daily out-of-body experience, as a witness to his own humiliation and loss for words, Spicer understood after a while—although he began to understand this beginning his first day on the job when dealing with the dispute about the inaugural audience numbers—that he had "gone down a rabbit hole." In this disorienting place, all public artifice, pretense, proportion, savvy, and self-awareness had been cast off, or—possibly another result of Trump never really intending to be president—never really figured into the state of being president.

On the other hand, constant hysteria did have one unintended political virtue. If every new event canceled out every other event, like some wacky news-cycle pyramid scheme, then you always survived another day.

* * *

Donald Trump's sons, Don Jr., thirty-nine, and Eric, thirty-three, existed in an enforced infantile relationship to their father, a role that embarrassed them, but one that they also professionally embraced. The role was to be Donald Trump's heirs and attendees. Their father took some regular pleasure in pointing out that they were in the back of the room when God handed out brains—but, then again, Trump tended to scorn anyone who might be smarter than he was. Their sister Ivanka, certainly no native genius, was the designated family smart person, her husband Jared the family's smooth operator. That left Don and Eric to errands and admin. In fact, the brothers had grown into reasonably competent family-owned-company executives (this is not saying all that much) because their father had little or no patience for actually running his company. Of course, quite a good amount of their professional time was spent on the whims, projects, promotions, and general way of life of DJT.

One benefit of their father's run for president was that it kept him away from the office. Still, the campaign's administration was largely their responsibility, so when the campaign went from caprice to a serious development in the Trump business and family, it caused a disruption in the family dynamic. Other people were suddenly eager to be Donald Trump's key lieutenants. There were the outsiders, like Corey Lewandowski, the campaign manager, but there was also the insider, brother-in-law Jared. Trump, not unusually for a family-run company, made everybody compete for his favor. The company was about him; it existed because of his name, personality, and charisma, so the highest standing in the company was reserved for those who could best serve him. There wasn't all that much competition for this role before he ran for president, but in early 2016, with the Republican Party collapsing and Trump rising, his sons faced a new professional and family situation.

Their brother-in-law had been slowly drawn into the campaign, partly at his wife's urging because her father's lack of constraint might actually affect the Trump business if they didn't keep an eye on him. And then he, with his brothers-in-law, was pulled in by the excitement of the campaign itself. By late spring 2016, when the nomination was all but clinched, the Trump campaign was a set of competing power centers with the knives out.

Lewandowski regarded both brothers and their brother-in-law with rolling-on-the-floor contempt: not only were Don Jr. and Eric stupid, and Jared somehow both supercilious and obsequious (the butler), but nobody knew a whit about politics—indeed, there wasn't an hour of political experience among them.

As time went on, Lewandowski became particularly close to the candidate. To the family, especially to Kushner, Lewandowski was an enabler. Trump's worst instincts flowed through Lewandowski. In early June, a little more than a month before the Republican National Convention, Jared and Ivanka decided that what was needed—for the sake of the campaign, for the sake of the Trump business—was an intervention.

Making common cause with Don Jr. and Eric, Jared and Ivanka pushed for a united front to convince Trump to oust Lewandowski. Don Jr., feeling squeezed not only by Lewandowski but by Jared, too, seized the opportunity. He would push out Lewandowski and become his replacement—and indeed, eleven days later Lewandowski would be gone.

All this was part of the background to one of the most preposterous meetings in modern politics. On June 9, 2016, Don Jr., Jared, and Paul Manafort met with a movieworthy cast of dubious characters in Trump Tower after having been promised damaging information about Hillary Clinton. Don Jr., encouraged by Jared and Ivanka, was trying to impress his father that he had the stuff to rise in the campaign.

When this meeting became public thirteen months later, it would, for the Trump White House, encapsulate both the case against collusion with the Russians and the case for it. It was a case, or the lack of one, not of masterminds and subterfuge, but of senseless and benighted people so guileless and unconcerned that they enthusiastically colluded in plain sight.

* * *

Walking into Trump Tower that June day were a well-connected lawyer from Moscow, who was a likely Russian agent; associates of the Azerbaijani Russian oligarch Aras Agalarov; a U.S. music promoter who managed Agalarov's son, a Russian pop star; and a Russian government lobbyist in Washington. Their purpose in visiting the campaign headquarters of a presumptive major party nominee for president of the United States was to meet with three of the most highly placed people on the campaign. This meeting was preceded by an email chain addressed to multiple recipients inside the Trump campaign of almost joyful intent: the Russians were offering a dump of negative or even incriminating information about their opponent.

Among the why-and-how theories of this imbecilic meeting:

- The Russians, in organized or freelance fashion, were trying to entrap the Trump campaign into a compromising relationship.
- The meeting was part of an already active cooperation on the part of the Trump campaign with the Russians to obtain and distribute damaging information about Hillary Clinton—and, indeed, within days of the Don Jr. meeting, WikiLeaks announced that it had obtained Clinton emails. Less than a month later, it started to release them.
- The wide-eyed Trump campaign, largely still playacting at running for president—and with no thought whatsoever of actually winning the election—was open to any and all entreaties and offers, because it had nothing to lose. Dopey Don Jr. (Fredo, as Steve Bannon would dub him, in one of his frequent *Godfather* borrowings) was simply trying to prove he was a player and a go-to guy.
- The meeting included the campaign chairman, Paul Manafort, and the campaign's most influential voice, Jared Kushner, because: (a) a

high-level conspiracy was being coordinated; (b) Manafort and Kushner, not taking the campaign very seriously, and without a thought of any consequence here, were merely entertained by the possibility of dirty tricks; (c) the three men were united in their plan to get rid of Lewandowski—with Don Jr. as the hatchet man—and, as part of this unity, Manafort and Kushner need to show up at Don Jr.'s silly meeting.

Whatever the reason for the meeting, no matter which of the above scenarios most accurately describes how this comical and alarming group came together, a year later, practically nobody doubted that Don Jr. would have wanted his father to know that he seized the initiative.

"The chance that Don Jr. did not walk these jumos up to his father's office on the twenty-sixth floor is zero," said an astonished and derisive Bannon, not long after the meeting was revealed.

"The three senior guys in the campaign," an incredulous Bannon went on, "thought it was a good idea to meet with a foreign government inside Trump Tower in the conference room on the twenty-fifth floor—with no lawyers. *They didn't have any lawyers.* Even if you thought that this was not treasonous, or unpatriotic, or bad shit, and I happen to think it's all of that, you should have called the FBI immediately. Even if you didn't think to do that, and you're totally amoral, and you wanted that information, you do it in a Holiday Inn in Manchester, New Hampshire, with your lawyers who meet with these people and go through everything and then they verbally come and tell another lawyer in a cut-out, and if you've got something, then you figure out how to dump it down to Breitbart or something like that, or maybe some other more legitimate publication. You never see it, you never know it, because you don't need to. . . . But that's the brain trust that they had."

All of the participants would ultimately plead that the meeting was utterly inconsequential, whatever the hope for it might have been, and admit that it was hapless. But even if that was true, a year later the revelation of the meeting had three profound and probably transformational effects:

First, the constant, ever repeated denials about there having been no discussion between campaign officials and the Russians connected to the Kremlin about the campaign, and, indeed, no meaningful contact between campaign officials and the Russian government, were exploded.

Second, the certainty among the White House staff that Trump himself would have not only been apprised of the details of this meeting, but have met the principals, meant that the president was caught out as a liar by those whose trust he most needed. It was another inflection point between hunkered-in-the-bunker and signed-on-for-the-wild-ride, and get-me-out-of-here.

Third, it was now starkly clear that everyone's interests diverged. The fortunes of Don Jr., Paul Manafort, and Jared Kushner hung individually in the balance. Indeed, the best guess by many in the West Wing was that the details of the meeting had been leaked by the Kushner side, thus sacrificing Don Jr. in an attempt to deflect responsibility away from themselves.

* * *

Even before word of the June 2016 meeting leaked out, Kushner's legal team—largely assembled in a rush since the appointment of Mueller, the special counsel—had been piecing together a forensic picture of both the campaign's Russian contacts and Kushner Companies' finances and money trail. In January, ignoring almost everybody's caution against it, Jared Kushner had entered the White House as a senior figure in the administration; now, six months later, he faced acute legal jeopardy. He had tried to keep a low profile, seeing himself as a behind-the-scenes counselor, but now his public position was not only endangering himself but the future of his family's business. As long as he remained exposed, his family was effectively blocked from most financial sources. Without access to this market, their holdings risked becoming distress debt situations.

Jared and Ivanka's self-created fantasylike life—two ambitious, well-mannered, well-liked young people living at the top of New York's social and financial world after having, in their version of humble fashion, accepted global power—had now, even with neither husband nor wife in office long enough to have taken any real action at all, come to the precipice of disgrace.

Jail was possible. So was bankruptcy. Trump may have been talking defiantly about offering pardons, or bragging about his power to give them, but that did not solve Kushner's business problems, nor did it provide a way to mollify Charlie Kushner, Jared's choleric and often irrational father. What's more, successfully navigating through the eye of the legal needle would require a careful touch and nuanced strategic approach on the part of the president—quite an unlikely development.

Meanwhile, the couple blamed everyone else in the White House. They blamed Priebus for the disarray that had produced a warlike atmosphere that propelled constant and damaging leaks, they blamed Bannon for leaking, and they blamed Spicer for poorly defending their virtue and interests.

They *needed* to defend themselves. One strategy was to get out of town (Bannon had a list of all the tense moments when the couple had taken a convenient holiday), and it happened that Trump would be attending the G20 summit Hamburg, Germany, on July 7 and 8. Jared and Ivanka accompanied the president on the trip, and while at the summit they learned that word of Don Jr.'s meeting with the Russians—and the couple kept pointedly presenting it as Don Jr.'s meeting—had leaked. Worse, they learned that the story was about to break in the *New York Times*.

Originally, Trump's staff was expecting details of the Don Jr. meeting to break on the website *Circa*. The lawyers, and spokesperson Mark Corallo, had been working to manage this news. But while in Hamburg, the president's staff learned that the *Times* was developing a story that had far more details about the meeting—quite possibly supplied by the Kushner side—which it would publish on Saturday, July 8. Advance knowledge of this article was kept from the president's legal team for the ostensible reason that it didn't involve the president.

In Hamburg, Ivanka, knowing the news would shortly get out, was presenting her signature effort: a World Bank fund to aid women entrepreneurs in developing countries. This was another instance of what White House staffers saw as the couple's extraordinarily off-message direction. Nowhere in the Trump campaign, nowhere on Bannon's white boards, nowhere in the heart of this president was there an interest in women entrepreneurs in developing countries. The daughter's agenda was singularly at odds with the father's—or at least the agenda that had elected him. Ivanka, in the view of almost every White House staffer, profoundly misunderstood the nature of her job and had converted traditional First Lady noblesse oblige efforts into White House staff work.

Shortly before boarding Air Force One for the return trip home, Ivanka—with what by now was starting to seem like an almost anarchic tone deafness—sat in for her father between Chinese president Xi Jinping and British prime minister Theresa May at the main G20 conference table. But this was mere distraction: as the president and his team huddled on the plane, the central subject was not the conference, it was how to respond to the *Times* story about Don Jr.'s and Jared's Trump Tower meeting, now only hours away from breaking.

En route to Washington, Sean Spicer and everybody else from the communications office was relegated to the back of the plane and excluded from the panicky discussions. Hope Hicks became the senior communications strategist, with the president, as always, her singular client. In the days following, that highest political state of being "in the room" was turned on its head. *Not* being in the room—in this case, the forward cabin on Air Force One—became an exalted status and get-out-of-jail-free card. "It used to hurt my feelings when I saw them running around doing things that were my job," said Spicer. "Now I'm glad to be out of the loop."

Included in the discussion on the plane were the president, Hicks, Jared and Ivanka, and their spokesperson, Josh Raffel. Ivanka, according to the later recollection of her team, would shortly leave the meeting, take a pill, and go to sleep. Jared, in the telling of his team, might have been there, but he was "not taking a pencil to anything." Nearby, in a small conference room watching the movie *Fargo*, were Dina Powell, Gary Cohn, Stephen Miller, and H. R. McMaster, all of whom would later insist that they were, however physically close to the unfolding crisis, removed from it. And, indeed, anyone "in the room" was caught in a moment that would shortly receive the special counsel's close scrutiny, with the relevant question being whether one or more federal employees had induced other federal employees to lie.

An aggrieved, unyielding, and threatening president dominated the discussion, pushing into line his daughter and her husband, Hicks, and Raffel. Kasowitz—the lawyer whose specific job was to keep Trump at arm's length from Russian-related matters—was kept on hold on the phone for an hour and then not put through. The president insisted that the meeting in Trump Tower was purely and simply about Russian adoption policy. That's what was discussed, period. Period. Even though it was likely, if not certain, that the *Times* had the incriminating email chain—in fact, it was quite possible that Jared and Ivanka and the lawyers *knew* the *Times* had this email chain—the president ordered that no one should let on to the more problematic discussion about Hillary Clinton.

It was a real-time example of denial and cover-up. The president believed, belligerently, what he believed. Reality was what he was convinced it was—or should be. Hence the official story: there was a brief courtesy meeting in Trump Tower about adoption policy, to no result, attended by senior aides and unaffiliated Russian nationals. The crafting of this manufactured tale was a rogue operation by rookies—always the two most combustible elements of a cover-up.

In Washington, Kasowitz and the legal team's spokesperson, Mark Corallo, weren't informed of either the *Times* article or the plan for how to respond to it until Don Jr.'s initial statement went out just before the story broke that Saturday.

Over the course of next seventy-two hours or so, the senior staff found itself wholly separate from—and, once again, looking on in astonishment at—the actions of the president's innermost circle of aides. In this, the relationship of the president and Hope Hicks, long tolerated as a quaint bond between the older man and a trustworthy young woman, began to be seen as anomalous and alarming. Completely devoted to accommodating him, she, his media facilitator, was the ultimate facilitator of unmediated behavior. His impulses and thoughts—unedited, unreviewed, unchallenged—not only passed through him, but, via Hicks, traveled out into the world without any other White House arbitration.

"The problem isn't Twitter, it's Hope," observed one communication staffer.

On July 9, a day after publishing its first story, the *Times* noted that the Trump Tower meeting was specifically called to discuss the Russian offer of damaging material about Clinton. The next day, as the *Times* prepared to publish the full email chain, Don Jr. hurriedly dumped it himself. There followed an almost daily count of new figures—all, in their own way, peculiar and unsettling—who emerged as participants in the meeting.

But the revelation of the Trump Tower meeting had another, perhaps even larger dimension. It marked the collapse of the president's legal strategy: the demise of Steve Bannon's Clinton-emulating firewall around the president.

The lawyers, in disgust and alarm, saw, in effect, each principal becoming a witness to another principal's potential misdeeds—all conspiring with one another to get their stories straight. The client and his family were panicking and running their own defense. Short-term headlines were overwhelming any sort of long-term strategy. "The worst thing you can do is lie to a prosecutor," said one member of the legal team. The persistent Trump idea that it is not a crime to lie to the media was regarded by the legal team as at best reckless and, in itself, potentially actionable: an explicit attempt to throw sand into the investigation's gears.

Mark Corallo was instructed not to speak to the press, indeed not to even answer his phone. Later that week, Corallo, seeing no good outcome—and privately confiding that he believed the meeting on Air Force One represented a likely obstruction of justice—quit. (The Jarvanka side would put it out that Corallo was fired.)

"These guys are not going to be second-guessed by the kids," said a frustrated Bannon about the firewall team.

Likewise, the Trump family, no matter its legal exposure, was not going to be run by its lawyers. Jared and Ivanka helped to coordinate a set of lurid leaks—drinking, bad behavior, personal life in disarray—about Marc Kasowitz, who had advised the president to send the couple home. Shortly after the presidential party returned to Washington, Kasowitz was out.

\* \* \*

Blame continued to flow. The odor of a bitter new reality, if not doom, that attached to the Comey-Mueller debacle was compounded by everyone's efforts not to be tagged by it.

The sides in the White House—Jared, Ivanka, Hope Hicks, and an increasingly ambivalent Dina Powell and Gary Cohn on one side, and almost everyone else, including Priebus, Spicer, Conway, and most clearly Bannon, on the other—were most distinguished by their culpability in or distance from the Comey-Mueller calamity. It was, as the non-Jarvanka side would unceasingly point out, a calamity *of their own making.* Therefore it became an effort of the Jarvankas not only to achieve distance for themselves from the causes of the debacle—such involvement as they had they now cast as strictly passive involvement or just following orders—but to suggest that their adversaries were at least equally at fault.

Shortly after the Don Jr. story broke, the president not unsuccessfully changed the subject by focusing the blame for the Comey-Mueller mess on Sessions, even more forcefully belittling and threatening him and suggesting that his days were numbered.

Bannon, who continued to defend Sessions, and who believed that he had militantly—indeed with scathing attacks on the Jarvankas for their stupidity—walled himself off from the Comey smashup, was now suddenly getting calls from reporters with leaks that painted him as an engaged participant in the Comey decision.

In a furious phone call to Hicks, Bannon blamed the leaks on her. In time, he had come to see the twenty-eight-year-old as nothing more than a hapless presidential enabler and poor-fish Jarvanka flunky—and he believed she had now deeply implicated herself in the entire disaster by participating in the Air Force One meeting. The next day, with more inquiries coming from reporters, he confronted Hicks inside the cabinet room, accusing her of doing Jared and Ivanka's dirty work. The face-off quickly escalated into an existential confrontation between the two sides of the White House—two sides on a total war footing.

*"You don't know what you're doing,"* shouted a livid Bannon at Hicks, demanding to know who she worked for, the White House or Jared and

Ivanka. "*You don't know how much trouble you are in,*" he screamed, telling her that if she didn't get a lawyer he would call her father and tell him he had better get her one. "*You are dumb as a stone!*" Moving from the cabinet room across the open area into the president's earshot, "a loud, scary, clearly threatening" Bannon, in the Jarvanka telling, yelled, "*I am going to fuck you and your little group!*" with a baffled president plaintively wanting to know, "What's going on?"

In the Jarvanka-side account, Hicks then ran from Bannon, hysterically sobbing and "visibly terrified." Others in the West Wing marked this as the high point of the boiling enmity between the two sides. For the Jarvankas, Bannon's rant was also a display that they believed they could use against him. The Jarvanka people pushed Priebus to refer the matter to the White House counsel, billing this as the most verbally abusive moment in the history of the West Wing, or at least certainly up among the most abusive episodes ever.

For Bannon, this was just more Jarvanka desperation—they were the ones, not him, saddled with Comey-Mueller. They were the ones panicking and out of control.

For the rest of his time in the White House, Bannon would not speak to Hicks again.

# 20

# MCMASTER AND SCARAMUCCI

Trump was impetuous and yet did not like to make decisions, at least not ones that seemed to corner him into having to analyze a problem. And no decision hounded him so much—really from the first moment of his presidency—as what to do about Afghanistan. It was a conundrum that became a battle. It involved not only his own resistance to analytic reasoning, but the left brain/right brain divide of his White House, the split between those who argued for disruption and those who wanted to uphold the status quo.

In this, Bannon became the disruptive and unlikely White House voice for peace—or anyway a kind of peace. In Bannon's view, only he and the not-too-resolute backbone of Donald Trump stood between consigning fifty thousand more American soldiers to hopelessness in Afghanistan.

Representing the status quo—and, ideally, a surge on top of the status quo—was H. R. McMaster, who, next to Jarvanka, had become Bannon's prime target for abuse. On this front, Bannon forged an easy bond with the president, who didn't much hide his contempt for the Power-Point general. Bannon and the president enjoyed trash-talking McMaster together.

McMaster was a protégé of David Petraeus, the former CENTCOM and Afghanistan commander who became Obama's CIA director before resigning in a scandal involving a love affair and the mishandling of classified information. Petraeus and now McMaster represented a kind of business-as-usual approach in Afghanistan and the Middle East. A stubborn McMaster kept proposing to the president new versions of the surge, but at each pitch Trump would wave him out of the Oval Office and roll his eyes in despair and disbelief.

The president's distaste and rancor for McMaster grew on pace with the approaching need to finally make a decision on Afghanistan, a decision he continued to put off. His position on Afghanistan—a military quagmire he knew little about, other than that it was a quagmire—had always been a derisive and caustic kiss-off of the sixteen-year war. Having inherited it did not make his feelings warmer or inspire him to want to dwell on it further. He knew the war was cursed and, knowing that, felt no need to know more. He put the responsibility for it on two of his favorite people to blame: Bush and Obama.

For Bannon, Afghanistan represented one more failure of establishment thinking. More precisely, it represented the establishment's inability to confront failure.

Curiously, McMaster had written a book on exactly this subject, a scathing critique of the unchallenged assumptions with which military leaders pursued the Vietnam War. The book was embraced by liberals and the establishment, with whom, in Bannon's view, McMaster had become hopelessly aligned. And now—ever afraid of the unknown, intent on keeping options open, dedicated to stability, and eager to protect his establishment cred—McMaster was recommending a huge troop surge in Afghanistan.

\* \* \*

By early July, the pressure to make a decision was approaching the boiling point. Trump had already authorized the Pentagon to deploy the troop resources it believed were needed, but Defense Secretary Mattis refused to act without a specific authorization from the president. Trump would finally have to make the call—unless he could find a way to put it off again.

Bannon's thought was that the decision could be made for the president—a way the president liked to have decisions made—if Bannon could get rid of McMaster. That would both head off the strongest voice for more troops and also avenge Bannon's ouster by McMaster's hand from the NSC.

With the president promising that he would make up his mind by August, and McMaster, Mattis, and Tillerson pressing for a decision as soon as possible, Bannon-inspired media began a campaign to brand McMaster as a globalist, interventionist, and all around not-our-kind-of-Trumper—and, to boot, soft on Israel.

It was a scurrilous, albeit partly true, attack. McMaster was in fact talking to Petraeus often. The kicker was the suggestion that McMaster was giving inside dope to Petraeus, a pariah because of his guilty plea regarding his mishandling of classified information. It was also the case that McMaster was disliked by the president and on the point of being dismissed.

It was Bannon, riding high again, enjoying himself in a moment of supreme overconfidence.

Indeed, in part to prove there were other options beyond more troops or humiliating defeat—and logically there probably weren't more options—Bannon became a sponsor of Blackwater-founder Erik Prince's obviously self-serving idea to replace the U.S. military force with private contractors and CIA and Special Operations personnel. The notion was briefly embraced by the president, then ridiculed by the military.

By now Bannon believed McMaster would be out by August. He was sure he had the president's word on this. Done deal. "McMaster wants to send more troops to Afghanistan, so we're going to send *him*," said a triumphal Bannon. In Bannon's scenario, Trump would give McMaster a fourth star and "promote" him to top military commander in Afghanistan.

As with the chemical attack in Syria, it was Dina Powell—even as she made increasingly determined efforts to get herself out of the White House, either on a Sheryl Sandberg trajectory or, stopping first at a way station, as ambassador to the United Nations—who struggled to help support the least disruptive, most keep-all-options-open approach. In this, both because the approach seemed like the safest course and because it was the opposite of Bannon's course, she readily recruited Jared and Ivanka.

The solution Powell endorsed, which was designed to put the problem and the reckoning off for another year or two or three, was likely to make the United States' position in Afghanistan even more hopeless. Instead of sending fifty or sixty thousand troops—which, at insupportable cost and the risk of national fury, might in fact win the war—the Pentagon would send some much lower number, one which would arouse little notice and merely prevent us from losing the war. In the Powell and Jarvanka view, it was the moderate, best-case, easiest-to-sell course, and it struck just the right balance between the military's unacceptable scenarios: retreat and dishonor or many more troops.

Before long, a plan to send four, five, six, or (tops) seven thousand troops became the middle-course strategy supported by the national security establishment and most everyone else save for Bannon and the president. Powell even helped design a PowerPoint deck that McMaster began using with the president: pictures of Kabul in the 1970s when it still looked something like a modern city. It could be like this again, the president was told, if we are resolute!

But even with almost everyone arrayed against him, Bannon was confident he was winning. He had a united right-wing press with him, and, he believed, a fed-up, working-class Trump base—its children the likely Afghanistan fodder. Most of all, he had the president. Pissed off that he was being handed the same problem and the same options that were handed Obama, Trump continued to heap spleen and mockery on McMaster.

Kushner and Powell organized a leak campaign in McMaster's defense. Their narrative was not a pro-troops defense; instead, it was about Bannon's leaks and his use of right-wing media to besmirch McMaster, "one of the most decorated and respected generals of his generation." The issue was not Afghanistan, the issue was Bannon. In this narrative, it was McMaster, a figure of stability, against Bannon, a figure of disruption. It was the *New York Times* and the *Washington Post*, who came to the defense of McMaster, against Breitbart and its cronies and satellites.

It was the establishment and never-Trumpers against the America-first Trumpkins. In many respects, Bannon was outgunned and outnumbered, yet he still thought he had it nailed. And when he won, not only would another grievously stupid chapter in the war in Afghanistan be avoided, but Jarvanka, and Powell, their factotum, would be further consigned to irrelevance and powerlessness.

* * *

As the debate moved toward resolution, the NSC, in its role as a presenter of options rather than an advocate for them (although of course it was advocating, too), presented three: withdrawal; Erik Prince's army of contractors; and a conventional, albeit limited, surge.

Withdrawal, whatever its merits—and however much a takeover of Afghanistan by the Taliban could be delayed or mitigated—still left Donald Trump with having lost a war, an insupportable position for the president.

The second option, a force of contractors and the CIA, was largely deep-sixed by the CIA. The agency had spent sixteen years successfully avoiding Afghanistan, and everyone knew that careers were not advanced in Afghanistan, they died in Afghanistan. So please keep us out of it.

That left McMaster's position, a modest surge, argued by Secretary of State Tillerson: more troops in Afghanistan, which, somehow, slightly, would be there on a different basis, somewhat, with a different mission, subtly, than that of troops sent there before.

The military fully expected the president to sign off on the third option. But on July 19, at a meeting of the national security team in the situation room at the White House, Trump lost it.

For two hours, he angrily railed against the mess he had been handed. He threatened to fire almost every general in the chain of command. He couldn't fathom, he said, how it had taken so many months of study to come up with this nothing-much-different plan. He disparaged the advice that came from generals and praised the advice from enlisted men. If we have to be in Afghanistan, he demanded, why can't we make money off it? China, he complained, has mining rights, but not the United States. (He was referring to a ten-year-old U.S.-backed deal.) This is just like the

21 Club, he said, suddenly confusing everyone with this reference to a New York restaurant, one of his favorites. In the 1980s, 21 closed for a year and hired a large number of consultants to analyze how to make the restaurant more profitable. In the end, their advice was: Get a bigger kitchen. *Exactly what any waiter would have said*, Trump shouted.

To Bannon, the meeting was a high point of the Trump presidency to date. The generals were punting and waffling and desperately trying to save face—they were, according to Bannon, talking pure "gobbledygook" in the situation room. "Trump was standing up to them," said a happy Bannon. "Hammering them. He left a bowel movement in the middle of their Afghan plans. Again and again, he came back to the same point: we're stuck and losing and nobody here has a plan to do much better than that."

Though there was still no hint of a viable alternative strategy in Afghanistan, Bannon, his Jarvanka frustration cresting, was sure he was the winner here. McMaster was toast.

* * *

Later on the day of the Afghanistan briefing, Bannon heard about yet another harebrained Jarvanka scheme. They planned to hire Anthony Scaramucci, aka "the Mooch."

After Trump had clinched the nomination more than a year before, Scaramucci—a hedge funder and go-to Trump surrogate for cable business news (mostly Fox Business Channel)—had become a reliable presence at Trump Tower. But then, in the last month of the campaign, with polls predicting a humiliating Trump defeat, he was suddenly nowhere to be seen. The question "Where's the Mooch?" seemed to be just one more indicator of the campaign's certain and pitiless end.

But on the day after the election, Steve Bannon—soon to be named chief strategist for the forty-fifth president-elect—was greeted as he arrived midmorning in Trump Tower by Anthony Scaramucci, holding a Starbucks coffee for him.

Over the next three months, Scaramucci, although no longer needed as a surrogate and without anything else particularly to do, became a constant hovering—or even lurking—presence at Trump Tower. Ever unflagging, he interrupted a meeting in Kellyanne Conway's office in early January just to make sure she knew that her husband's firm, Wachtell, Lipton, was representing him. Having made that point, name-dropping and vastly praising the firm's key partners, he then helped himself to a chair in Conway's meeting and, for both Conway's and her visitor's benefit, offered a stirring testimonial to the uniqueness and sagacity of Donald Trump and the working-class people—speaking of which, he took the opportunity to provide a résumé of his own Long Island working-class bona fides—who had elected him.

Scaramucci was hardly the only hanger-on and job seeker in the building, but his method was among the most dogged. He spent his days looking for meetings to be invited into, or visitors to engage with—this was easy because every other job seeker was looking for someone with whom to chat it up, so he soon became something like the unofficial official greeter. Whenever possible, he would grab a few minutes with any senior staffer who would not rebuff him. As he waited to be offered a high White House position, he was, he seemed personally certain, reaffirming his loyalty and team spirit and unique energy. He was so confident about his future that he made a deal to sell his hedge fund, Skybridge Capital, to HNA Group, the Chinese megaconglomerate.

Political campaigns, substantially based on volunteer help, attract a range of silly, needy, and opportunistic figures. The Trump campaign perhaps scraped lower in the barrel than most. The Mooch, for one, might not have been the most peculiar volunteer in the Trump run for president, but many figured him to be among the most shameless.

It was not just that before he became a dedicated supporter of Donald Trump, he was a dedicated naysayer, or that he had once been an Obama and Hillary Clinton supporter. The problem was that, really, nobody liked him. Even for someone in politics, he was immodest and incorrigible, and followed by a trail of self-serving and often contradictory statements made to this person about that person, which invariably made it back to whatever person was being most negatively talked about.

He was not merely a shameless self-promoter; he was a *proud* self-promoter. He was, by his own account, a fantastic networker. (This boast was surely true, since Skybridge Capital was a fund of funds, which is less a matter of investment acumen than of knowing top fund managers and being able to invest with them.) He had paid as much as half a million dollars to have his firm's logo appear in the movie *Wall Street 2* and to buy himself a cameo part in the film. He ran a yearly conference for hedge funders at which he himself was the star. He had a television gig at Fox Business Channel. He was a famous partier every year at Davos, once exuberantly dancing alongside the son of Muammar Gaddafi.

As for the presidential campaign, when signing on with Donald Trump—after he had bet big against Trump—he billed himself as a version of Trump, and he saw the two of them as a new kind of showman and communicator set to transform politics.

Although his persistence and his constant on-the-spot personal lobbying might not have endeared him to anybody, it did prompt the "What to do with Scaramucci?" question, which somehow came to beg an answer. Priebus, trying to deal with the Mooch problem and dispose of him at the same time, suggested that he take a money-raising job as finance director of the RNC—an offer Scaramucci rebuffed in a blowup in Trump Tower, loudly bad-mouthing Priebus in vivid language, a mere preview of what was to come.

While he wanted a job with the Trump administration, the Mooch specifically wanted one of the jobs that would give him a tax break on the sale of his business. A federal program provides for deferred payment of capital gains in the event of a sale of property to meet ethical requirements. Scaramucci needed a job that would get him a "certificate of divestiture," which is what an envious Scaramucci knew Gary Cohn had received for the sale of his Goldman stock.

A week before the inaugural he was finally offered such a job: director of the White House Office of Public Engagement and Intergovernmental Affairs. He would be the president's representative and cheerleader before Trump-partial interest groups.

But the White House ethics office balked—the sale of his business would take months to complete and he would be directly negotiating with an entity that was at least in part controlled by the Chinese government. And because Scaramucci had little support from anybody else, he was effectively blocked. It was, a resentful Scaramucci noted, one of the few instances in the Trump government when someone's business conflicts interfered with a White House appointment.

And yet with a salesman's tenacity, the Mooch pressed on. He appointed himself a Trump ambassador without portfolio. He declared himself Trump's man on Wall Street, even if, practically speaking, he wasn't a Trump man and he was exiting his firm on Wall Street. He was also in constant touch with anybody from the Trump circle who was willing to be in touch with him.

The "What to do with the Mooch" question persisted. Kushner, with whom Scaramucci had exercised a rare restraint during the campaign, and who had steadily heard from other New York contacts about Scaramucci's continued loyalty, helped push the question.

Priebus and others held Scaramucci at bay until June and then, as a bit of a punch line, Scaramucci was offered and, degradingly, had to accept, being named senior vice president and chief strategy officer for the U.S. Export-Import Bank, an executive branch agency Trump had long vowed to eliminate. But the Mooch was not ready to give up the fight: after yet more lobbying, he was offered, at Bannon's instigation, the post of ambassador to the Organization for Economic Co-operation and Development. The job came with a twenty-room apartment on the Seine, a full staff, and—Bannon found this part particularly amusing—absolutely no influence or responsibilities.

* * *

Meanwhile, another persistent question, "What to do with Spicer," seemed to somehow have been joined to the disaster involving the bungled response to the news of the June 2016 meeting between Don Jr., Jared, and the Russians. Since the president, while traveling on Air Force One, had actually dictated Don Jr.'s response to the initial *Times* report about the meeting, the blame for this should have been laid at the feet of Trump and Hope Hicks: Trump dictated, Hicks transcribed. But because no disasters could be laid at the president's feet, Hicks herself was spared. And, even though he had been pointedly excluded from the Trump Tower crisis, the blame for the episode was now put at Spicer's feet, precisely because, his loyalty in doubt, he and the communications staff *had* to be excluded.

In this, the comms team was judged to be antagonistic if not hostile to the interests of Jared and Ivanka; Spicer and his people had failed to mount an inclusive defense for them, nor had the comms team adequately defended the White House. This of course homed in on the essential and obvious point: although the junior first couple were mere staffers and not part of the institutional standing of the White House, they thought and acted as if they were part of the presidential entity. Their ire and increasing bitterness came from some of the staff's reluctance—really, a deep and intensifying resistance—to treat them as part and parcel of the presidency. (Once Priebus had to take Ivanka aside to make sure she understood that in her official role, she was just a staffer. Ivanka had insisted on the distinction that she was a staffer-slash-First Daughter.)

Bannon was their public enemy; they expected nothing of him. But Priebus and Spicer they regarded as functionaries, and their job was to support the White House's goals, which included their goals and interests.

Spicer, ever ridiculed in the media for his cockamamie defense of the White House and a seeming dumb loyalty, had been judged by the president, quite from the inauguration, to be not loyal enough and not nearly as aggressive as he should be in Trump's defense. Or, in Jared and Ivanka's view, in his family's defense. "What does Spicer's forty-member comm staff actually *do*?" was a persistent First Family question.

* * *

Almost from the beginning, the president had been interviewing potential new press secretaries. He appeared to have offered the job to various people, one of whom was Kimberly Guilfoyle, the Fox News personality and cohost of *The Five*. Guilfoyle, the former wife of California Democrat Gavin Newsom, was also rumored to be Anthony Scaramucci's girlfriend. Unbeknownst to the White House, Scaramucci's personal life was in dramatic free fall. On July 9, nine months pregnant with their second child, Scaramucci's wife filed for divorce.

Guilfoyle, knowing that Spicer was on his way out but having decided not to take his job—or, according to others in the White House, never having been offered it—suggested Scaramucci, who set to work convincing Jared and Ivanka that theirs was largely a PR problem and that they were ill served by the current communications team.

Scaramucci called a reporter he knew to urge that an upcoming story about Kushner's Russian contacts be spiked. He followed up by having another mutual contact call the reporter to say that if the story was spiked it would help the Mooch get into the White House, whereupon the reporter would have special Mooch access. The Mooch then assured Jared and Ivanka that he had, in this clever way, killed the story.

Now Scaramucci had their attention. *We need some new thinking,* the couple thought; *we need somebody who is more on our side.* The fact that Scaramucci was from New York, and Wall Street, and was rich, reassured them that he understood what the deal was. And that he would understand the stakes and know that an aggressive game needed to be played.

On the other hand, the couple did not want to be perceived as being heavy-handed. So, after bitterly accusing Spicer of not defending them adequately, they suddenly backed off and suggested that they were just looking to add a new voice to the mix. The job of White House communications director, which had no precise purview, had been vacant since May, when Mike Dubke, whose presence at the White House had hardly registered, resigned. Scaramucci could take this job, the couple figured, and in that role he could be their ally.

"He's good on television," Ivanka told Spicer when she explained the rationale for hiring a former hedge fund manager as White House communications director. "Maybe he can help us."

It was the president who, meeting with Scaramucci, was won over by the Mooch's cringeworthy Wall Street hortatory flattery. ("I can only hope to realize a small part of your genius as a communicator, but you are my example and model" was one report of the gist of the Scaramucci supplication.) And it was Trump who then urged that Scaramucci become the true communications chief, reporting directly to the president.

On July 19, Jared and Ivanka, through intermediaries, put a feeler out to Bannon: What would he think about Scaramucci's coming on board in the comms job?

So preposterous did this seem to Bannon—it was a cry of haplessness, and certain evidence that the couple had become truly desperate—that he refused to consider or even reply to the question. Now he was sure: Jarvanka was losing it.

# 21

# BANNON AND SCARAMUCCI

**B**annon's apartment in Arlington, Virginia, a fifteen-minute drive from downtown Washington, was called the "safe house." This seemed somehow to acknowledge his transience and to nod, with whatever irony, to the underground and even romantic nature of his politics—the roguish and *joie de guerre* alt-right. Bannon had decamped here from the Breitbart Embassy on A Street on Capitol Hill. It was a one-bedroom graduate-student sort of apartment, in a mixed-use building over a mega-McDonald's—quite belying Bannon's rumored fortune—with five or six hundred books (emphasis on popular history) stacked against the wall without benefit of shelving. His lieutenant, Alexandra Preate, also lived in the building, as did the American lawyer for Nigel Farage, the right-wing British Brexit leader who was part of the greater Breitbart circle.

On the evening on Thursday, July 20, the day after the contentious meeting about Afghanistan, Bannon was hosting a small dinner—organized by Preate, with Chinese takeout. Bannon was in an expansive, almost celebratory, mood. Still, Bannon knew, just when you felt on top of the world in the Trump administration, you could probably count on getting cut down. That was the pattern and price of one-man leadership—insecure-man leadership. The other biggest guy in the room always had to be reduced in size.

Many around him felt Bannon was going into another bad cycle. In his first run around the track, he'd been punished by the president for his *Time* magazine cover and for the *Saturday Night Live* portrayal of "President Bannon"—that cruelest of digs to Trump. Now there was a new book, *The Devil's Bargain*, and it claimed, often in Bannon's own words, that Trump could not have done it without him. The president was again greatly peeved.

Still, Bannon seemed to feel he had broken through. Whatever happened, he had clarity. It was such a mess inside in the White House that, if nothing else, this clarity would put him on top. His agenda was front and center, and his enemies sidelined. Jared and Ivanka were getting blown up every day and were now wholly preoccupied with protecting themselves. Dina Powell was looking for another job. McMaster had screwed himself on Afghanistan. Gary Cohn, once a killer enemy, was now desperate to be named Fed chairman and currying favor with Bannon—"licking my balls," Bannon said with a quite a cackle. In return for supporting Cohn's campaign to win the Fed job, Bannon was extracting fealty from him for the right-wing trade agenda.

The geniuses were fucked. Even POTUS might be fucked. But Bannon had the vision and the discipline—he was sure he did. "I'm cracking my shit every day. The nationalist agenda, we're fucking owning it. I'll be there for the duration."

Before the dinner, Bannon had sent around an article from the *Guardian*—though one of the leading English-language left-leaning newspapers, it was nevertheless Bannon's favorite paper—about the backlash to globalization. The article, by the liberal journalist Nikil Saval, both accepted Bannon's central populist political premise—"the competition between workers in developing and developed countries . . . helped drive down wages and job security for workers in developed countries"—and elevated it to the epochal fight of our time. Davos was dead and Bannon was very much alive. "Economists who were once ardent proponents of globalization have become some of its most prominent critics," wrote Saval. "Erstwhile supporters now concede, at least in part, that it has produced inequality, unemployment and downward pressure on wages. Nuances and criticisms that economists only used to raise in private seminars are finally coming out in the open."

"I'm starting to get tired of winning" was all that Bannon said in his email with the link to the article.

Now, restless and pacing, Bannon was recounting how Trump had dumped on McMaster and, as well, savoring the rolling-on-the-floor absurdity of the geniuses' Scaramucci gambit. But most of all he was incredulous about something else that had happened the day before.

Unbeknownst to senior staff, or to the comms office—other than by way of a pro forma schedule note—the president had given a major interview to the *New York Times*. Jared and Ivanka, along with Hope Hicks, had set it up. The *Times*'s Maggie Haberman, Trump's bête noire ("very mean, and not smart") and yet his go-to journalist for some higher sort of approval, had been called in to see the president with her colleagues Peter Baker and Michael Schmidt. The result was one of the most peculiar and ill-advised interviews in presidential history, from a president who had already, several times before, achieved that milestone.

In the interview, Trump had done his daughter and son-in-law's increasingly frantic bidding. He had, even if to no clear end and without certain strategy, continued on his course of threatening the attorney general for recusing himself and opening the door to a special prosecutor. He openly pushed Sessions to resign—mocking and insulting him and daring him to try to stay. However much this seemed to advance no one's cause, except perhaps that of the special prosecutor, Bannon's incredulity— "Jefferson Beauregard Sessions is not going to go anywhere"—was most keenly focused on another remarkable passage in the interview: the president had admonished the special counsel not to cross the line into his family's finances.

"*Ehhh . . . ehhh . . . ehhh!*" screeched Bannon, making the sound of an emergency alarm. "Don't look here! Let's tell a prosecutor what *not* to look at!"

Bannon then described the conversation he'd had with the president earlier that day: "I went right into him and said, 'Why did you say that?' And he says, 'The Sessions thing?' and I say, 'No, that's bad, but it's another day at the office.' I said, 'Why did you say it was off limits to go after your family's finances?' And he says, 'Well, it is . . . .' I go, 'Hey, they are going to determine their mandate. . . . You may not like it, but you just guaranteed if you want to get anybody else in [the special counsel] slot, every senator will make him swear that the first thing he's going to do is come in and subpoena your fucking tax returns.'"

Bannon, with further disbelief, recounted the details of a recent story from the *Financial Times* about Felix Sater, one of the shadiest of the shady Trump-associated characters, who was closely aligned with Trump's longtime personal lawyer, Michael Cohen (reportedly a target of the Mueller investigation), and a key follow-the-money link to Russia. Sater, "get ready for it—I know this may shock you, but wait for it"—had had major problems with the law before, "caught with a couple of guys in Boca running Russian money through a boiler room." And, it turns out, "Brother Sater" was prosecuted by—"wait"—*Andrew Weissmann*. (Mueller had recently hired Weissmann, a high-powered Washington lawyer who headed the DOJ's criminal fraud division.) "You've got the LeBron James of money laundering investigations on you, Jarvanka. My asshole just got so tight!"

Bannon quite literally slapped his sides and then returned to his conversation with the president. "And he goes, 'That's not their mandate.' Seriously, dude?"

Preate, putting out the Chinese food on a table, said, "It wasn't their mandate to put Arthur Andersen out of business during Enron, but that didn't stop Andrew Weissmann"—one of the Enron prosecutors.

"You realize where this is going," Bannon continued. "This is all about *money laundering*. Mueller chose Weissmann first and he is a money laundering guy. Their path to fucking Trump goes right through Paul Manafort, Don Jr., and Jared Kushner . . . It's as plain as a hair on your face. . . . It goes through Deutsche Bank and all the Kushner shit. The Kushner shit is greasy. They're going to go right through that. They're going to roll those two guys up and say play me or trade me. But . . . 'executive privilege!'" Bannon mimicked. "'We've got executive privilege!' There's no executive privilege! We proved that in Watergate."

An expressive man, Bannon seemed to have suddenly exhausted himself. After a pause, he added wearily: "They're sitting on a beach trying to stop a Category Five."

With his hands in front of him, he mimed something like a force field that would isolate him from danger. "It's not my deal. He's got the five geniuses around him: Jarvanka, Hope Hicks, Dina Powell, and Josh Raffel." He threw up his hands again, this time as if to say *Hands off.* "I know no Russians, I don't know nothin' about nothin'. I'm not being a witness. I'm not hiring a lawyer. It is not going to be my ass in front of a microphone on national TV answering questions. Hope Hicks is so fucked she doesn't even know it. They are going to lay her out. They're going to crack Don Junior like an egg on national TV. Michael Cohen, cracked like an egg. He"—the president—"said to me everybody would take that Don Junior meeting with the Russians. I said, 'Everybody would *not* take that meeting.' I said, 'I'm a naval officer. I'm not going to take a meeting with Russian nationals, and do it in headquarters, are you fucking insane?' and he says, 'But he's a good boy.' There were no meetings like that after I took over the campaign."

Bannon's tone veered from ad absurdum desperation to resignation.

"If he fires Mueller it just brings the impeachment quicker. Why not, let's do it. Let's get it on. Why not? What am I going to do? Am I going to go in and save him? He's Donald Trump. He's always gonna do things. He wants an unrecused attorney general. I told him if Jeff Sessions goes, Rod Rosenstein goes, and then Rachel Brand"—the associate attorney general, next in line after Rosenstein—"goes, we'll be digging down into Obama career guys. An Obama guy will be acting attorney general. I said you're not going to get Rudy"—Trump had again revived a wish for his loyalists Rudy Giuliani or Chris Christie to take the job—"because he was on the campaign and will have to recuse himself, and Chris Christie, too, so those are masturbatory fantasies, get those out of your brain. And, for anybody to get confirmed now, they are going to have to swear and ensure that things will go ahead and they won't fire anybody, because you said yesterday—*Ehhh . . . ehhh . . . . ehhh!*—'my family finances are off limits,' and they're going to demand that, whoever he is, he promises and commits to make the family finances part of this investigation. I told him as night follows day that's a lock, so you better hope Sessions stays around."

"He was calling people in New York last night asking what he should do," added Preate. (Almost everybody in the White House followed Trump's thinking by tracking whom he had called the night before.)

Bannon sat back and, with steam-rising frustration—almost a cartoon figure—he outlined his Clinton-like legal plan. "They went to the mattresses with amazing discipline. They ground through it." But that *was* about discipline, he emphasized, and Trump, said Bannon, noting the obvious, was the least disciplined man in politics.

It was clear where Mueller and his team were going, said Bannon: they would trace a money trail through Paul Manafort, Michael Flynn, Michael Cohen, and Jared Kushner and roll one or all of them on the president.

*It's Shakespearean*, he said, enumerating the bad advice from his family circle: "It's the geniuses, the same people who talked him into firing Comey, the same people on Air Force One who cut out his outside legal team, knowing the email was out there, knowing that email existed, put the statement out about Don Junior, that the meeting was all about adoptions . . . the same geniuses trying to get Sessions fired.

"Look, Kasowitz has known him for twenty-five years. Kasowitz has gotten him out of all kinds of jams. Kasowitz on the campaign—what did we have, a hundred women? Kasowitz took care of all of them. And now he lasts, what, four weeks? He's in the mumble tank. This is New York's toughest lawyer, broken. Mark Corallo, toughest motherfucker I ever met, just can't do it."

Jared and Ivanka believe, said Bannon, that if they advocate prison reform and save DACA—the program to protect the children of illegal immigrants—the liberals will come to their defense. He digressed briefly to characterize Ivanka Trump's legislative acumen, and her difficulty—which had become quite a White House preoccupation—in finding sponsorship for her family leave proposal. "Here's why, I keep telling her: there's no political constituency in it. You know how easy it is to get a bill sponsored, any schmendrick can do it. You know why your bill has no sponsorship? Because people realize how *dumb* it is." In fact, said, Bannon, eyes rolling and mouth agape, it was the Jarvanka idea to try to trade off amnesty for the border wall. "If not the dumbest idea in Western civilization, it's up there in the top three. Do these geniuses even know who we are?"

Just then Bannon took a call, the caller telling him that it looked as if Scaramucci might indeed be getting the job of communications director. "Don't fuck with me, dude," he laughed. "Don't fuck with me like that!"

He got off the phone expressing further wonder at the fantasy world of the geniuses—and added, for good measure, an extra dollop of dripping contempt for them. "I literally do not talk to them. You know why? I'm doing my shit, and they got nothing to do with it, and I don't care what they're doing . . . I don't care. . . . I'm not going to be alone with them, I'm not going to be in a room with them. Ivanka walked into the Oval today . . . [and] as soon as she walked in, I looked at her and walked right out. . . . I won't be in a room . . . don't want to do it. . . . Hope Hicks walked in, I walked out."

"The FBI put Jared's father in jail," said Preate. "Don't they understand you don't mess—"

"Charlie Kushner," said Bannon, smacking his head again in additional disbelief. "He's going crazy because they're going to get down deep in his shit about how he's financed everything. . . . The rabbis with the diamonds and all the shit coming out of Israel . . . and all these guys coming out of Eastern Europe . . . all these Russian guys . . . and guys in Kazakhstan. . . . And he's frozen on 666 [Fifth Avenue], when it goes under next year, the whole thing's cross-collateralized . . . he's wiped, he's gone, he's done, it's over. . . . Toast."

He held his face in his hands for a moment and then looked up again.

"I'm pretty good at coming up with solutions, I came up with a solution for his broke-dick campaign in about a day, but I don't see this. I don't see a plan for getting through. Now, I gave him a plan, I said you seal the Oval Office, you send those two kids home, you get rid of Hope, all these deadbeats, and you listen to your legal team—Kasowitz, and Mark Dowd, and Jay Sekulow, and Mark Corallo, these are all professionals who have done this many times. You listen to those guys and never talk about this stuff again, you just conduct yourself as commander in chief and then you can be president for eight years. If you don't, you're not, simple. But he's the president, he gets a choice, and he's clearly choosing to go down another path . . . and you can't stop him. The guy is going to call his own plays. He's Trump. . . ."

And then another call came, this one from Sam Nunberg. He, too, was calling about Scaramucci, and his words caused something like stupefaction in Bannon: "No fucking, fucking way."

Bannon got off the phone and said, "Jesus. Scaramucci. I can't even respond to this. It's Kafkaesque. Jared and Ivanka needed somebody to represent their shit. It's madness. He'll be on that podium for two days and he'll be so chopped he'll bleed out everywhere. He'll literally blow up in a week. This is why I don't take this stuff seriously. Hiring Scaramucci? He's not qualified to do anything. He runs a fund of funds. Do you know what a fund of funds is? It's not a fund. Dude, it's sick. We look like buffoons."

* * *

The ten days of Anthony Scaramucci, saw, on the first day, July 21, the resignation of Sean Spicer. Oddly, this seemed to catch everyone unawares. In a meeting with Scaramucci, Spicer, and Priebus, the president—who in his announcement of Scaramucci's hire as communications director had promoted Scaramucci not only over Spicer, but in effect over Priebus, his chief of staff—suggested that the men ought to be able to work it out together.

Spicer went back to his office, printed out his letter of resignation, and then took it back to the nonplussed president, who said again that he really wanted Spicer to be a part of things. But Spicer, surely the most mocked man in America, understood that he had been handed a gift. His White House days were over.

For Scaramucci, it was now payback time. Scaramucci blamed his six humiliating months out in the cold on nobody so much as Reince Priebus—having announced his White House future, having sold his business in anticipation of it, he had come away with nothing, or at least nothing of any value. But now, in a reversal befitting a true master of the universe—befitting, actually, Trump himself—Scaramucci was in the White House, bigger, better, and grander than even he had had the gall to imagine. And Priebus was dead meat.

That was the signal the president had sent Scaramucci—deal with the mess. In Trump's view, the problems in his tenure so far were just prob-

lems about the team. If the team went, the problems went. So Scaramucci
had his marching orders. The fact that the president had been saying the
same stuff about his rotten team from the first day, that this riff had been
a constant from the campaign on, that he would often say he wanted
everybody to go and then turn around and say he *didn't* want everybody
to go—all that rather went over Scaramucci's head.

Scaramucci began taunting Priebus publicly, and inside the West
Wing he adopted a tough-guy attitude about Bannon—"I won't take
his bullshit." Trump seemed delighted with this behavior, which led Scaramucci to feel that the president was urging him on. Jared and Ivanka
were pleased, too; they believed they had scored with Scaramucci and
were confident that he would defend them against Bannon and the rest.

Bannon and Priebus remained not just disbelieving but barely able
not to crack up. For both men, Scaramucci was either a hallucinatory
episode—they wondered whether they ought to just shut their eyes while
it passed—or some further march into madness.

* * *

Even as measured against other trying weeks in the Trump White
House, the week of July 24 was a head-slammer. First, it opened the next
episode in what had become a comic-opera effort to repeal Obamacare in
the Senate. As in the House, this had become much less about health
care than a struggle both among Republicans in Congress and between
the Republican leadership and the White House. The signature stand for
the Republican Party had now become the symbol of its civil war.

On that Monday, the president's son-in-law appeared at the micro-
phones in front of the West Wing to preview his statement to Senate
investigators about the Trump campaign's connections to Russia. Having almost never spoken before in public, he now denied culpability in
the Russian mess by claiming feckless naïveté; speaking in a reedy, self-
pitying voice, he portrayed himself as a Candide-like figure who had
become disillusioned by a harsh world.

And that evening, the president traveled to West Virginia to deliver a
speech before the Boy Scouts of America. Once more, his speech was ton-
ally at odds with time, place, and good sense. It prompted an immediate

apology from the Boy Scouts to its members, their parents, and the country at large. The quick trip did not seem to improve Trump's mood: the next morning, seething, the president again publicly attacked his attorney general and—for good measure and no evident reason—tweeted his ban of transgender people in the military. (The president had been presented with four different options related to the military's transgender policy. The presentation was meant to frame an ongoing discussion, but ten minutes after receiving the discussion points, and without further consultation, Trump tweeted his transgender ban.)

The following day, Wednesday, Scaramucci learned that one of his financial disclosure forms seemed to have been leaked; assuming he'd been sabotaged by his enemies, Scaramucci blamed Priebus directly, implicitly accusing him of a felony. In fact, Scaramucci's financial form was a public document available to all.

That afternoon, Priebus told the president that he understood he should resign and they should start talking about his replacement.

Then, that evening, there was a small dinner in the White House, with various current and former Fox News people, including Kimberly Guilfoyle, in attendance—and this was leaked. Drinking more than usual, trying desperately to contain the details of the meltdown of his personal life (being linked to Guilfoyle wasn't going to help his negotiation with his wife), and wired by events beyond his own circuits' capacity, Scaramucci called a reporter at the *New Yorker* magazine and unloaded.

The resulting article was surreal—so naked in its pain and fury, that for almost twenty-four hours nobody seemed to be able to quite acknowledge that he had committed public suicide. The article quoted Scaramucci speaking bluntly about the chief of staff: "Reince Priebus—if you want to leak something—he'll be asked to resign very shortly." Saying that he had taken his new job "to serve the country" and that he was "not trying to build my brand," Scaramucci also took on Steve Bannon: "I'm not Steve Bannon. I'm not trying to suck my own cock." (In fact, Bannon learned about the piece when fact-checkers from the magazine called him for comment about Scaramucci's accusation that he sucked his own cock.)

Scaramucci, who had in effect publicly fired Priebus, was behaving so bizarrely that it wasn't at all clear who would be the last man standing. Priebus, on the verge of being fired for so long, realized that he might have agreed to resign too soon. He might have gotten the chance to fire Scaramucci!

On Friday, as health care repeal cratered in the Senate, Priebus joined the president on board Air Force One for a trip to New York for a speech. As it happened, so did Scaramucci, who, avoiding the *New Yorker* fallout, had said he'd gone to New York to visit his mother but in fact had been hiding out at the Trump Hotel in Washington. Now here he was, with his bags (he would indeed now stay in New York and visit his mother), behaving as though nothing had happened.

On the way back from the trip, Priebus and the president talked on the plane and discussed the timing of his departure, with the president urging him to do it the right way and to take his time. "You tell me what works for you," said Trump. "Let's make it good."

Minutes later, Priebus stepped onto the tarmac and an alert on his phone said the president had just tweeted that there was a new chief of staff, Department of Homeland Security chief John Kelly, and that Priebus was out.

The Trump presidency was six months old, but the question of who might replace Priebus had been a topic of discussion almost from day one. Among the string of candidates were Powell and Cohn, the Jarvanka favorites; OMB director Mick Mulvaney, one of the Bannon picks; and Kelly.

In fact, Kelly—who would soon abjectly apologize to Priebus for the basic lack of courtesy in the way his dismissal was handled—had not been consulted about his appointment. The president's tweet was the first he knew of it.

But indeed there was no time to waste. Now the paramount issue before the Trump government was that somebody would have to fire Scaramucci. Since Scaramucci had effectively gotten rid of Priebus— the person who logically should have fired *him*—the new chief of staff was needed, more or less immediately, to get rid of the Mooch.

And six days later, just hours after he was sworn in, Kelly fired Scaramucci.

Chastened themselves, the junior first couple, the geniuses of the Scaramucci hire, panicked that they would, deservedly, catch the blame for one of the most ludicrous if not catastrophic hires in modern White House history. Now they rushed to say how firmly they supported the decision to get rid of Scaramucci.

"So I punch you in the face," Sean Spicer noted from the sidelines, "and then say, 'Oh my god, we've got to get you to a hospital!'"

# 22

# GENERAL KELLY

On August 4, the president and key members of the West Wing left for Trump's golf club in Bedminster. The new chief of staff, General Kelly, was in tow, but the president's chief strategist, Steve Bannon, had been left behind. Trump was grouchy about the planned seventeen-day trip, bothered by how diligently his golf dates were being clocked by the media. So this was now dubbed a "working" trip—another piece of Trump vanity that drew shrugs, eye rolling, and head shaking from a staff that had been charged with planning events that looked like work even as they were instructed to leave yawning expanses of time for golf.

During the president's absence, the West Wing would be renovated—Trump, the hotelier and decorator, was "disgusted" by its condition. The president did not want to move over to the nearby Executive Office Building, where the West Wing business would temporarily be conducted—and where Steve Bannon sat waiting for his call to go to Bedminster.

He was about to leave for Bedminster, Bannon kept telling everyone, but no invitation came. Bannon, who claimed credit for bringing Kelly into the administration in the first place, was unsure where he stood with the new chief. Indeed, the president himself was unsure about where he himself stood; he kept asking people if Kelly liked him. More generally,

Bannon wasn't entirely clear *what* Kelly was doing, other than his duty. Where exactly did the new chief of staff fit in Trumpworld?

While Kelly stood somewhere right of center on the political spectrum and had been a willing tough immigration enforcer at Homeland Security, he was not anywhere near so right as Bannon or Trump. "He's not hardcore" was Bannon's regretful appraisal. At the same time, Kelly was certainly not close in any way to the New York liberals in the White House. But politics was not his purview. As director of Homeland Security he had watched the chaos in the White House with disgust and thought about quitting. Now he had agreed to try to tame it. He was sixty-seven, resolute, stern, and grim. "Does he ever smile?" asked Trump, who had already begun to think that he had somehow been tricked into the hire.

Some Trumpers, particularly those with over-the-transom access to the president, believed that he had been tricked into some form of very-much-not-Trump submission. Roger Stone, one of those people whose calls Kelly was now shielding the president from, spread the dark scenario that Mattis, McMaster, and Kelly had agreed that no military action would ever be taken unless the three were in accord—and that at least one of them would always remain in Washington if the others were away.

After Kelly dispatched Scaramucci, his two immediate issues, now on the table in Bedminster, were the president's relatives and Steve Bannon. One side or the other obviously had to go. Or perhaps both should go.

It was far from clear whether a White House chief of staff who saw his function as establishing command process and enforcing organizational hierarchy—directing a decision funnel to the commander in chief—could operate effectively or even exist in a White House where the commander in chief's children had special access and overriding influence. As much as the president's daughter and son-in-law were now offering slavish regard for the new command principals, they would, surely, by habit and temperament, override Kelly's control of the West Wing. Not only did they have obvious special influence with the president, but important members of the staff saw them as having this juice, and hence believed that they were the true north of West Wing advancement and power.

Curiously, for all their callowness, Jared and Ivanka had become quite a fearsome presence, as feared by others as the two of them feared Bannon. What's more, they had become quite accomplished infighters and leakers—they had front-room *and* back-channel power—although, with great woundedness, they insisted, incredibly, that they never leaked. "If they hear someone talking about them, because they are so careful about their image and have crafted this whole persona—it's like anyone who tries to pierce it or say something against it is like a big problem," said one senior staffer. "They get very upset and will come after you."

On the other hand, while "the kids" might make Kelly's job all but impossible, keeping Bannon on board didn't make a lot of sense, either. Whatever his gifts, he was a hopeless plotter and malcontent, bound to do an end run around any organization. Besides, as the Bedminster hiatus—working or otherwise—began, Bannon was once more on the president's shit list.

The president continued to stew about *The Devil's Bargain*, the book by Joshua Green that gave Bannon credit for the election. Then, too, while the president tended to side with Bannon against McMaster, the campaign to defend McMaster, supported by Jared and Ivanka, was having an effect. Murdoch, enlisted by Jared to help defend McMaster, was personally lobbying the president for Bannon's head. Bannonites felt they had to defend Bannon against an impulsive move by the president: so now, not only did they brand McMaster as weak on Israel, they persuaded Sheldon Adelson to lobby Trump—Bannon, Adelson told the president, was the only person he trusted on Israel in the White House. Adelson's billions and implacability always impressed Trump, and his endorsement, Bannon believed, significantly strengthened his hand.

But overriding the management of the harrowing West Wing dysfunction, Kelly's success—or even relevance, as he was informed by almost anyone who was in a position to offer him an opinion—depended on his rising to the central challenge of his job, which was how to manage Trump. Or, actually, how to live with not managing him. His desires, needs, and impulses had to exist—*necessarily* had to exist—outside the organizational structure. Trump was the one variable that, in management terms, simply could not be controlled. He was like a recalcitrant two-year-old. If you tried to control him, it would only have the opposite effect. In this, then, the manager had to most firmly manage his own expectations.

In an early meeting with the president, General Kelly had Jared and Ivanka on his agenda—how the president saw their role; what he thought was working and not working about it; how he envisioned it going forward. It was all intended to be a politic way of opening a discussion about getting them out. But the president was, Kelly soon learned, delighted with all aspects of their performance in the West Wing. Maybe at some point Jared would become secretary of state—that was the only change the president seemed to foresee. The most Kelly could do was to get the president to acknowledge that the couple should be part of a greater organizational discipline in the West Wing and should not so readily jump the line.

This, at least, was something that the general could try to enforce. At a dinner in Bedminster—the president dining with his daughter and son-in-law—the First Family were confused when Kelly showed up at the meal and joined them. This, they shortly came to understand, was neither an attempt at pleasant socializing nor an instance of unwarranted over-familiarity. It was enforcement: Jared and Ivanka needed to go through him to talk to the president.

But Trump had made clear his feeling that the roles played by the kids in his administration needed only minor adjustment, and this now presented a significant problem for Bannon. Bannon really had believed that Kelly would find a way to send Jarvanka home. How could he not? Indeed, Bannon had convinced himself that they represented the largest danger to Trump. They would take the president down. As much, Bannon believed that *he* could not remain in the White House if they did.

Beyond Trump's current irritation with Bannon, which many believed was just the usual constant of Trump resentment and complaint, Bannonites felt that their leader had, at least policywise, gained the upper hand. Jarvanka was marginalized; the Republican leadership, after health care, was discredited; the Cohn-Mnuchin tax plan was a hash. Through one window, the future looked almost rosy for Bannon.

Sam Nunberg, the former Trump loyalist who was now wholly a Bannon loyalist, believed that Bannon would stay in the White House for two years and then leave to run Trump's reelection campaign. "If you can get this idiot elected twice," Nunberg marveled, you would achieve something like immortality in politics.

But through another window, Bannon couldn't possibly remain in place. He seemed to have moved into a heightened state that allowed him to see just how ridiculous the White House had become. He could barely hold his tongue—indeed, he couldn't hold it. Pressed, he could not see the future of the Trump administration. And, while many Bannonites argued the case for Jarvanka ineffectiveness and irrelevance—just ignore them, they said—Bannon, with mounting ferocity and pubic venom, could abide them less and less every day.

Bannon, continuing to wait for his call to join the president in Bedminster, decided that he would force the situation and offered his resignation to Kelly. But this was in fact a game of chicken: he wanted to stay. On the other hand, he wanted Jarvanka to go. And that became an effective ultimatum.

* * *

At lunch on August 8, in the Clubhouse at Bedminster—amid Trumpish chandeliers, golf trophies, and tournament plaques—the president was flanked by Tom Price, the secretary of health and human services, and his wife, Melania. Kellyanne Conway was at the lunch; so were Kushner and several others. This was one of the "make-work" events—over lunch, there was a discussion of the opioid crisis, which was then followed by a statement from the president and a brief round of questions from reporters. While reading the statement in a monotone, Trump kept his head down, propping it on his elbows.

After taking some humdrum questions about opioids, he was suddenly asked about North Korea, and, quite as though in stop-action animation, he seemed to come alive.

North Korea had been a heavy-on-detail, short-on-answers problem that that he believed was the product of lesser minds and weaker resolve—and that he had trouble paying attention to. What's more, he had increasingly personalized his antagonism with North Korean leader Kim Jong-un, referring to him often with derogatory epithets.

His staff had not prepared him for this, but, in apparent relief that he could digress from the opioid discussion, as well as sudden satisfaction at the opportunity to address this nagging problem, he ventured out, in language that he'd repeated often in private—as he repeated everything often—to the precipice of an international crisis.

"North Korea best not make any more threats to the United States. They will be met with the fire and the fury like the world has never seen. He has been very threatening beyond a normal state, and as I said they will be met with fire and fury and frankly power, the likes of which this world has never seen before. Thank you."

\* \* \*

North Korea, a situation the president had been consistently advised to downplay, now became the central subject of the rest of the week—with most senior staff occupied not so much by the topic itself, but by how to respond to the president, who was threatening to "blow" again.

Against this background, almost no one paid attention to the announcement by the Trump supporter and American neo-Nazi Richard Spencer that he was organizing a protest at the University of Virginia, in Charlottesville, over the removal of a statue of Robert E. Lee. "Unite the Right," the theme of the rally called for Saturday, August 12, was explicitly designed to link Trump's politics with white nationalism.

On August 11, with the president in Bedminster continuing to threaten North Korea—and also, inexplicably to almost everyone on his staff, threatening military intervention in Venezuela—Spencer called for an evening protest.

At 8:45 p.m.—with the president in for the night in Bedminster—about 250 young men dressed in khaki pants and polo shirts, quite a Trump style of dress, began an organized parade across the UVA campus while carrying kerosene torches. Parade monitors with headsets directed the scene. At a signal, the marchers began chanting official movement slogans: "Blood and soil!" "You will not replace us!" "Jews will not replace us!" Soon, at the center of campus, near a statue of UVA's founder, Thomas Jefferson, Spencer's group was met by a counterprotest. With virtually no police presence, the first of the weekend's melees and injuries ensued.

Beginning again at eight o'clock the next morning, the park near the Lee statue became the battleground of a suddenly surging white racist movement, with clubs, shields, mace, pistols, and automatic rifles (Virginia is an "open carry" state)—a movement seemingly, and to liberal horror, born out of the Trump campaign and election, as in fact Richard Spencer intended it to seem. Opposing the demonstrators was a hardened, militant left called to the barricades. You could hardly have better set an end-times scene, no matter the limited numbers of protesters. Much of the morning involved a series of charges and countercharges—a rocks-and-bottles combat, with a seemingly hands-off police force standing by.

In Bedminster, there was still little awareness of the unfolding events in Charlottesville. But then, at about one o'clock in the afternoon, James Alex Fields Jr., a twenty-year-old would-be Nazi, plunged his Dodge Charger into a group of counterprotesters, killing thirty-two-year-old Heather Heyer and injuring a score of others.

In a tweet hurriedly composed by his staff, the president declared: "We ALL must be united & condemn all that hate stands for. There is no place for this kind of violence in America. Lets come together as one!"

Otherwise, however, it was largely business as usual for the president—Charlottesville was a mere distraction, and indeed, the staff's goal was to keep him off North Korea. The main event in Bedminster that day was the ceremonial signing of an act extending the funding of a program that let veterans obtain medical care outside VA hospitals. The signing was held in a big ballroom at the Clubhouse two hours after Alex Field's attack.

During the signing, Trump took a moment to condemn the "hatred, bigotry, and violence on many sides" in Charlottesville. Almost immediately, the president came under attack for the distinction he had appeared to refuse to draw between avowed racists and the other side. As Richard Spencer had correctly understood, the president's sympathies were muddled.

However easy and obvious it was to condemn white racists—even self-styled neo-Nazis—he instinctively resisted.

It wasn't until the next morning that the White House finally tried to clarify Trump's position with a formal statement: "The President said very strongly in his statement yesterday that he condemns all forms of violence, bigotry, and hatred. Of course that includes white supremacists, KKK neo-Nazi and all extremist groups. He called for national unity and bringing all Americans together."

But in fact he hadn't condemned white supremacists, KKK, and neo-Nazis—and he continued to be stubborn about not doing it.

In a call to Bannon, Trump sought help making his case: "Where does this all end? Are they going to take down the Washington Monument, Mount Rushmore, Mount Vernon?" Bannon—still not receiving his summons to Bedminster—urged this to be the line: the president should condemn violence and misfits and also defend history (even with Trump's weak grasp of it). Stressing the literal issue of monuments would bedevil the left and comfort the right.

But Jared and Ivanka, with Kelly backing them, urged presidential behavior. Their plan was to have Trump return to the White House and address the issue with a forceful censure of hate groups and racial politics—exactly the unambiguous sort of position Richard Spencer had strategically bet Trump would not willingly take.

Bannon, understanding these same currents in Trump, lobbied Kelly and told him that the Jarvanka approach would backfire: *It will be clear his heart's not in it*, said Bannon.

The president arrived shortly before eleven o'clock on Monday morning at a White House under construction and a wall of shouted questions about Charlottesville: "Do you condemn the actions of neo-Nazis? Do you condemn the actions of white supremacists?" Some ninety minutes later he stood in the Diplomatic Reception Room, his eyes locked on to the teleprompter, and delivered a six-minute statement.

Before getting to the point: "Our economy is now strong. The stock market continues to hit record highs, unemployment is at a sixteen-year low, and businesses are more optimistic than ever before. Companies are moving back to the United States and bringing many thousands of jobs with them. We have already created over one million jobs since I took office."

And only then: "We must love each other, show affection for each other and unite together in condemnation of hatred, bigotry and violence. . . . We must rediscover the bonds of love and loyalty that bring us together as Americans. . . . Racism is evil. And those who cause violence in its name are criminals and thugs including the KKK, neo-Nazis, white supremacists, and other hate groups that are repugnant to everything we hold dear as Americans."

It was a reluctant mini-grovel. It was something of a restaging of the take-it-back birther speech about Obama during the campaign: much distraction and obfuscation, then a mumbled acknowledgment. Similarly, he looked here, trying to tow the accepted line on Charlottesville, like a kid called on the carpet. Resentful and petulant, he was clearly reading forced lines.

And in fact he got little credit for these presidential-style remarks, with reporters shouting questions about why it had taken him so long to address the issue. As he got back on Marine One to head to Andrews Air Force Base and on to JFK and then into Manhattan and Trump Tower, his mood was dark and I-told-you-so. Privately, he kept trying to rationalize why someone would be a member of the KKK—that is, they might not actually believe what the KKK believed, and the KKK probably does not believe what it used to believe, and, anyway, who really knows what the KKK believes now? In fact, he said, his own father was accused of being involved with the KKK—not true. (In fact, yes, true.)

The next day, Tuesday, August 15, the White House had a news conference scheduled at Trump Tower. Bannon urged Kelly to cancel it. It was a nothing conference anyway. Its premise was about infrastructure—about undoing an environmental regulation that could help get projects started faster—but it was really just another effort to show that Trump was working and not just on a holiday. So why bother? What's more, Bannon told Kelly, he could see the signs: the arrow on the Trump pressure cooker was climbing, and before long he'd blow.

The news conference went ahead anyway. Standing at the lectern in the lobby of Trump Tower, the president stayed on script for mere minutes.

Defensive and self-justifying, he staked out a contrition-is-bunk, the-fault-lies-everywhere-else position and then dug in deep. He went on without an evident ability to adjust his emotions to political circumstance or, really, even to make an effort to save himself. It was yet one more example, among his many now, of the comic-absurd, movielike politician who just says whatever is on his mind. Unmediated. Crazylike.

"What about the alt-left that came charging at the, as you say, alt-right? Do they have any semblance of guilt? What about the fact they came charging with clubs in their hands? As far as I'm concerned that was a horrible, horrible day. . . . I think there's blame on both sides. I have no doubt about it, you don't have any doubt about it. If you reported it accurately, you would see."

Steve Bannon, still waiting in his temporary office in the EOB, thought, *Oh my god, there he goes. I told you so.*

* * *

Outside of the portion of the electorate that, as Trump once claimed, would let him shoot someone on Fifth Avenue, the civilized world was pretty much universally aghast. Everybody came to a dumbfounded moral attention. Anybody in any position of responsibility remotely tied to some idea of establishment respectability had to disavow him. Every CEO of a public company who had associated him- or herself with the Trump White House now needed to cut the ties. The overriding issue might not even be what unreconstructed sentiments he actually seemed to hold in his heart—Bannon averred that Trump was not in fact anti-Semitic, but on the other count he wasn't sure—but that he flat-out couldn't control himself.

In the wake of the immolating news conference, all eyes were suddenly on Kelly—this was his baptism of Trump fire. Spicer, Priebus, Cohn, Powell, Bannon, Tillerson, Mattis, Mnuchin—virtually the entire senior staff and cabinet of the Trump presidency, past and present, had traveled through the stages of adventure, challenge, frustration, battle, self-justification, and doubt, before finally having to confront the very real likelihood that the president they worked for—whose presidency they bore some official responsibility for—didn't have the wherewithal to adequately function in his job. Now, after less than two weeks on the job, it was Kelly's turn to stand at that precipice.

The debate, as Bannon put it, was not about whether the president's situation was bad, but whether it was Twenty-Fifth-Amendment bad.

* * *

To Bannon, if not to Trump, the linchpin of Trumpism was China. The story of the next generation, he believed, had been written, and it was about war with China. Commercial war, trade war, cultural war, diplomatic war—it would be an all-encompassing war that few in the United States now understood needed to be fought, and that almost nobody was prepared to fight.

Bannon had compiled a list of "China hawks" that crossed political lines, going from the Breitbart gang, to former *New Republic* editor Peter Beinart—who regarded Bannon only with scorn—and orthodox liberal-progressive stalwart Robert Kuttner, the editor of the small, public policy magazine *American Prospect*. On Wednesday, August 16, the day after the president's news conference in Trump Tower, Bannon, out of the blue, called Kuttner from his EOB office to talk China.

By this point, Bannon was all but convinced that he was on the way out of the White House. He had received no invitation to join the president in Bedminster, a withering sign. That day, he had learned of the appointment of Hope Hicks as interim communications director—a Jarvanka victory. Meanwhile, the steady whisper from the Jarvanka side continued about his certain demise; it had become a constant background noise.

He was still not sure he would be fired, yet Bannon, in only the second on-the-record interview he had given since the Trump victory, called Kuttner and in effect sealed his fate. He would later maintain that the conversation was not on the record. But this was the Bannon method, in which he merely tempted fate.

If Trump was helplessly Trump in his most recent news conference, Bannon was helplessly Bannon in his chat with Kuttner. He tried to prop up what he made sound like a weak Trump on China. He corrected, in mocking fashion, the president's bluster on North Korea—"ten million people in Seoul" will die, he declared. And he insulted his internal enemies—"they're wetting themselves."

If Trump was incapable of sounding like a president, Bannon had matched him: he was incapable of sounding like a presidential aide.

* * *

That evening, a group of Bannonites gathered near the White House for dinner. The dinner was called for the bar at the Hay-Adams hotel, but Arthur Schwartz, a Bannonite PR man, got into an altercation with the Hay-Adams bartender about switching the television from CNN to Fox, where his client, Blackstone's Stephen Schwarzman, the chairman of one of the president's business councils, was shortly to appear. The business council was hemorrhaging its CEO members after the president's Charlottesville news conference, and Trump, in a tweet, had announced that he was disbanding it. (Schwarzman had advised the president that the council was collapsing and that the president ought to at least make it look as if shutting it down was his decision.)

Schwartz, in high dudgeon, announced that he was checking out of the Hay-Adams and moving to the Trump Hotel. He also insisted that the dinner be moved two blocks away to Joe's, an outpost of Miami's Joe's Stone Crab. Matthew Boyle, the Washington political editor of Breitbart News, was swept into Schwartz's furious departure, with Schwartz upbraiding the twenty-nine-year-old for lighting a cigarette. "I don't know anyone who smokes," he sniffed. Although Schwartz was firmly in the Bannon camp, this seemed to be a general dig at the Breitbart people for being low-class.

Both dedicated Bannonites debated the effect of Bannon's interview, which had caught everybody in the Bannon universe off guard. Neither man could understand why he would have given an interview.

Was Bannon finished?

*No, no, no,* argued Schwartz. He might have been a few weeks ago when Murdoch had ganged up with McMaster and gone to the president and pressed him to dump Bannon. But then Sheldon had fixed it, Schwartz said.

"Steve stayed home when Abbas came," said Schwartz. "He wasn't going to breathe the air that a terrorist breathed." This was the precise line Schwartz would hand out to reporters in the coming days in a further effort to establish Bannon's right-wing virtue.

Alexandra Preate, Bannon's lieutenant, arrived at Joe's out of breath. Seconds later, Jason Miller, another PR man in the Bannon fold, arrived. During the transition, Miller had been slated to be the communications director, but then it had come out that Miller had had a relationship with another staff member who announced in a tweet she was pregnant by Miller—as was also, at this point, Miller's wife. Miller, who had lost his promised White House job but continued serving as an outside Trump and Bannon voice, was now, with the recent birth of the child—with the recent birth of both of his children by different women—facing another wave of difficult press. Still, even he was obsessively focused on what Bannon's interview might mean.

By now the table was buzzing with speculation.

How would the president react?

How would Kelly react?

Was this curtains?

For a group of people in touch with Bannon on an almost moment-by-moment basis, it was remarkable that nobody seemed to understand that, forcibly or otherwise, he would surely be moving out of the White House. On the contrary, the damaging interview was, by consensus, converted into a brilliant strategic move. Bannon was not going anywhere—not least because there was no Trump without Bannon.

It was an excited dinner, a revved-up occasion involving a passionate group of people all attached to the man who they believed was the most compelling figure in Washington. They saw him as some sort of irreducible element: Bannon was Bannon was Bannon.

As the evening went on, Matt Boyle got in a furious text-message fight with Jonathan Swan, a White House reporter who had written a story about Bannon being on the losing side in the Bannon-McMaster showdown. Soon almost every well-connected reporter in the city was checking in with somebody at the table. When a text came in, the recipient would hold up his or her phone if it showed a notable reporter's name.

At one point, Bannon texted Schwartz some talking points. Could it be that this was just one more day in the endless Trump drama?

Schwartz, who seemed to regard Trump's stupidity as a political given, offered a vigorous analysis of why Trump could not do without Bannon. Then, seeking more proof of his theory, Schwartz said he was texting Sam Nunberg, generally regarded as the man who understood Trump's whims and impulses best, and who had sagely predicted Bannon's survival at each doubtful moment in the past months.

"Nunberg always knows," said Schwartz.

Seconds later, Schwartz looked up. His eyes widened and for a moment he went silent. Then he said: "Nunberg says Bannon's dead."

And, indeed, unbeknownst to the Bannonites, even those closest to him, Bannon was at that moment finalizing his exit with Kelly. By the next day, he would be packing up his little office, and on Monday, when Trump would return to a refurbished West Wing—a paint job, new furniture, and new rugs, its look tilting toward the Trump Hotel—Steve Bannon would be back on Capitol Hill at the Breitbart Embassy, still, he was confident, the chief strategist for the Trump revolution.

# EPILOGUE:
# BANNON AND TRUMP

On a sweltering morning in October 2017, the man who had more or less single-handedly brought about the U.S. withdrawal from the Paris climate accord, stood on the steps of the Breitbart town house and said, with a hearty laugh, "I guess global warming is real."

Steve Bannon had lost twenty pounds since his exit from the White House six weeks before—he was on a crash all-sushi diet. "That building," said his friend David Bossie, speaking about all White Houses but especially the Trump White House, "takes perfectly healthy people and turns them into old, unhealthy people." But Bannon, who Bossie had declared on virtual life support during his final days in the West Wing, was again, by his own description, "on fire." He had moved out of the Arlington "safe house" and reestablished himself back at the Breitbart Embassy, turning it into a headquarters for the next stage of the Trump movement, which might not include Trump at all.

Asked about Trump's leadership of the nationalist-populist movement, Bannon registered a not inconsiderable change in the country's political landscape: "*I* am the leader of the national-populist movement."

One cause of Bannon's boast and new resolve was that Trump, for no reason that Bannon could quite divine, had embraced Mitch McConnell's establishment candidate in the recent Republican run-off in Alabama rather than support the nat-pop choice for the Senate seat vacated by now attorney general Jeff Sessions. After all, McConnell and the president were barely on speaking terms. From his August "working holiday" in Bedminster, the president's staff had tried to organize a makeup meeting with McConnell, but McConnell's staff had sent back word that it wouldn't be possible because the Senate leader would be getting a haircut.

But the president—ever hurt and confused by his inability to get along with the congressional leadership, and then, conversely, enraged by their refusal to get along with him—had gone all-in for the McConnell-backed Luther Strange, who had run against Bannon's candidate, the right-wing firebrand Roy Moore. (Even by Alabama standards, Moore was far right: he had been removed as chief justice of the Alabama Supreme Court for defying a federal court order to take down a monument of the Ten Commandments in the Alabama judicial building.)

For Bannon, the president's political thinking had been obtuse at best. He was unlikely to get anything from McConnell—and indeed Trump had demanded nothing for his support for Luther Strange, which came via an unplanned tweet in August. Strange's prospects were not only dim, but he was likely to lose in a humiliating fashion. Roy Moore was the clear candidate of the Trump base—and he was Bannon's candidate. Hence, that would be the contest: Trump against Bannon. In fact, the president really didn't have to support anyone—no one would have complained if he'd stayed neutral in a primary race. Or, he could have tacitly supported Strange and not doubled down with more and more insistent tweets.

For Bannon, this episode was not only about the president's continuing and curious confusion about what he represented, but about his mercurial, intemperate, and often cockamamie motivations. Against all political logic, Trump had supported Luther Strange, he told Bannon, because "Luther's my friend."

"He said it like a nine-year-old," said Bannon, recoiling, and noting that there was no universe in which Trump and Strange were actually friends.

For every member of the White House senior staff this would be the lasting conundrum of dealing with President Trump: the "why" of his often baffling behavior.

"The president fundamentally wants to be liked" was Katie Walsh's analysis. "He just fundamentally needs to be liked so badly that it's always . . . everything is a struggle for him."

This translated into a constant need to win something—anything. Equally important, it was essential that he *look* like a winner. Of course, trying to win without consideration, plan, or clear goals had, in the course of the administration's first nine months, resulted in almost nothing but losses. At the same time, confounding all political logic, that lack of a plan, that impulsivity, that apparent *joie de guerre*, had helped create the disruptiveness that seemed to so joyously shatter the status quo for so many.

But now, Bannon thought, that novelty was finally wearing off.

For Bannon, the Strange-Moore race had been a test of the Trump cult of personality. Certainly Trump continued to believe that people were following *him*, that he was the movement—and that his support was worth 8 to 10 points in any race. Bannon had decided to test this thesis and to do it as dramatically as possible. All told, the Senate Republican leadership and others spent $32 million on Strange's campaign, while Moore's campaign spent $2 million.

Trump, though aware of Strange's deep polling deficit, had agreed to extend his support in a personal trip. But his appearance in Huntsville, Alabama, on September 22, before a Trump-size crowd, was a political flatliner. It was a full-on Trump speech, ninety minutes of rambling and improvisation—the wall would be built (now it was a see-through wall), Russian interference in the U.S. election was a hoax, he would fire anybody on his cabinet who supported Moore. But, while his base turned out en masse, still drawn to Trump the novelty, his cheerleading for Luther Strange drew at best a muted response. As the crowd became restless, the event threatened to become a hopeless embarrassment.

Reading his audience and desperate to find a way out, Trump suddenly threw out a line about Colin Kaepernick taking to his knee while the national anthem played at a National Football League game. The line got a standing ovation. The president thereupon promptly abandoned Luther Strange for the rest of the speech. Likewise, for the next week he continued to whip the NFL. Pay no attention to Strange's resounding defeat five days after the event in Huntsville. Ignore the size and scale of Trump's rejection and the Moore-Bannon triumph, with its hint of new disruptions to come. Now Trump had a new topic, and a winning one: the Knee.

*  *  *

The fundamental premise of nearly everybody who joined the Trump White House was, *This can work. We can help make this work.* Now, only three-quarters of the way through just the first year of Trump's term, there was literally not one member of the senior staff who could any longer be confident of that premise. Arguably—and on many days indubitably—most members of the senior staff believed that the sole upside of being part of the Trump White House was to help prevent worse from happening.

In early October, Secretary of State Rex Tillerson's fate was sealed—if his obvious ambivalence toward the president had not already sealed it—by the revelation that he had called the president "a fucking moron."

This—insulting Donald Trump's intelligence—was both the thing you could not do and the thing—drawing there-but-for-the-grace-of-God guffaws across the senior staff—that everybody was guilty of. Everyone, in his or her own way, struggled to express the baldly obvious fact that the president did not know enough, did not know what he didn't know, did not particularly care, and, to boot, was confident if not serene in his unquestioned certitudes. There was now a fair amount of back-of-the-classroom giggling about who had called Trump what. For Steve Mnuchin and Reince Priebus, he was an "idiot." For Gary Cohn, he was "dumb as shit." For H. R. McMaster he was a "dope." The list went on.

Tillerson would merely become yet another example of a subordinate who believed that his own abilities could somehow compensate for Trump's failings.

Aligned with Tillerson were the three generals, Mattis, McMasters, and Kelly, each seeing themselves as representing maturity, stability, and restraint. And each, of course, was resented by Trump for it. The suggestion that any or all of these men might be more focused and even tempered than Trump himself was cause for sulking and tantrums on the president's part.

The daily discussion among senior staffers, those still there and those now gone—all of whom had written off Tillerson's future in the Trump administration—was how long General Kelly would last as chief of staff. There was something of a virtual office pool, and the joke was that Reince Priebus was likely to be Trump's longest-serving chief of staff. Kelly's distaste for the president was open knowledge—in his every word and gesture he condescended to Trump—the president's distaste for Kelly even more so. It was sport for the president to defy Kelly, who had become the one thing in his life he had never been able to abide: a disapproving and censorious father figure.

*　*　*

There really were no illusions at 1600 Pennsylvania Avenue. Kelly's long-suffering antipathy toward the president was rivaled only by his scorn for the president's family—"Kushner," he pronounced, was "insubordinate." Cohn's derisive contempt for Kushner as well as the president was even greater. In return, the president heaped more abuse on Cohn—the former president of Goldman Sachs was now a "complete idiot, dumber than dumb." In fact, the president had also stopped defending his own family, wondering when they would "take the hint and go home."

But, of course, this was still politics: those who could overcome shame or disbelief—and, despite all Trumpian coarseness and absurdity, suck up to him and humor him—might achieve unique political advantage. As it happened, few could.

By October, however, many on the president's staff took particular notice of one of the few remaining Trump opportunists: Nikki Haley, the UN ambassador. Haley—"as ambitious as Lucifer," in the characterization of one member of the senior staff—had concluded that Trump's tenure would last, at best, a single term, and that she, with requisite submission, could be his heir apparent. Haley had courted and befriended Ivanka, and Ivanka had brought her into the family circle, where she had become a particular focus of Trump's attention, and he of hers.

Haley, as had become increasingly evident to the wider foreign policy and national security team, was the family's pick for secretary of state after Rex Tillerson's inevitable resignation. (Likewise, in this shuffle, Dina Powell would replace Haley at the UN.)

The president had been spending a notable amount of private time with Haley on Air Force One and was seen to be grooming her for a national political future. Haley, who was much more of a traditional Republican, one with a pronounced moderate streak—a type increasingly known as a Jarvanka Republican—was, evident to many, being mentored in Trumpian ways. The danger here, offered one senior Trumper, "is that she is so much smarter than him."

What now existed, even before the end of the president's first year, was an effective power vacuum. The president, in his failure to move beyond daily chaos, had hardly seized the day. But, as sure as politics, someone would.

In that sense, the Trumpian and Republican future was already moving beyond this White House. There was Bannon, working from the outside and trying to take over the Trump movement. There was the Republican leadership in Congress, trying to stymie Trumpism—if not slay it. There was John McCain, doing his best to embarrass it. There was the special counsel's office, pursuing the president and many of those around him.

The stakes were very clear to Bannon. Haley, quite an un-Trumpian figure, but by far the closest of any of his cabinet members to him, might, with clever political wiles, entice Trump to hand her the Trumpian revolution. Indeed, fearing Haley's hold on the president, Bannon's side had—the very morning that Bannon had stood on the steps of the Breitbart town house in the unseasonable October weather—gone into overdrive to push the CIA's Mike Pompeo for State after Tillerson's departure.

This was all part of the next stage of Trumpism—to protect it from Trump.

* * *

General Kelly was conscientiously and grimly trying to purge the West Wing chaos. He had begun by compartmentalizing the sources and nature of the chaos. The overriding source, of course, was the president's own eruptions, which Kelly could not control and had resigned himself to accepting. As for the ancillary chaos, much of it had been calmed by the elimination of Bannon, Priebus, Scaramucci, and Spicer, with the effect of making it quite a Jarvanka-controlled West Wing.

Now, nine months in, the administration faced the additional problem that it was very hard to hire anyone of stature to replace the senior people who had departed. And the stature of those who remained seemed to be more diminutive by the week.

Hope Hicks, at twenty-eight, and Stephen Miller, at thirty-two, both of whom had begun as effective interns on the campaign, were now among the seniormost figures in the White House. Hicks had assumed command of the communications operation, and Miller had effectively replaced Bannon as the senior political strategist.

After the Scaramucci fiasco, and the realization that the position of communications director would be vastly harder to fill, Hicks was assigned the job as the "interim" director. She was given the interim title partly because it seemed implausible that she was qualified to run an already battered messaging operation, and partly because if she *was* given the permanent job everyone would assume that the president was effectively calling the daily shots. But by the middle of September, interim was quietly converted to permanent.

In the larger media and political world, Miller—who Bannon referred to as "my typist"—was a figure of ever increasing incredulity. He could hardly be taken out in public without engaging in some screwball, if not screeching, fit of denunciation and grievance. He was the de facto crafter of policy and speeches, and yet up until now he had largely only taken dictation.

Most problematic of all, Hicks and Miller, along with everyone on the Jarvanka side, were now directly connected to actions involved in the Russian investigation or efforts to spin it, deflect it, or, indeed, cover it up. Miller and Hicks had drafted—or at least typed—Kushner's version of the first letter written at Bedminster to fire Comey. Hicks had joined with Kushner and his wife to draft on Air Force One the Trump-directed press release about Don Jr. and Kushner's meeting with the Russians in Trump Tower.

In its way, this had become the defining issue for the White House staff: who had been in what inopportune room. And even beyond the general chaos, the constant legal danger formed part of the high barrier to getting people to come work in the West Wing.

Kushner and his wife—now largely regarded as a time bomb inside the White House—were spending considerable time on their own defense and battling a sense of mounting paranoia, not least about what members of the senior staff who had already exited the West Wing might now say about them. Kushner, in the middle of October, would, curiously, add to his legal team Charles Harder, the libel lawyer who had defended both Hulk Hogan in his libel suit against Gawker, the Internet gossip site, and Melania Trump in her suit against the *Daily Mail*. The implied threat to media and to critics was clear. Talk about Jared Kushner at your peril. It also likely meant that Donald Trump was yet managing the White House's legal defense, slotting in his favorite "tough guy" lawyers.

Beyond Donald Trump's own daily antics, here was the consuming issue of the White House: the ongoing investigation directed by Robert Mueller. The father, the daughter, the son-in-law, his father, the extended family exposure, the prosecutor, the retainers looking to save their own skins, the staffers who Trump had rewarded with the back of his hand— it all threatened, in Bannon's view, to make Shakespeare look like Dr. Seuss.

Everyone waited for the dominoes to fall, and to see how the president, in his fury, might react and change the game again.

* * *

Steve Bannon was telling people he thought there was a 33.3 percent chance that the Mueller investigation would lead to the impeachment of the president, a 33.3 percent chance that Trump would resign, perhaps in the wake of a threat by the cabinet to act on the Twenty-Fifth Amendment (by which the cabinet can remove the president in the event of his incapacitation), and a 33.3 percent chance that he would limp to the end of his term. In any event, there would certainly not be a second term, or even an attempt at one.

"He's not going to make it," said Bannon at the Breitbart Embassy. "He's lost his stuff."

Less volubly, Bannon was telling people something else: he, Steve Bannon, was going to run for president in 2020. The locution, "If I were president . . ." was turning into, "When I am president . . ."

The top Trump donors from 2016 were in his camp, Bannon claimed: Sheldon Adelson, the Mercers, Bernie Marcus, and Peter Thiel. In short order, and as though he had been preparing for this move for some time, Bannon had left the White House and quickly thrown together a rump campaign organization. The heretofore behind-the-scenes Bannon was methodically meeting with every conservative leader in the country— doing his best, as he put it, to "kiss the ass and pay homage to all the gray-beards." And he was keynoting a list of must-attend conservative events.

"Why is Steve speaking? I didn't know he spoke," the president remarked with puzzlement and rising worry to aides.

Trump had been upstaged in other ways as well. He had been scheduled for a major *60 Minutes* interview in September, but this was abruptly canceled after Bannon's *60 Minutes* interview with Charlie Rose on September 11. The president's advisers felt he shouldn't put himself in a position where he would be compared with Bannon. The worry among staffers—all of them concerned that Trump's rambling and his alarming repetitions (the same sentences delivered with the same expressions minutes apart) had significantly increased, and that his ability to stay focused, never great, had notably declined—was that he was likely to suffer by such a comparison. Instead, the interview with Trump was offered to Sean Hannity—with a preview of the questions.

Bannon was also taking the Breitbart opposition research group— the same forensic accountant types who had put together the damning *Clinton Cash* revelations—and focusing it on what he characterized as the "political elites." This was a catchall list of enemies that included as many Republicans as Democrats.

Most of all, Bannon was focused on fielding candidates for 2018. While the president had repeatedly threatened to support primary challenges against his enemies, in the end, with his aggressive head start, it was Bannon who would be leading these challenges. It was Bannon spreading fear in the Republican Party, not Trump. Indeed, Bannon was willing to pick outré if not whacky candidates—including former Staten Island congressman Michael Grimm, who had done a stint in federal prison—to demonstrate, as he had demonstrated with Trump, the scale, artfulness, and menace of Bannon-style politics. Although the Republicans in the 2018 congressional races were looking, according to Bannon's numbers, at a 15-point deficit, it was Bannon's belief that the more extreme the right-wing challenge appeared, the more likely the Democrats would field left-wing nutters even less electable than right-wing nutters. The disruption had just begun.

Trump, in Bannon's view, was a chapter, or even a detour, in the Trump revolution, which had always been about weaknesses in the two major parties. The Trump presidency—however long it lasted—had created the opening that would provide the true outsiders their opportunity. Trump was just the beginning.

Standing on the Breitbart steps that October morning, Bannon smiled and said: "It's going to be wild as shit."

# ACKNOWLEDGMENTS

I am grateful to Janice Min and Matthew Belloni at the *Hollywood Reporter*, who, eighteen months ago, got me up one morning to jump on a plane in New York and that evening interview the unlikely candidate in Los Angeles. My publisher, Stephen Rubin, and editor, John Sterling, at Henry Holt have not only generously supported this book but shepherded it with enthusiasm and care on an almost daily basis. My agent, Andrew Wylie, made this book happen, as usual, virtually overnight.

Michael Jackson at Two Cities TV, Peter Benedek at UTA, and my lawyers, Kevin Morris and Alex Kohner, have patiently pushed this project forward.

A libel reading can be like a visit to the dentist. But in my long experience, no libel lawyer is more nuanced, sensitive, and strategic than Eric Rayman. Once again, almost a pleasure.

Many friends, colleagues, and generous people in the greater media and political world have made this a smarter book, among them Mike Allen, Jonathan Swan, John Homans, Franklin Foer, Jack Shafer, Tammy Haddad, Leela de Kretser, Stevan Keane, Matt Stone, Edward Jay Epstein, Simon Dumenco, Tucker Carlson, Joe Scarborough, Piers Morgan, Juleanna Glover, Niki Christoff, Dylan Jones, Michael Ledeen, Mike Murphy, Tim Miller, Larry McCarthy, Benjamin Ginsberg, Al

From, Kathy Ruemmler, Matthew Hiltzik, Lisa Dallos, Mike Rogers, Joanna Coles, Steve Hilton, Michael Schrage, Matt Cooper, Jim Impoco, Michael Feldman, Scott McConnell, and Mehreen Maluk.

My appreciation to fact-checkers Danit Lidor, Christina Goulding, and Joanne Gerber.

My greatest thanks to Victoria Floethe, for her support, patience, and insights, and for her good grace in letting this book take such a demanding place in our lives.

# INDEX

# ABOUT THE AUTHOR

MICHAEL WOLFF has received numerous awards for his work, including two National Magazine Awards. He has been a regular columnist for *Vanity Fair*, *New York*, *The Hollywood Reporter*, British *GQ*, *USA Today*, and *The Guardian*. He is the author of six prior books, including the bestselling *Burn Rate* and *The Man Who Owns the News*. He lives in Manhattan and has four children.